HERALDRY
AND THE
heralds

by the same author

THE HERALDIC IMAGINATION

HERALDRY
AND THE
heralds

RODNEY DENNYS

JONATHAN CAPE
THIRTY BEDFORD SQUARE LONDON

First published 1982
Reprinted 1984
Copyright © 1982 by Rodney Dennys

Jonathan Cape Ltd, 30 Bedford Square, London WC1

British Library Cataloguing in Publication Data

Dennys, Rodney
Heraldry and the heralds.
1. Heraldry
I. Title
929.6   CR21
ISBN 0-224-01643-1

Printed in Great Britain by Butler & Tanner Ltd,
Frome and London

To
Miles, Duke of Norfolk and Earl Marshal,
who has done much to encourage and guide the
Heralds of England to cope with the modern world

CONTENTS

Contents

ILLUSTRATIONS

COLOUR PLATES

between pages 158 and 159

between pages 174 and 175

between pages 206 and 207

FIGURES

ACKNOWLEDGMENTS

HERE SO many people have been so generous with advice, assistance and friendly criticism, it is difficult to express one's gratitude adequately because the tally is so long. If I mention only a few by name it does not mean that my gratitude to the others is any the less, but only that I have badgered some of my friends like a persistent bluebottle and I owe them apologies as well as thanks for taking up so much of their time.

First of all my thanks are due to the Earl Marshal for permission to consult and use papers in the muniment room at Arundel Castle dealing with certain Ceremonies of State and, in particular, with the Churchill Funeral. To my brother heralds collectively as the Chapter of the College of Arms my warmest thanks are due for permission to use material from the records and collections of the College, which is individually acknowledged in the footnotes. The copyright in them belongs to the College of Arms.

Lt.-Col. A. Colin Cole, Garter King of Arms, John Brooke-Little, Norroy & Ulster King of Arms, Conrad Swan, York Herald, Michael Maclagan, Richmond Herald, and George Squibb, Norfolk Herald, have read various chapters and made invaluable comments. Any views expressed are my own, nor can I avoid paternity for any errors of fact or interpretation — for those the responsibility is mine. Another colleague,

Mary Rose Rogers, Clerk to Norroy & Ulster for many years, produced the original idea for this book. Like all embryos it altered considerably between conception and birth. Her long experience of the College of Arms and those connected with it has been of great help in writing Part III, on the modern work of the heralds.

Without the Herald Painters of the College of Arms and other associated artists this would have been a much duller book. Again, the list is long, so I will mention here only those Herald Painters (an official designation) who have collaborated with me. Gerald Cobb, the doyen of them, must come first, and Geoffrey Mussett and Norman Manwaring are close runners up, while Alison Urwick has done more than any other of those outside the College stable to make this book agreeable to look at; to all of them my sincere thanks.

While one obviously does a certain amount of original research in manuscript sources, it would have been impossible to write this book without consulting the works of others in the fields of heraldry, armory and genealogy. The names of their authors will be found in the notes at the end of this book. Nevertheless I must make special mention of a few, still living, whose scholarly and well documented books have been and will long remain invaluable to all of us. The first that springs to mind is Sir Anthony Wagner, Clarenceux King of Arms (formerly Garter), whose *Heralds of England*, and *Heralds and Heraldry in the Middle Ages*, are landmarks in heraldic scholarship, while his many other productions have also proved quarries for a number of subsequent writers. Major Francis Jones, Wales Herald, is one of the foremost scholars on the early heraldry of Wales and his articles, monographs and books have proved most valuable, in particular *The Princes and Principality of Wales*. Mr C. W. Scott-Giles's *Shakespeare's Heraldry* provides an endless source of information of much wider importance than its title indicates, and I am grateful for the opportunity of grazing in this field and in his other works. Mr G. D. Squibb's *High Court of Chivalry* is a 'must' for anyone interested in the subject; while the many productions which have flowed from the busy pen of Mr John Brooke-Little, Norroy & Ulster King of Arms, leave us all in his debt.

Without our secretaries we should be pretty poor fish and I am very conscious of the debt I owe to Carol Hartley for the patience and skill with which she has coped with this book. Its punctuation, spelling and syntax would have been much worse without her watchful eye, while it would never have got finished without the time she devoted to typing and re-typing it. I am grateful. Finally I should like to thank Mary Banks of Jonathan Cape for all the many hours of editorial work she has put in to bring this book to life.

1981   R.D

Acknowledgments

We are grateful to the following for permission to reproduce the colour plates: Her Majesty The Queen, by gracious permission (VII); Associated Press (XI); Chapter of the College of Arms (II); Reginald Davis (V); Garter King of Arms (IV, IX, X); Directors of The Guardian Royal Exchange Assurance Ltd (III); courtesy of the National Portrait Gallery (I); John Scott (VIII); Universal Pictorial Press and Agency Ltd (VI).

The text figures were drawn by the following artists: John Bainbridge (63); Gerald Cobb (5, 25); A. Colin Cole (28); John Hawes (12, 13, 68); David Hopkinson (30, 39, 54, 66); Norman Manwaring (1, 2, 4, 6, 7, 14, 15, 16, 20, 29 right, 31, 32, 33, 34, 35, 36, 55, 56 centre, 59, 60, 61, 69); Geoffrey Mussett (3, 8, 45, 56 bottom, 64); Alison Urwick (9, 10, 11, 17, 18, 19, 22, 23, 24, 26, 27, 29 left, 37, 38, 40, 41, 44, 47, 48, 49, 50, 51, 52, 53, 57, 58, 62, 67, 70, 71 and Pedigree); Linda West (46).

PREFACE

S A HERALD one is constantly being asked what heraldry is about, how heralds are created and what they do and what is the place of the College of Arms in the world of today. Indeed, some people wonder whether it is not just a colourful and improbable anachronism, serving no particular purpose. The child is father of the man, and any organisation or body of people which has grown and developed over some eight hundred years can only be understood in the light of its history. To appreciate the College of Arms today it is, therefore, necessary to take a look at the realities of heraldry during the centuries which formed it.

Some knowledge of the basic rules of armory, as that part of a herald's duties which concerns coats of arms is called, is necessary because otherwise it is difficult to discuss individual coats of arms or, indeed, to describe them accurately. One also needs a nodding acquaintance with the way in which armory developed over the centuries; but this is not a textbook or 'grammar' of armory, because many excellent books on the subject are readily available. We begin, therefore, in Part I with no more than a little basic heraldry, enough to whet the appetite and provide a compass to steer the reader through the rest of the book. This is followed by chapters showing how armory has played a part in many different aspects of life; bringing the deft touch of imagination to illuminate concepts or events which are, in essence, rather ordinary.

Armory is a lively and living thing which can exist only in the context of people, so the second part of this book is about some famous coats of arms and the people who used them, particularly during the last two centuries of feudalism, to serve their dynastic ambitions and the cut-throat politics of a glittering and ruthless age – a period during which the English heralds came into their own, culminating in the first formation of the College of Arms in 1484 and its second formation in 1555, a time in which heraldry and politics were inextricably mixed. There is, however, more to armory than its sparkle, as historians are now beginning to realise. A knowledge of heraldry can throw light into many a shady corner of past politics by illuminating family, tenurial and political connections and affiliations hitherto unexplained, or even suspected. The second part of this book seeks, therefore, to describe not only the more obvious aspects of heraldry, but also some unusual details of armory, from the late Middle Ages and more modern times.

Finally, we try to answer the recurrent question, 'But what actually do the heralds do?' In fact, when one sits down and thinks about it, one is surprised by the number and variety of the things we do today. The third part of this book tries to illustrate these numerous activities, and show how the heralds have adapted to the modern world.

In recent years there has been a remarkable revival of interest in every aspect of heraldry, not only in Britain and Europe, but for some time in Canada, America, Australia and New Zealand, and new societies have now been formed in many of the British universities and schools, which is indication enough of the growing popular interest in it.

The visual aspects of heraldry are a major part of its fascination – the colour of armory and the romance associated with it, the deeds of valour commemorated by certain coats of arms, or the entertaining associations of its symbolism. While heraldic art has a unique vigour and significance, it can also hold its own with the contemporary art of its period. The drawings in this book are in most cases based on, or copies of, early originals, intended both to show what functional heraldry looked like and how it was used, and to give a good idea of how people in former times envisaged the creatures depicted in armory.

I

Some
Aspects of
Armory

ONE

SOME DEFINITIONS

ANY PEOPLE get a little muddled over the differences between arms, crests, supporters and badges, so it is essential to sort these out straight away. We will take as our illustration the full 'achievement', a term which embraces all these elements of armorial bearings, of the College of Arms (Figure 1). These are drawn in 'trick', that is, an open line drawing in ink with the colours indicated by their names, either in full or, more usually, abbreviated. This has been a very common way of illustrating arms for many centuries.

The central and most important part is the shield and the designs on it and these, properly speaking, are called the 'arms', although nowadays the term is often used loosely as a synonym for the whole achievement; the context usually makes clear what is intended. Another synonym for arms is 'coat of arms', which has a respectable antiquity. By the later twelfth century it became customary to wear a loose linen surcoat over the body armour, on which was painted the knight's arms, which was then often referred to as his 'coat armour'. One may be entitled to arms alone, and this is by no means uncommon, but one cannot have a crest, supporters or badge without arms. Among the earliest paintings of arms, dating from 1244–59, are the Matthew Paris shields.

The crest was worn on top of the helm. In the early Middle Ages it usually consisted of the same design as the arms, painted upon a fan-like

3

Figure 1   Armorial Bearings of the College of Arms.

piece of metal or stiffened leather, but as early as the twelfth century we find three-dimensional ones carved in wood or made of boiled leather, and usually different from the arms. Crests were normally used in the gay and ostentatious display of heraldry at tournaments and jousts, but not in the stern business of war, where they would only have got in the way. Around the base of the crest was the crest-wreath or torse, originally two pieces of silk twisted together into a circlet, possibly to hide the join with the helm, but as often as not the token of some lady in whose honour the knight was jousting. Sometimes the crest is set upon a cap of maintenance, as was done by the Black Prince and sometimes upon a coronet, as with the College of Arms or the Earl of Salisbury. Below the crest and hanging down behind the helm is the mantling, a piece of cloth probably for keeping the heat of the sun off the back of the helm; in real use originally very simple, but in later heraldic art it is often drawn in wildly flowing shapes. Where the crest was feathered, as with a swan's head and neck, the later heraldic artists carried the feathering down on to the mantling.

Supporters, which came into heraldry during the later Middle Ages, are the human or semi-human figures, or real or imaginary beasts and birds, that are depicted standing on either side of a shield and holding it up — supporting it, in fact (see Figure 1). It follows that inanimate objects or trees and the like cannot reasonably be used as supporters, although there are a few horrid exceptions. In the Middle Ages trees were sometimes shown on seals, with the owner's shield hanging from a branch, but this was purely decorative, and the tree was not a 'supporter'.

The badge is quite different and separate from the arms, crest or supporters, and is never shown on a shield or crest-wreath, but stands free and alone. A badge can, however, be shown on a banner of the livery colours, on a standard or on a roundel of the colours. Whilst arms and crests are personal to their owners and should be borne only by them, badges may be worn by their adherents and employees or by whom they please.

Many of us find it difficult to distinguish between flags of various kinds. The British Union Flag (the Union Jack) as flown on government offices and on naval and merchant ships, as well as by the public, normally has the length, from hoist to fly, twice the breadth. The Army form of Union Flag is more nearly square. So too are naval signalling flags, while numeral pendants are narrow and tapering, and burgees triangular.

The principal flags of heraldry are the gonfanon, pennoncel, banner, and standard. The Bayeux Tapestry shows William the Conqueror at the Battle of Hastings, accompanied by Count Eustace of Boulogne holding a lance with William's gonfanon at its head. This is a small square flag with three tails streaming from the fly (Figure 2). In the eleventh century gonfanons appear to have been mostly used by the commanders, and they

5

Figure 2   Duke William, during the Battle of Hastings, raises his helm to show his followers that he is still alive.

Figure 3   Seal (*c.* 1141–2) of Waleran, Count of Meulan and Lord of Worcester.

continued in use into the following century. While William's gonfanon bore only a rudimentary kind of armorial device upon it, the later gonfanons were certainly used for the display of armorial ensigns. One of the earliest examples is the seal (*c.* 1141–2) of Waleran, Count of Meulan and Lord of Worcester (Figure 3).

The pennoncel, or pennon, was a small, triangular, pennon-shaped lance-flag, and became the distinctive flag of the ordinary knight or knight bachelor, more usually referred to in the records as just bachelor, or someone's bachelor, such as the King's bachelor. On the knight bachelor's pennoncel would be painted his arms, and a splendid example is to be seen in the Luttrell Psalter (Figure 4).

During the thirteenth century gonfanons, which were the particular ensigns of barons, faded out and were superseded by banners. When the knight bachelor was promoted to command a larger formation the point of his pennoncel was ceremoniously cut off, thus symbolising its conversion into a banner, from which such senior knights became known as knights banneret, or more simply and usually, bannerets. These were usually knights who were following a regular military career and were frequently referred to as 'strenuous knights', and their pay was double that of a bachelor. So it can be seen that a banner was not just a pretty armorial flag, but denoted a commander of some seniority. For a long time the height of banners along the staff was approximately twice the length from hoist to fly, but by the fifteenth century they had become approximately square, and this is their shape today. The size may vary to suit the occasion and place. The banners of Knights of the Garter, which hang above their stalls in St George's Chapel, Windsor, are five feet square; those of Knights Grand Cross of the Order of the Bath are six feet square; the banners of heralds, which we hang outside the College of Arms to show which of the heralds is on duty as Officer in Waiting, are three feet square.

Standards are long flags, narrowing towards the fly and terminating in a rounded end or a double rounded end. Although beginning to come into use earlier, they became popular in the late fifteenth century and well into the sixteenth. It was the growing popularity of badges and crests which caused the development of standards, as they proved a wonderfully ostentatious means of displaying them. During this period English standards had the cross of St George next the hoist, with the crest usually between two representations of the badge. Nowadays the family arms have replaced St George's Cross. By Tudor times these flamboyant flags had reached fantastic lengths and in the reign of Henry VIII it was ordained that the Great Standard, when borne in battle with the King, should be eight or nine yards long; that of a duke seven yards, the end to be slit; an earl six yards; a baron five yards; a banneret four and a half; and a knight four yards long. Although still allowed today the standard is rarely used, except in paintings, when it can be very decorative.

There are two further definitions which should be made before we move on. Many people find it rather puzzling that the terms 'heraldry' and 'armory' seem to be used rather indiscriminately in a synonymous way. So they may be, because as early as 1285 armory, the special skill of the heralds in the science of individual devices and the rules and conventions governing their use, had become known as 'hiraudie', while the earliest known English treatise on armory, probably compiled before 1300, was called *De Heraudie*. As a rule 'heraldry' can be taken to embrace all the duties of a herald, which are many and various and which of course include those concerning armorial devices, while 'armory' applies to the narrower meaning. However, both terms are used in this book and it is hoped that the context will make their meaning clear.

Figure 4   Sir Geoffrey Luttrell being armed for a tournament.

TWO

THE LANGUAGE OF HERALDRY

I T BECAME CLEAR at a very early stage in the development of heraldry that armorial charges on shields, pennoncels and banners must follow internationally recognised rules if chaos were to be avoided. It is important, therefore, to have some idea of the basic rules and conventions, so that when arms are blazoned in the following chapters they will be understood.

When blazoning arms, one begins with the colour or tincture of the field, that is to say the shield itself. Sometimes this is all of one colour, or metal, or fur, and sometimes the field may be of two tinctures divided by a party line. The principal object or *charge* on the field is next given, followed by charges of lesser importance, then any minor objects or figures which may be placed upon the ordinary or the principal charge, ending with any marks of distinction or difference. It sounds very complicated, but one gets the hang of it pretty quickly, as the illustrations in this chapter will show.

A shield may be divided in a number of different ways, as Figure 5 demonstrates, and in such cases it is blazoned as, for example, *party per pale*, or *party per fess*, and so on, with the tinctures then stated. By turning these party lines into broad bands one gets the *ordinaries*, the basic geometrical charges used in armory, which are named after the party lines, such as the *pale*, the *fess*, the *cross*, the *bend*, the *bend sinister*, the *saltire*, the *chevron* and so on (see Figure 6). There are also several diminutives for each of them.

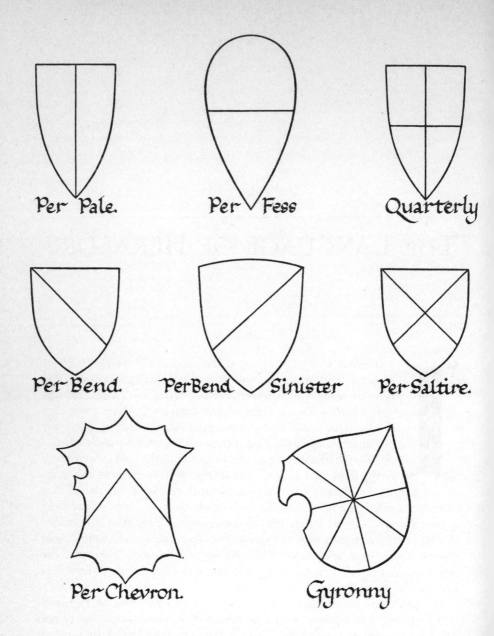

Per Pale.

Per Fess

Quarterly

Per Bend.

Per Bend Sinister

Per Saltire.

Per Chevron.

Gyronny

Figure 5   Party lines dividing shields.
Figure 6   (*opposite*) The principal ordinaries.

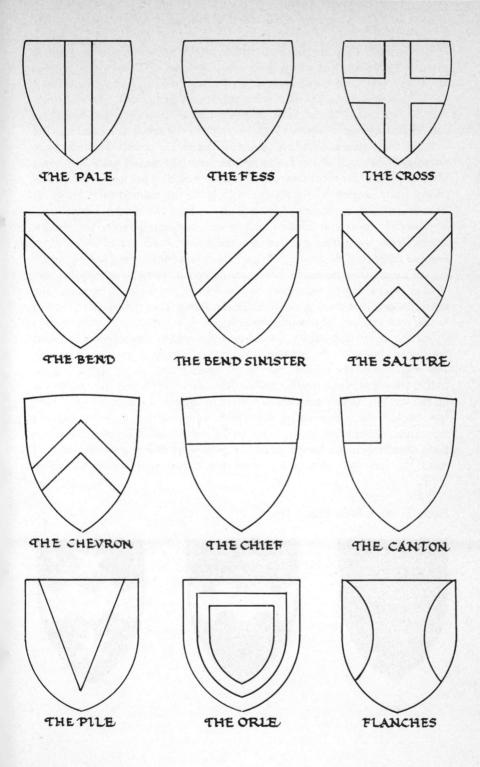

THE PALE   THE FESS   THE CROSS

THE BEND   THE BEND SINISTER   THE SALTIRE

THE CHEVRON   THE CHIEF   THE CANTON

THE PILE   THE ORLE   FLANCHES

Let us take fairly simple arms, those of Sir Francis Drake of glorious memory, who first circumnavigated the world in 1577 and was granted arms and crest to commemorate it. Sir Francis had been using the arms of the Drakes of Ashe in Devon, a red wyvern on a silver field. The story goes that Sir Bernard Drake of Ashe, meeting him at Court one day, boxed his ears, declaring him an upstart with no right to the arms, as indeed was the case for they were not related. Queen Elizabeth, it is said, hearing of the summary treatment of her favourite, declared she would grant him arms which would be far more famous. These were *Sable a fess wavy between two estoiles [stars] argent.* The wavy fess alludes to the sea and the stars to Sir Francis's skill in navigation. Figure 7 shows how the blazon is built up.

A slightly more complicated coat is that of Samuel Pepys, the famous diarist: *Sable, on a bend gold between two horses' heads erased argent three fleurs de lys of the field* (that is, of the first colour mentioned; see Figure 8). Erased means that the horses' heads are ragged at the neck, as if pulled off.

One final thing to remember: when looking at a shield of arms, one must imagine that there is a man behind holding it, so the left of the shield as you look at it will be towards the holder's right, which is why that side is called the *dexter* in heraldry, while the right side to the onlooker is called the *sinister*, being on the holder's left. In the Middle Ages the dexter side was regarded as the nobler. Bartolo di Sassoferrato, in his day a famous Italian lawyer, wrote a treatise on heraldry about 1354, and has this to say on the subject: 'When arms are depicted on shields, the nobler part should face towards the part of the shield which, when carried, is on the bearer's right side. When arms are depicted on the caparisons of horses, the nobler parts should face the horse's head.' (Figure 4, p. 8 is a good example of this.) He also said that 'when arms are borne on clothing the more

Figure 7   Arms of Sir Francis Drake.

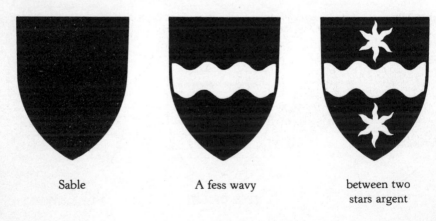

Sable   A fess wavy   between two
                                                 stars argent

important part should be towards the head and the inferior towards the feet', but 'arms are painted in any manner on the coverings of beds, on walls and on other fixtures', so you can let yourself go in your own home.

In the later Middle Ages people 'quartered' arms, that is, they combined two or more separate arms in the same shield, to show the lordships they owned, and they often marshalled the quarterings in the order of importance of these lordships. The best known example is that of Edward III, who in 1340 marshalled the royal arms with France in the first and fourth quarters and England in the second and third, because France, which he claimed unsuccessfully, was generally regarded as the more prestigious kingdom (see Pedigree, pp. 100–1).

The practical approach of the Middle Ages to the uses of heraldry had much to be said for it. Modern conventions and rules regarding the marshalling of arms have tended to fossilise a practice which should be flexible. The practice in England since Tudor times has been to marshal the arms of heiresses to show heirships in blood; that is to say that, in the absence of male heirs, the daughters become the representatives of their father, whether they own property or not. So, to keep the memory of their family alive, they can transmit their family arms to their children, providing they have taken the precaution of marrying an armorial husband.

It should be explained that the term the *quarterings* of a shield does not necessarily mean that there are only four. Very often there are only four quarterings, as in the British Royal Arms, but it is equally correct to add as many as one may be entitled to. For instance, some years ago the family of Lloyd of Stockton registered at the College of Arms a scheme of quarterings to which they were legally entitled. This embraced 323 quarterings and looks like a gaily coloured patchwork quilt.[1] The present

Figure 8 Arms of Samuel Pepys.

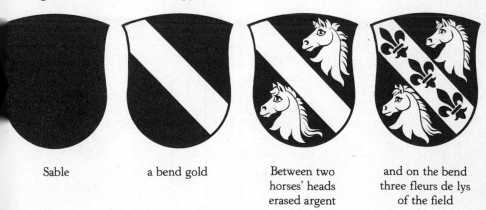

Sable a bend gold Between two horses' heads erased argent and on the bend three fleurs de lys of the field

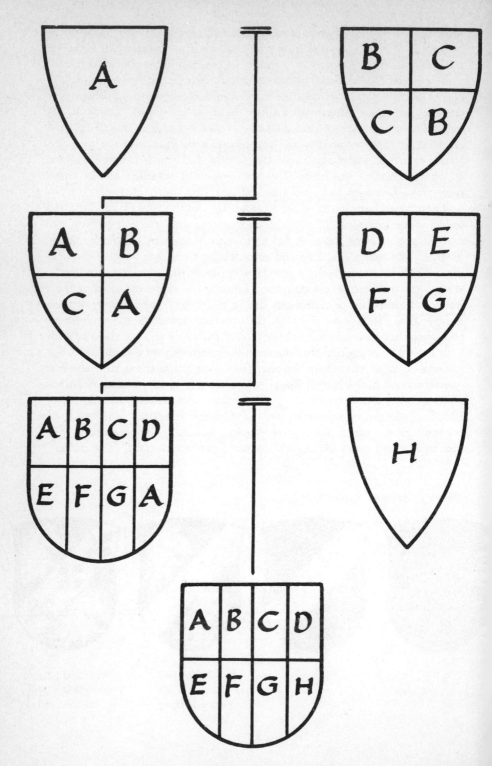

Figure 9   English method of quartering.

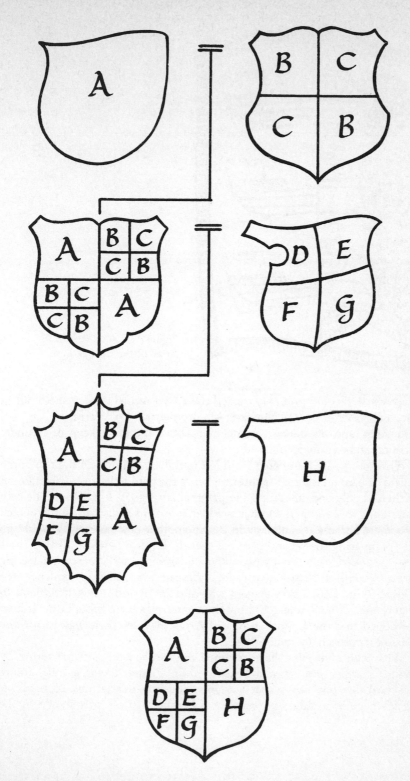

Figure 10   Scottish method of quartering.

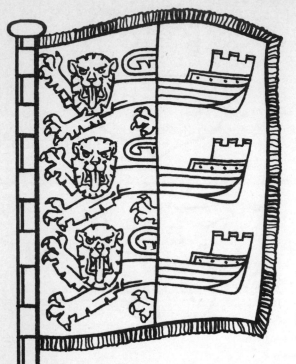

Figure 11
Arms of the Cinque Ports.

Earl Marshal could probably exceed the Lloyd record if he wished, but in fact only uses four: (1) Howard, (2) Brotherton, (3) Warrenne, and (4) Fitz-Alan; and his banner, flying high above the great keep of Arundel Castle, can be easily recognised.

Quarterings are numbered from left to right, beginning at the top of the shield or banner, the first quartering being the paternal arms of the family. If there is only one quartering the paternal arms go in 1 and 4 and the new quartering in 2 and 3; if another is added it goes in 3, displacing that which was there because it is already in 2, and another new quartering would go in 4, displacing the second paternal coat. In English heraldry further coats may be added, each occupying a whole quartering, and if a new quartering brings in with it further quarterings, they are just added in sequence (see Figure 9). It is not a very elegant way of doing it and makes it difficult to determine, without research, how the quarterings were brought in. It is to be hoped that the English Kings of Arms may see their way to a more flexible approach to quartering.

The Scots, however, have retained the early system of quartering by grand quarters and, as will be seen from Figure 10, it is much more practical, for one can see at a glance how the quarterings accrued.

Marriage to a lady who was not a heraldic heiress was shown in the

16

earlier Middle Ages by *dimidiating* the arms of husband and wife. The arms of husband and wife were literally cut in half vertically and joined together, usually producing bizarre or inartistic results. The arms of the Cinque Ports, although not those of an individual, are one of the best known examples of dimidiation (Figure 11). This unworkable system was soon abandoned in favour of *impaling*, combining side by side in the same shield the entire arms of husband and wife; although there still lingers an echo of dimidiation where there is a *bordure* or *orle* around the arms, in which case the side next to the join is omitted. The arms of John de Balliol are an interesting example and also an exception to the rule, for the arms of his wife are placed in the dexter, probably because Dervorguilla was co-heir to the great lordship of Galloway. Their son was John Balliol, King of Scotland from 1292 to 1296, and they were joint founders of Balliol College, Oxford, which has used these arms ever since, in memory of its founders (Figure 12).

A further example of unusual impaling is Richard II's placing of the Royal Arms of England (France Ancient and England quarterly) side by side with the attributed arms of Edward the Confessor. Richard's second wife, Isabel, the daughter of King Charles VI of France, whom he married in 1396 when she was aged only seven, impaled her own Arms of France with her husband's already impaled arms (Figure 13).

Figure 12
Arms of Dervorguilla, Lady of Galloway, impaling Balliol.

Figure 13
Triple impalement of Queen Isabel.

In the Middle Ages eldest sons, during their father's lifetime, usually differenced the family arms with a 'label' across the top of the shield. This is still the practice today. The shield of the Black Prince, now in Canterbury Cathedral, is a good example. His two shields were described by him as his 'shield for war' and his 'shield for peace', the latter no doubt being used in jousts (Figure 14).

As younger sons would not succeed to the paternal title, unless the heir died, they would be founding new families, so the differences introduced into their arms were intended to be permanent. For this reason fairly substantial alterations were made, sometimes by changing the colours, at other times by incorporating a bordure round the arms or adding one or more charges to the original coat. The famous case between Sir Richard Scrope and Sir Robert Grosvenor, which occupied the Court of Chivalry for many years towards the end of the fourteenth century, when both parties claimed the coat *Azure a bend or*, is an interesting example of the medieval view of family differencing. The Court of Chivalry suggested that Grosvenor should difference his arms with a bordure round them, but Richard II ruled that this was not sufficient difference for a stranger in blood, as it was the recognised difference for a junior or cadet branch of the same family.

Figure 14 The Black Prince's shields for war and peace.

The modern English system of differencing (which is permissive rather than mandatory) was certainly in use by the middle of the fifteenth century, and is believed to have been invented by John Wrythe, Garter King of Arms (died 1504). It is a system in which a number of small charges, a crescent for a second son, a mullet for a third son, a martlet for a fourth, and so on, are placed fairly inconspicuously at some convenient point in the shield. As this is not now insisted upon by the English Kings of Arms, few people do it, so one is unlikely to find such differences piled one upon the other. In Scotland, however, differencing is mandatory, but is effected by means of a variety of different bordures, the arms being *rematriculated*, or regranted in each case.[2]

One area in which differencing of arms is mandatory in England concerns bastards and adopted children. The reason for this is that in all western European countries bastards have been regarded from the Middle Ages onwards as being ineligible to succeed to dignities, titles and land and thus they have had to found new families, often with the assistance of their fathers, and have needed new arms to difference them from the elder or legitimate line. The Legitimacy Acts of 1926 and 1959, while legitimating bastards on the subsequent marriage of their parents and making them eligible to inherit property, expressly exempted the inheritance of peerages, titles and dignities. As arms are in the nature of a dignity and not a kind of property, legitimated bastards continue to be debarred from succeeding to their father's arms.

In the fourteenth century bastards sometimes placed their paternal arms upon a bend. Thus Sir Roger de Clarendon, the illegitimate son of the Black Prince, bore a gold shield with a black bend, on which were three white ostrich feathers (Figure 15). John Beaufort, the illegitimate son of John of Gaunt, Duke of Lancaster, by Katherine Swinford, bore for his arms *Party per pale argent and azure a bend of Lancaster* (Figure 16). After John of Gaunt's children were legitimated, they bore the Royal Arms within a bordure gobony argent and azure (Figure 17), which are still borne by the Dukes of Beaufort today.

Nowadays when a bastard wishes to use his father's arms, with his father's consent, a petition is prepared by the College of Arms and addressed to The Sovereign, praying for a Royal Licence for the petitioner to bear his paternal arms duly differenced. This petition is sent to the Home Office (which has, of course, been consulted in advance), where a Royal Licence is prepared, and this is signed by The Sovereign. It is then sent to the officer of arms dealing with the matter. The licence is recorded in the official registers of the College of Arms, and it is also published in the *London Gazette*. After this, the Earl Marshal is enabled to issue his warrant to the Kings of Arms authorising them to grant the paternal arms, suitably differenced, to the petitioner. The difference in England usually

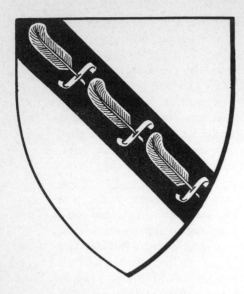

takes the form of a bordure wavy of some suitable tincture, as the baton sinister (bend couped at each end) is now reserved for royal bastards. Quite a number of people have taken advantage of this procedure in recent years to tidy up their offspring. The procedure for adopted children is the same, because they cannot automatically inherit the armorial dignity of their adoptive father as they are not of his blood. In this case the Royal Licence enables the Kings of Arms to grant the adoptive father's arms, differenced with two linked annulets, placed at some convenient point on the shield.

Badges and supporters became popular in England only in the fifteenth century, with the flamboyant flowering of heraldic conceits, themselves products of the age of livery and maintenance, and they were given further impetus by the new men of the sixteenth century, with their love of display. While the sovereigns of England have used badges since the time of Henry II, the magnates of the realm only began using them much later, and they did not spread to the greater country gentry until the golden sunset of the Middle Ages and feudal chivalry. Badges were and are quite separate from the arms, crest and supporters of an armorial achievement, and are used and depicted by themselves, without any crest-wreath or other form of support. They may be depicted on a roundel or banner of the two principal livery colours of the owner, parted per pale.

The cross was the earliest badge used by the rank and file of European armies, being assumed by all those who took the vow to go on the First Crusade of 1098, which liberated the Holy Sepulchre in 1100. The crosses, made of cloth of every colour, were sewn on the right shoulders of the crusaders' clothes. In 1189, when Henry II of England, Philip Augustus of

Figure 15 (*far left*)
Arms of Sir Roger Clarendon.

Figure 16 (*left*)
Arms of Beaufort before
legitimation.

Figure 17 (*right*)
Arms of Beaufort after
legitimation.

France, and Philip, Count of Flanders, and lords and prelates met on the Norman frontier to confer on undertaking a crusade to rescue the Kingdom of Jerusalem, they agreed that the French were to wear red crosses, the English white crosses, and the Flemish green crosses.[3] Henry died before the Third Crusade finally started and the English contingent was commanded by Richard Coeur de Lion. It is interesting to note that the red cross was never adopted as a French national badge, though it later became the English national badge. Richard I, after a spell in captivity in Austria on his way home, returned to England. He died in 1199. Although the Third Crusade achieved only limited success, it was a famous crusade and the veterans of the English army would have looked on their white crosses with pride, and many of them would have lived for long after Richard's untimely death.

In the disastrous crusade of 1270, Louis IX of France, was accompanied by a small English army commanded by the Prince Edward, son and heir of Henry III. After the main armies had turned back for home, Prince Edward decided to take his small contingent on alone to the Holy Land, although they achieved nothing of importance, for the English army was much too small, Edward gained much fame for having continued and it was a political success. By this time the cult of St George had become very popular in the Holy Land and it is probable that this saint's fabulous victory over the dragon of evil made a considerable impression on the young Prince, and may have led him to adopt St George as the protector of his little crusading army. His father died while he was abroad and he succeeded to the throne as King Edward I.

The Welsh wars which occupied so much of the reign of Edward I led

Broom badge of the Plantagenets.

Genet badge of Henry II.

Badge of the Heir to the Throne of
England.

Welsh Dragon badge of the Prince
of Wales.

White Hart badge of Richard II.

White Boar badge of Richard III.

Figures 18 to 23

that able and energetic king to abandon reliance on feudal levies and to build up a paid army, stiffened with contingents of professional officers and soldiers, and this inevitably led him to dress them in a common uniform. In the last quarter of the thirteenth century, we find in some accounts relating to the mustering of his army an order for cloth from which arm-bands were to be made for the infantry, and these bands were to be marked with the cross of St George.[4] Successive English armies wore it in campaigns thereafter, the most well-known reference being the order of King Henry V before the Battle of Agincourt in 1415, that all the English soldiers must 'wear a bande of St George sufficient large' upon their clothes.[5] St George's Cross was used as a battle flag by the English until the Union Flag was devised in 1707.

Henry II was the first English King to use a personal badge, the sprig of broom with pods (Figure 18), the *planta genista*, which flourishes in Anjou, and from which the Plantagenet dynasty derived its name. The badge was probably also used by his father Geoffrey, Count of Anjou, as it can be seen on the decoration of his tomb. Henry II also used as a personal badge a genet (a kind of civet cat) standing between two erect branches of broom (Figure 19). This is a double pun on the name.

Much has been written about the royal badges of England, so a selection only are shown here as illustrating the wide variety used by the sovereigns of England. As badges are heritable like arms, Queen Elizabeth II is entitled, should she wish, to use any of her predecessors' badges. The three white ostrich feathers encircled by a gold coronet, used since the time of the Black Prince by the heir to the throne, is not the badge of the Prince of Wales, as is commonly supposed, but the badge of the heir (Figure 20). His badge as Prince of Wales is the red Dragon of Cadwalader, with a white label of three points around its neck (Figure 21).

Many royal badges have been used as inn signs, two of the commonest being the White Hart of Richard II (Figure 22) and the rarer White Boar badge of Richard III (Figure 23), more often found in the north of England, which was where the centre of his power lay, than the south. As an able and courageous soldier Richard III no doubt chose the boar because it was regarded as brave beyond measure.

After Richard had been killed at the Battle of Bosworth in 1485, the victorious Henry VII celebrated the event by adopting as a badge a hawthorn tree crowned, alluding to the fact that after the battle the coronet which Richard had worn around his helmet had been found under a hawthorn bush (Figure 24). Henry VII also used a badge which combined the red rose of Lancaster and the white rose of York, but in his case the two were dimidiated. He also used the crowned Portcullis badge of the Beauforts, which he inherited through his mother. This is still used as the official badge of the Palace of Westminster and is the badge of office of

Somerset Herald of Arms (Figure 25). The Royal Badge for Scotland is St Andrew's Cross encircled by a crown (Figure 26).

The most romantic of all medieval legends, that of the Swan Knight, is reflected in the badge of the great family of Bohun, Earls of Hereford and Essex. A White Swan was also used as a badge or crest by the Beauchamps and Staffords. One version of the ancient European story relates that the Duke of Saxony was about to seize the castle and lands of the widowed Duchess of Bouillon, who appealed for help. There arrived an unknown knight in a boat drawn by a white swan, who defended the castle and slew the wicked Duke. The 'Swan Knight' thereafter married the Duchess's daughter Beatrice and they lived happily and produced a daughter, Ida. The Swan Knight had, however, made Beatrice take an oath that she would never question him about his antecedents or birth. After some years she could no longer restrain her curiosity, and asked the fatal question. The Swan Knight must obey his destiny, and sorrowfully he went to the riverside, after taking leave of his wife and vassals, and departed in his boat drawn by the same swan, never to be seen again. Ida subsequently married Count Eustace I of Boulogne. It is from their distinguished son Eustace III of Boulogne, and also his illegitimate half-brother Geoffrey, that many of the great families of Europe trace their descent, most of whom in the fourteenth century and later used a white swan as their badge.[6]

The White Swan of the Bohuns is usually depicted with a gold coronet about its neck, from which hangs a gold chain (Figure 27), but there are other variations. The Courtenays and the Luttrells inherited the badge from the Bohuns, as did Henry V of England, who used it as one of his badges, and also the Staffords. One of the most charming renderings of the badge is to be seen on the tomb in Exeter Cathedral of Margaret (died 1391), daughter of Humphrey de Bohun, Earl of Hereford and Essex, and wife of Hugh Courtenay, Earl of Devon, where two mourning swans, with necks entwined and their heads resting on the ground, stand at her feet.

While arms were regarded as the *alter ego* of their owner and were normally used in some obvious connection with him, his acts or his personal property, his badges were used much more widely. Indeed, he could, within reason, authorise anyone to use them. The last will and inventory of John de Vere, 13th Earl of Oxford, who died in March 1512/13, gives us some idea of the ways in which a great nobleman then used his badges.[7] A staunch Lancastrian, he played a very active part in the Wars of the Roses, being Captain-General of Henry Tudor's army, commanding the archers at the Battle of Bosworth. Thereafter honours and offices showered upon him, including the Garter. His will and inventory show that he used a number of badges and other emblems in a most sumptuous way, on gold and silver plate and on tapestries, hangings and cushions.

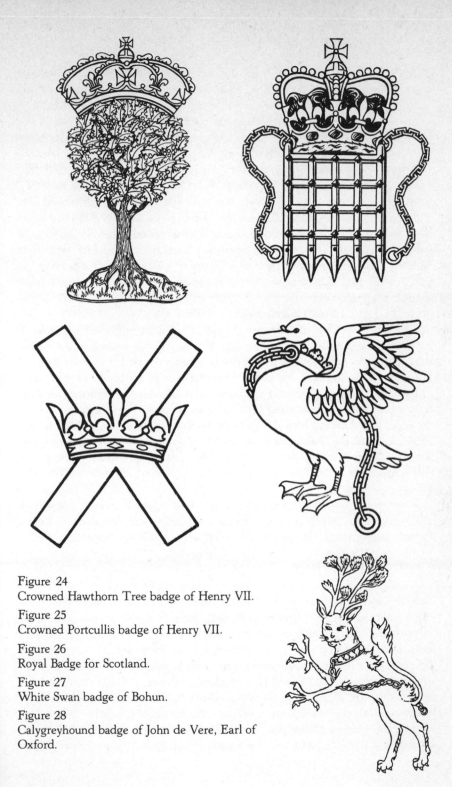

Figure 24
Crowned Hawthorn Tree badge of Henry VII.

Figure 25
Crowned Portcullis badge of Henry VII.

Figure 26
Royal Badge for Scotland.

Figure 27
White Swan badge of Bohun.

Figure 28
Calygreyhound badge of John de Vere, Earl of
Oxford.

The Blue Boar was one of the most widely used of the Vere badges, and was clearly a rebus or pun on their name, for a boar in Old French is *ver*; another widely used badge was the molet (a kind of five-pointed star, originally a spur-rowel), which was a charge borne in the first quarter of the Vere arms; and the badge of a calygreyhound, a creature otherwise unknown to heraldry, was often used on the Vere plate and furnishings. Earl John was clearly very fond of this badge, for he also used two calygreyhounds as supporters of his arms on his last three seals (Figure 28). Another badge he used extensively was an eagle with wings displayed and with 'an angel's face', and not, therefore, a harpy. Obviously this was highly regarded by him, for we find one example inventoried as 'a splayde Egle of gold with an angell face with six dyamoundes and eleven perles, with four Rubies'. Other badges used by Earl John about his house were a cranket, an instrument used by soldiers to stretch crossbows; an ox crossing a ford, again a play upon his title; and a Chair of Estate, being the badge of his office of Lord Great Chamberlain.

The creatures depicted on either side of a shield in a medieval seal of arms were essentially a decorative way of filling in the spaces, and not true supporters. As often as not they were the 'beast' or badge of the owner of the arms. It is, however, noticeable that the beasts, birds and reptiles used as badges during the fifteenth century often became the armorial supporters of the family arms during the sixteenth century. For example, Edward de Vere, 17th Earl of Oxford (1550–1604) used the Blue Boar for his dexter supporter and the 'Eagle with an Angel's Face' for his sinister supporter. The Blue Boar is still to be seen as the sign of many an inn in Essex, where the ruins of their seat, Castle Hedingham, remains a memorial to the family's power.

It is a very long way from the Bear and Ragged Staff badge of Warwick the Kingmaker, which he used extensively during the Wars of the Roses, to the present-day badge of the Football League (Figure 29), but it underlines the continuing vitality of heraldry.

Colour was everywhere in the Middle Ages. When we stand today in our cathedrals and parish churches, with their plain stone walls, it is difficult to imagine the exciting colours our ancestors saw there. Then the walls would have been plastered and painted with scenes from sacred history, with figures of archangels and saints, the seven deadly sins and many an allegorical lesson, displayed like a modern strip-cartoon, for the education of the faithful. The glory of colour, the bright reds, blues, greens and golds, would grip their imaginations. While the peasantry wore plain homespun clothes those not much further up the social ladder wore colourful garments, and the brilliantly illuminated manuscripts which

Figure 29   Badges of the Football League (*left*) and Warwick the Kingmaker (*right*).

beguiled the leisure hours of the nobility and gentry attested, too, to their love of colour. Jousts and tournaments were the occasion for the flamboyant display of heraldic emblems on banners, shields and horse-trappers, and people also made full use of armory in the decoration of clothes as well as houses.

The earliest existing heraldic manuscript is the *Historia Anglorum*, written by Matthew Paris, a monk of St Albans Abbey, about 1244, and copiously illustrated by him with painted shields of arms. From then onwards there is a magnificent series of painted rolls of arms, mostly compiled by heralds. Some are 'general rolls', many beginning with foreign sovereigns or the Nine Worthies of the World, and continuing with English lords, bannerets, knights and squires, with several foreign nobles; others are 'occasional rolls' recording the names and arms of those who were present on a particular occasion, such as a battle, siege or tournament. Sometimes, as in the *Military Roll of Arms*, they are illustrated with mounted knights jousting.[9] The magnificent armorial history of the Earls of Warwick, known as the *Warwick* or *Rous Roll*, was drawn and painted between 1477 and 1491 by John Rous, a chantry priest;[10] and the *Livre des Tournois* of good King René, complied a few years earlier, is a beautifully illustrated book.

As each artist made and mixed his own colours in the Middle Ages there was, naturally, no standard tint or shade of colour used in heraldic art, and it is this which has given it such a lively variety. To this day no special shade of colour is laid down and the artist is at liberty to use such tint as seems most appropriate for the particular purpose, so long as it is a good clear colour which cannot be mistaken for any other.

The principal tinctures of heraldry consist of two metals (gold and silver), four colours (red, blue, black and green) and two furs (ermine and vair). There are some rarer colours, such as purple, and some complicated variations on the two furs, which we need not bother about here. The colours and furs are discussed in more detail in the Glossary (pp. 242–60).

One of the more important rules of armory is never to put metal on a metal or a colour on a colour. This is a common-sense rule because, for example, a blue charge on a black field would be very difficult to make out at a distance. As with all rules there are, however, one or two exceptions. The arms of the crusader Kingdom of Jerusalem are the most famous exception and they are quoted in almost every book on armory written since the early Middle Ages. The anonymous herald who wrote *De Heraudie* shortly before 1300 mentions them, adding that it is normally a bad practice to put the colour gold on argent.[11] The Kingdom of Jerusalem's arms were *Argent, a cross potent between four crosslets or.*

Heraldic art has naturally been influenced by the cultural trends of its period, from the primitive simplicity of the twelfth century, through the romantic revival of the fourteenth, when 'round tables' became popular with the Arthurian revival, to the extravagantly flamboyant fifteenth and sixteenth centuries, and it reflected the art of all of these periods. The rot set in with the age of reason and heraldic art in England went into a decline which brought it well-earned discredit until recent times. The invigorating artistic challenge of today has led the present generation of officers of arms to encourage our herald painters to try out new ideas in the painting and presentation of the armorial artwork now being produced by the College of Arms. There are some eight artists working full time for the College, and the officers can also call on the assistance of several outside artists. But in no case will an officer of arms sign and certify a painting of an armorial achievement unless it is on record in the official registers of the College of Arms. There are many firms who advertise that they will produce paintings of 'arms for your name', but this is misleading. For example, there are dozens of different arms for different families of Smith, but unless a descent from a particular armigerous Smith can be proved a painting of those arms is no more than a piece of decoration.

THREE

THE BIRTH OF HERALDRY

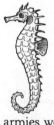N THE VERY EARLIEST times armies were remarkably small and tactics were of the most rudimentary kind, and the leader of a war-band had only to tell his followers what the objective was and then order them to follow him and get on with it. The Laws of Ine, King of Wessex (668–95), defined an army as being over thirty-five men, although this was an already archaic concept, based no doubt on the crew of an early longship, for English armies were larger than that by Ine's time. Even so, after battle was joined orders would probably have been given by voice or by hand signals. Battle fought on foot is a more static affair than one fought on horseback, and is thus somewhat easier for the commander to control.

By the time of the Battle of Hastings, in 1066, armies had increased considerably in size. The English were some 8,000 strong, all fighting on foot, although they used horses to get there. The greater numbers involved made even foot soldiers difficult to control, and King Harold was unable to stop two contingents of his army from breaking ranks to pursue bodies of Normans who had recoiled from the attack. The Normans were some 7,000 strong, of which about 2,000 were mounted knights and men-at-arms, and the rest foot soldiers and archers. William and his subordinate commanders had much difficulty in controlling their cavalry, for the early medieval knight was frequently rashly impetuous.

The introduction of the stirrup into western Europe made it possible to fight even more effectively from horseback, and this coincided with the beginning of feudalism. The feudal obligation, by which a landed estate was held of the king or an overlord by the service of one or more fully equipped and mounted knights, led to the formation of many independent military units of varying size, each under its immediate lord, and grouped under a ruler or greater baron as commander-in-chief. It soon became apparent that it gave a boost to *esprit de corps* if these feudal units had some emblem with which they could regard themselves as being particularly associated.

As the size of the armies increased, the voice would have only a very limited range in the din of battle and hand signals would not be easy to see. It seems reasonable to assume, therefore, that devices of an emblematic nature were first borne on pennons, gonfanons and banners, affixed to the head of a lance. In the mêlée of the medieval battle a flag held aloft would be readily seen by a lord's men, whereas devices painted on shields, which would be facing the enemy, would be invisible to them. The object of displaying emblems in battle, then as now, was not to assist the enemy by telling him who you were, but to give your followers a rallying point, to enable them to keep an eye on their commander and watch for his signals. There are several references to banners being used by inclining them one way or another, to convey orders. Banners and pennons thus became associated with particular lordships as well as with their owners.

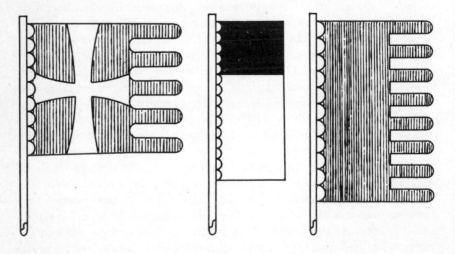

Figure 30
(i) Gonfanon of the Hospital of St John of Jerusalem

(ii) Banner of the Knights Templar

(iii) The Oriflamme of France

At first these battle flags seem to have been of one colour only. The most famous of all was the Oriflamme—red without any charges on it—which was kept in the Abbey of St Denis and only unfurled when the French declared war on a foreign enemy. However, there is only a limited range of colours suitable for flags and the possibility of single-colour banners being duplicated and thereby causing confusion, led to banners being differentiated by dividing them or placing inanimate or animate objects on them (Figure 30). In time this gave rise to a more systematic treatment of these emblems and, because people tend to be conservative, they became hereditary. Thus heraldry, as western Europeans have known it for the last eight hundred years or so, came about.

What I am suggesting is that it was on banners, gonfanons and pennons that emblems of a heraldic nature were first depicted, and that these devices were subsequently used on seals, which were important for authenticating charters and deeds of gift. It was, I suggest, the rise in popularity of tournaments during the later years of the eleventh and during the twelfth centuries that led to knights having their devices painted on their shields; for in a tournament the identification of one's opponents and friends was important.

Because of the social significance of tournaments, people have tended to regard shields as more important than banners, and to assume that the latter were merely a reflection of the former. While there are innumerable examples throughout the Middle Ages of the same device borne on both shield and banner, there are many examples where the two differ markedly. The one most often quoted in books on heraldry, and thus best known, is the case of the de Montfort family. The members of this famous family, which included Simon de Montfort, Earl of Leicester, bore a lion rampant with a forked tail for their family arms — although the tinctures seem to have varied a little between the branches — while they bore banners *Party per pale indented gules and argent*; here again there seems to have been some variation in the tinctures. It has been thought that the Earls of Leicester bore it for their Honour of Hinkley, but in fact the French de Montforts also bore this banner (Figure 31).

Interest has been attracted to the ceremony of knighting because it carried with it military and social advancement and, except on the field of battle, was accompanied by impressive ceremonial and followed by martial displays and much junketing. A man who held no land could be knighted providing he qualified militarily and socially. The enfeoffment of someone with a barony or knight's fee was a different matter. There is reason to think that enfeoffment with a barony, however small, was signalled by the overlord handing to his knightly tenant a lance with a banner or pennon at its head symbolising the land being granted. It might well be that the design of the banner had been associated, since 'a time beyond which the memory of man runneth not', with that particular fief. There are also cases of barons who had inherited a second barony or an earldom using in battle the banner of the arms traditionally associated with it, as the men from the newly accrued barony would be used to fighting under those colours. This is a subject which deserves much further study.

Figure 31
Arms and banner of de Montfort, drawn from a window in Chartres Cathedral.

FOUR

HERALDRY AND THE KNIGHT

ERALDRY has been defined by Sir Anthony Wagner as a systematic use of hereditary devices centred on the shield, but we can do little more than speculate about its origins. What is clear is that its development was greatly influenced by the development of armour and battle tactics, so it is as well to have some idea of what knights of various periods looked like. The standard equipment of a knight in the early Middle Ages was simple. The Assize of Arms, promulgated by Henry II of England in 1181, laid down that 'whoever possesses one knight's fee shall have a hauberk [shirt of chain-mail], a helmet, a shield and a lance; and every knight shall have as many hauberks, helms, shields and lances as he possesses knight's fees in demesne.'[1] A knight's fee was the estate or manor from which the service of a fully armed knight was due to the King or overlord.

The Assize of Arms obviously lays down the minimal equipment for a knight. The sword was taken for granted – no well-dressed knight would be seen without one. He would also probably have two war-horses and a small following of some five or six men from his manor; a couple of grooms to look after the horses and victualling, a squire or two to look after his armour and weapons, and a man-at-arms and possibly an archer. About half of these were non-combatant. Their number would vary and so would their equipment, depending on the wealth of the knight. As with modern warfare, you needed a large administrative tail to keep the knight battle-worthy.

Armour and equipment changed very little during the eleventh and twelfth centuries, so our first examples have come from the Bayeux Tapestry, which was made a few years after the Battle of Hastings. It will be seen that the knights wore chain-mail hauberks, which reached down to the knee, split up the skirts to make them more convenient for riding. They must have been pretty heavy, as the Bayeux Tapestry shows two men carrying each hauberk on poles threaded through the arms, when loading the ships of the expeditionary army. To protect their heads, the knights wore steel helms with nose-guards. Although quite a lot of the face was exposed, it was already becoming difficult to identify them when they were wearing their helms, so Duke William had to lift up his helm to show his followers that he was still alive, when a rumour arose in the middle of the battle that he had been killed (Figure 2, p. 6).

One gets a clearer idea of the armour of this period from another picture in the Bayeux Tapestry showing Earl Harold of Wessex being knighted by Duke William (Figure 32), a custom which was not used in Anglo-Saxon England. Defensive armour was completed with a long, pointed shield with rounded top. The usual weapons were the sword and lance, although Duke William and Bishop Odo of Bayeux used a mace, a kind of iron-headed club. The lance was fairly light, and would either be couched under the arm and used for thrusting, or thrown overarm.

If it was difficult to distinguish one knight from another at the time of the Conquest, it became more difficult as time went on and the armour covered more and more of the face, and so some means had to be devised to identify knights. From the very earliest times flags or pennons of one kind or another had been borne in battle, so that the whereabouts of the commander could be seen. At the Battle of Hastings we see Duke William's gonfanon, borne on the end of a lance by Count Eustace of Boulogne riding beside him. Although the Norman shields are depicted with wavy lines or curious, rather dragon-like creatures painted on them, they were not recognisably heraldic in character, nor were any charges remotely resembling them borne by any of their descendants.

By the time of the First Crusade, which began in 1098, the leaders of the different contingents were certainly using banners which could readily be identified, such as those of Bohemond of Taranto, one of the leaders, and his nephew Tancred, soon to become Prince of Galilee, Count Raymond of Toulouse, and others. The army which set out so hopefully to wrest the Holy City from paynim hands was made up of contingents of varying size from all over western Europe. Those from the Norman principalities and lordships in southern Italy and from the Duchy of Normandy played a leading part in this hazardous enterprise.

Figure 32
Duke William knights Earl Harold in Normandy.

Robert Guiscard, a son of Tancred of Hauteville-le-Guichard, near Coutances in Normandy, began his remarkable career in Italy in 1047, the same year in which the young Duke William ended his minority and began his effective reign in Normandy. Robert's career carried him to the Dukedom of Apulia, and his younger brother Roger, 'the Great Count', to what later became the Kingdom of Sicily. Robert's son, Bohemond of Taranto, was commander-in-chief of the First Crusade and founded the Principality of Antioch, while Duke William had conquered the Kingdom of England.

In the regions which were to be specially affected by the Normans the developments which occured during these years were wholly remarkable ... Indeed it might reasonably be suggested that the alteration to the balance of power consequent upon the Norman impact upon England was among the causes of the special characteristics of the culture of Western Europe in the twelfth century. The Normans, by linking England more closely to Latin Europe, may have helped the Romance-speaking lands to achieve that dominance in western culture which they exercised during that brilliant and productive period.[2]

The association between the Normans of southern Italy and the Papacy, which was to have such far-reaching consequences, also resulted in the Pope being regarded as a kind of spiritual overlord, symbolised by the presentation by him of consecrated banners, in the same way as a feudal lord would hand to his vassal, on enfeoffing him, a lance, to the head of which was affixed a pennon or gonfanon with an appropriate device. In 1061/2 Pope Alexander II gave his blessing and a banner to the Normans fighting in Sicily. Just before the invasion of England, the Pope gave Duke William a consecrated banner, while in 1081 Robert Guiscard fought under a papal banner when he captured Durazzo.

We know that recognisably heraldic devices were already in use by 1127, when Henry I knighted Geoffrey of Anjou prior to his marriage to Henry's daughter, the Empress Matilda. The King invested Geoffrey with a mail hauberk and shoes of mail, and hung about his neck a blue shield painted with six little golden lions; he then handed Geoffrey a lance, a sword and a war-horse. Now it is obvious that armory did not emerge fully developed, like Aphrodite from the sea. It must have been evolving for at least a generation. One cannot help thinking, therefore, that the Normans, possibly of the south, might provide pointers to the origin of European armory.

Armorial devices were at first only used by rulers and greater barons. Anna Comnena described the shields of the crusader knights which she saw in 1096 as being 'smooth and shiny', and makes no mention of any designs being painted on them. It would seem that the fanciful, non-armorial designs on the shields of the Normans, carried at the Battle of Hastings and illustrated in the Bayeux Tapestry, were being abandoned by this time but had not yet been replaced by truly armorial designs. In 1136 the ordinary knights were not yet using armorial devices on their shields and surcoats, for the author of the *Gesta Stephani* said that at the siege of Exeter Castle 'among so many clad in mail it was impossible easily to distinguish one from another'.[3]

We know that in the First Crusade the commanders of the various contingents had banners which could be readily recognised as being personal to themselves. The author of the *Gesta Francorum* tells us that:

When the amir who was in charge of the citadel [of Antioch] saw Karbuga and all the others fleeing from the battlefield before the Frankish army, he was much afraid, and he came in a great hurry to ask for a Frankish banner [as a sign of protection]. The Count of St Gilles, who was there keeping watch outside the citadel, ordered his own banner to be delivered to the amir, who took it and was careful to display it upon his tower. Some men from southern Italy, who were standing by, said at once, 'This is not Bohemond's banner.' The amir questioned them, saying, 'Whose is it?', and they replied, 'It belongs to the Count of St Gilles.' The amir came and took the banner and gave it back to the Count, and just then the noble Bohemond [commander-in-chief of the army] came up and gave him his own banner, which he accepted with great joy.[4]

In view of this, it would seem unlikely that Hugh of Vermandois, son of Henri I of France and most illustrious of the commanders of the First Crusade (even if he was an arrogant man, with a pretty indifferent military record), did not also have his personal banner.

This brings us to the important analysis of associated arms made by Sir Anthony Wagner, now Clarenceux King of Arms.[5] Hugh's son Ralph, Count of Vermandois, bore checky arms on his seal. His nephew, the lord of Beaugency, also bore a checky shield, and so did the descendants of his other sister, Isabel, with minor variations. The problem is whether Ralph's relations bore checky shields because they wanted to show solidarity with him, or whether these families adopted similar checky coats in order to commemorate and emphasise their descent from one of the (by that time) most famous commanders of the First Crusade. Common sense indicates the latter, particularly as Ralph was not exceptionally distinguished, and this leads to the presumption that Hugh of Vermandois may well have borne checky arms on his banner, if not on his shield.

To take another case, that of the quarterly coat borne, with differences, by the descendants of Aubrey II de Vere (born probably before 1090; died 1141): it is interesting to speculate as to who was the first to bear this coat. If it was the ruffianly and murderous Geoffrey de Mandeville, Earl of Essex (died 1144) who first bore it, then one might suppose that his relations adopted it to demonstrate their solidarity with him. Yet his brother-in-law, Aubrey III de Vere, 1st Earl of Oxford, was in some respects more important than Geoffrey de Mandeville. In 1142 Aubrey joined Geoffrey in a plot against King Stephen, but it was crushed and the two earls were arrested the next year. Aubrey soon afterwards switched sides to join Stephen. Geoffrey would seem to be altogether too turbulent and unreliable a man for anyone to wish to advertise an association with him instead of with the successful Earl of Oxford. These circumstances might well indicate that Aubrey II de Vere was the fount of these arms; but in the lack of firm evidence this is purely speculation and rests only on probable human behaviour.

There are other cases of early associated arms which would repay study. One such concerns the arms of the Earls of Chester, adduced by M. Léon Jéquier in his new edition of the *Manuel du Blason*.[6] The famous wheatsheaf arms, borne by the Earls of Chester, were also borne by the

Figure 33
William Longespée, Earl of Salisbury, drawn from his tomb in Salisbury Cathedral.

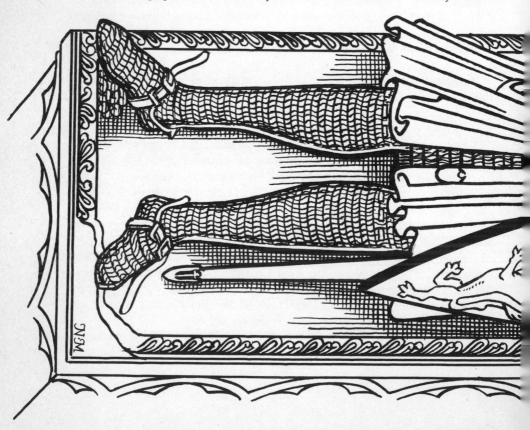

Seigneurs de Gerberoy and other families, who were all descended from Hugh II, Count of Clermont (d. 1103) whose daughter, Ermentrude, married Hugh d'Avranches, 1st Earl of Chester.

There are two theories which might explain these associated arms: one, the perpendicular theory, that arms were adopted in the earliest times to emphasise descent, in the male or female line, from an illustrious ancestor; the other, the horizontal theory, that a group of related barons adopted, pretty well simultaneously, similar arms to emphasise family solidarity. I incline to the former, on common-sense grounds, though I cannot prove it.

Henry II did not use the arms granted to his father, Geoffrey Plantagenet, but his illegitimate grandson William Longespée, Earl of Salisbury, Henry's bastard son by the Fair Rosamund, did adopt them. He died in 1226 and his splendid tomb can still be seen in Salisbury Cathedral. William's effigy gives one a good idea of how armour had developed by this time. Chain mail was still worn, but now it covered hands and feet as well as the main part of the body. William would have worn a steel helm in battle, which would completely conceal his face. Shields were still pretty large and designed for combatants to use when mounted. They were made of wood covered with boiled leather, which becomes remarkably hard

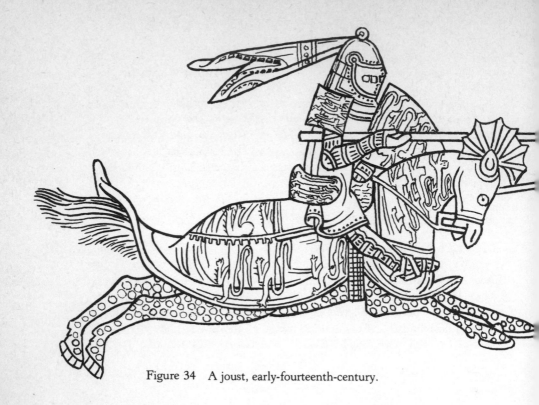

Figure 34   A joust, early-fourteenth-century.

when it dries; the Bayeux Tapestry has many pictures of knights with their shields stuck full of arrows. William's shield was painted with his arms, *Azure, six lioncels gold* (when there are more than three lions, they are called Lioncels). As will be seen, the surcoat has now come into use, and the arms would almost certainly have been painted on it. As, however, the colours have entirely faded from the effigy the surcoat has been left plain in the drawing (Figure 33).

John, Lord of Joinville and Seneschal of Champagne, in his lively and perceptive *Histoire de St Louis*, has some interesting things to say about the heraldic practices of his day. He accompanied Louis IX of France in 1248 on his crusade to the Holy Land, and was on active service there until 1254. De Joinville recounts a conversation with Louis, in the course of which the King remarked that 'men ought to clothe and arm their bodies in such wise that men of worth and age would never say, this man has done too much, nor young men say, this man has done too little.' De Joinville goes on to say that he repeated this to Philip III (1270–85), Louis's son and successor,

the father of the King that now is, when speaking of the embroidered coats of arms that are made nowadays; and I told him that never, during

40

our voyage overseas, had I seen embroidered coats, either belonging to the King or to anyone else. And the King that now is [1309, when Philip IV was on the throne] told me that he had such coats with arms embroidered, as had cost him 800 *livres parisis*. And I told him he would have employed the money to better purpose if he had given it to God, and had had his coats made of good taffeta ornamented with his arms as his father had done.

From this it would seem that before the fourteenth century arms were painted on surcoats and horse-trappers, but de Joinville earlier mentions at a banquet which he attended at Saumur in 1241 'there were a great quantity of serjeants bearing on their clothing the arms of the Count of Poitiers embroidered in taffeta'. As de Joinville was aged eighty-five when he wrote his chronicle, his memory may have slipped a little. Another incident, which took place during the invasion of Egypt and which gives a lively picture of the use of heraldry at that time, is graphically described by de Joinville. He was ordered by King Louis to 'land by the ensign of St Denis, which was being borne in another vessel before the King.' This was, of course, the Oriflamme, the famous scarlet battle flag of the French. He goes on to recount that:

at my left hand landed the Count of Jaffa ... of the lineage of Joinville. It was he who landed in the greatest pride, for his galley came all painted, within and without, with escutcheons of his arms, which are, *or, a cross gules patée*. He had at least three hundred rowers on his galley, and for each rower there was a targe with the Count's arms thereon and to each targe was a pennon attached with his arms wrought in gold.[7]

Chain-mail continued to be worn in battle and tournaments until the latter part of the fourteenth century. Our next example shows Sir Geoffrey Luttrell, of Irnham in Lincolnshire, who died in 1345 and for whom the beautiful Luttrell Psalter was made, about 1320–40, which is now in the British Library (see Figure 4, p. 8).[8] Sir Geoffrey is getting ready to take part in a tournament. Most of his armour is chain-mail, but now steel greaves have been added to protect his legs, and he is also probably wearing a steel rerebrace to protect the upper arms. His great helm is being handed to him by his wife, together with his lance with its triangular pennoncel bearing his arms. This indicates that he was an ordinary knight, or bachelor. The more senior commanders, knights bannerets, barons and upwards, had rectangular banners. Sir Geoffrey's surcoat is painted or embroidered with his family arms, *Azure, a bend between six martlets argent*, as is his horse-trapper, the cloth covering the horse. His arms are also painted on the fan-like crests on his great helm and on his horse's head. His wife's dress is embroidered with the arms of Luttrell impaling those of Sutton, her father's arms, *Or, a lion rampant vert*. His daughter-in-law Beatrix has her dress embroidered with Luttrell impaling Scrope, *Azure, a bend gold*, her father's arms. She is handing Sir Geoffrey his shield bearing the Luttrell arms. It will be seen that shields are becoming much smaller.

The kind of joust in which Sir Geoffrey took part is also illustrated in the Luttrell Psalter and the spirited picture shown as Figure 34 gives a good idea of it. By this time the lance had become longer and heavier and was only used couched under the arm, the combined weight of horse and rider behind it being relied upon to break up an enemy formation.

The last example is of Sir Thomas Montagu, Earl of Salisbury and Knight of the Garter. He was as famous a soldier as William Longespée (from whom he was not, however, directly descended), and one of the great generals of the Hundred Years War. He was killed in 1428 during a campaign against Joan of Arc. The picture shown here was done some years later, about 1488, for the *Wrythe Garter Book*,[9] so it shows Sir Thomas in the kind of plate armour that was worn during the Wars of the Roses. By about 1360 shields were no longer used in battle, but only in tournaments. The knight was by now completely encased in plate armour, from top to toe. This was enormously expensive, so that only the wealthy could afford to take part in tournaments. In this case the Earl of Salisbury is dressed for the joust, with his tilting helm beside him. The coat of arms and his banner show the arms of Montagu quartering Monthermer (Figure 35).

As the penetrating power of the English long-bow and the Continental cross-bow increased, armour became thicker and heavier, so that there came a time when a knight who had fallen down had the greatest difficulty in regaining his feet. By Tudor times armour was being rapidly discarded, except for jousts, so that the need for armorial emblems also diminished. The growth of professional armies, which eventually superseded the indentured troops of the later Middle Ages, finally removed the need for personal devices in war.

Figure 35
Thomas Montagu, Earl of Salisbury.

FIVE

'WHAT DO THEY MEAN?'

O MANY PEOPLE expect a coat of arms to tell a story and feel cheated if the herald to whom they put this question has to reply that he does not know why a particular design was selected for the arms of a particular family. Yet more often than not there is no clue at all. In the very early days of heraldry the barons selected simple, geometrical devices because these were easy to distinguish on gonfanon or shield in the mêlée of battle, with the dust kicked up by the horses' hooves and the sweat running into men's eyes. Before long punning, or 'canting', arms became popular. John de Bado Aureo, whose *Tractatus de Armis* was written about 1395, said that it was important to study the characteristics of heraldic charges because these should recall the qualities of the original possessor of the arms. In another place, he says, 'whenever a man makes a petition for arms or some device, it is necessary to know about the man's habits, and thus can arms be suggested for him.'[1] Nicholas Upton, writing in 1446, gives two instances of squires whose valour in battle was rewarded by grants of arms. During the Battle of Verneuil in 1424 a household squire of the Earl of Salisbury (whose portrait is depicted in Figure 35, p. 43), had been 'maymed so in his privi partes that he was unable for generation', so Upton therefore granted him *Argent, three ox heads caboshed sable*, because plough-oxen were gelded and 'therefore oxen or theyr heddes batokeneth that the berer of theym fyrste was gelded.'[2]

It would, of course, be wrong to think that every coat of arms tells its story and that the charges on a shield have a special significance. Many obviously do not but it is surprising how many ancient arms have some kind of punning allusion to their owner's name. For instance, the three sharply pointed red fusils in fess of the Montagues are a play on the name Montaigu, the pointed hill which provided the place name of the manor in France after which they were called. The medieval English family of Hopwell who derived from the manor of that name in Derbyshire bore for their arms *Argent, three conies* [rabbits] *gules each playing a pipe*, as charming an armorial conceit as one could wish (Figure 36).[3] There are many other examples of canting or allusive arms, also termed *armes parlantes*, but there is only space to touch here on a few of them. Sir Thomas Lucy of Charlecote in Warwickshire, whose principal claim to fame is that he imprisoned the young Shakespeare for poaching his deer,

Figure 36 (*right*)
Arms of Hopwell.
Figure 37 (*below left*)
Arms of Lucy of Charlecote.

Figure 38 (*below right*)
Arms of the Kingdom of Castile and Leon.

bore *Gules, semée of cross crosslets three luces* [pike] *hauriant argent* (Figure 37). Sir Robert de Setvans, whose brass memorial of about 1305 is to be seen in Chartham Church, Kent, bore winnowing fans for his arms. Ferdinand III, King of Castile (1217) and Leon (1230–52) was the first to quarter the triple-towered castle of Castile with the lion of Leon, *Quarterly 1 and 4, gules a triple-towered castle or, and 2 and 3, argent a lion purpure,*[4] a beautiful coat which says it all simply and neatly (Figure 38). These two arms first appear about the middle of the twelfth century and are thus some of the oldest of the European royal arms.

Where medieval arms are concerned we must rely on conjecture, supported by long experience, to identify the point of an armorial allusion. Some are so obvious that they jump out at you, but many others are subtle and require some acquaintance with the medieval sense of humour, robust and much given to punning. The following examples are taken from the fifteenth century to modern times and demonstrate the remarkable flexibility and vitality of heraldry.

During the Middle Ages trade had been the occupation of the bourgeoisie, while the magnates and the country gentry lived off their lands and rents, sending their younger sons to the Inns of Court to become lawyers, or arranging other official appointments for them. Towards the end of the Middle Ages younger sons were being apprenticed to the great merchants of London, York and the main centres of trade. This was unheard of in France and most western European countries, where to engage in trade meant loss of the privileges enjoyed by the *noblesse*, loss of status and consequent loss of arms, and loss of exemption from many forms of taxation. In England it was not regarded as reprehensible for a gentleman to engage in trade and this explains why, down to modern times, so many have gone into business, made their money and bought estates in the country to which they have returned. The mayors and aldermen of the City of London, for example, have always been armigerous. The earliest existing English grant of arms is that by William Bruges, the first Garter King of Arms, to the Worshipful Company of Drapers of the City of London, on March 10th, 1438/9. Throughout medieval Europe the burghers formed societies, known as guild-merchants, which governed the towns. In time these gave way to craft guilds, which were concerned with a particular craft or trade. Those in London, like the Drapers, exercised considerable power.

A parallel mercantile development, with its origins in the reign of Edward I, was the 'Staple', a term applied to those towns appointed by the King as the centres for the trade of those merchants who had been granted a monopoly in the export of the staple commodities of England, wool, leather, tin and lead. With the opening up of the sea routes to the Levant and to Africa, to Russia, the East Indies, and especially to the New World, the Staple with its archaic monopolistic practices proved unsuitable to finance the trading voyages across the world, or to handle the greatly enlarged two-way trade. The Merchants of the Staple of Calais were incorporated by Edward III and bore for their arms *Barry nebuly of six argent and azure, on a chief gules a leopard or.*[5] The barry field clearly alludes to their maritime interests and the leopard, from the English Royal Arms, to the fact of royal patronage, no doubt obtained at a price.

By Tudor times the restless English merchants found their acquisitive enterprises better served by the formation of chartered companies, each having monopoly rights to trade with a particular country or region, rather than being confined to a particular commodity. Through the sixteenth and seventeenth centuries one chartered company after another was being incorporated, with a consequent grant of arms.

The Worshipful Company and Fellowship of the Merchant Adventurers Trading to Muscovia, commonly called the Muscovy Company or the Russia Merchants, were incorporated in 1555, and were granted arms of some complexity but much allusive significance.[6] One of the most important of the great trading companies was the Company of Merchant Adventurers trading to the Levant, otherwise called the Turkey Merchants. Granted a royal charter in 1579 by Queen Elizabeth, they flourished down to modern times. The arms they were granted on their incorporation bear comparison with some of the more deplorable nineteenth-century grants, and demonstrate the armorial dangers of trying to paint a picture on a shield, instead of using it as a vehicle for allegory and allusion. Their arms were *Azure, on a sea in base proper a ship with three square rigged masts or, the sails banner and pennants argent each charged with a cross gules, sailing between two rocky cliffs or, in base a seahorse proper, a chief invected argent* (Figure 39).[7]

Figure 39
Arms of the Levant Company.

The most famous of all the trading companies was the East India Company, which was incorporated by a royal charter dated December 31st, 1600, and 'the Governor and Company of Merchants of London trading into the East Indies' were granted sole trading rights in the area east of the Cape of Good Hope and west of the Straits of Magellan—in short all the countries bordering the Indian and Pacific Oceans. Unauthorised interlopers were liable, if captured, to forfeit their ships and cargo. It speaks worlds for the wonderful self-confidence of the Elizabethans that they could think in such sweeping terms. The first Governor was Sir Thomas Smith and there were 145 shareholders, with a capital of £72,000. Sir Thomas was the grandson of Sir Andrew Judd, one of the founders of the Muscovy Company, and he was himself a considerable figure in the City of London and promoter of several voyages of discovery, including that for the North-West Passage. He was also one of the founders of the Virginia Company, whose arms were later adopted by the State of Virginia.

In their Letters Patent, dated February 6th, 1600, the English Kings of Arms recited the fact that the 'Worshipful Company of the Merchants of India, who lately have to their great charges, with hazard of their ships, goods and lives [been made] a body politicke and incorporated ... by the name of The Governor and Company of Merchants of London trading into the East Indies', and granted them the following arms: *Azure, three ships gold, under all their sails garnished with crosses gules, and upon a chief or between two roses proper an additament out of the Arms of England, quarterly azure and gules in the first and last one flower de luce or, and in the second and third a lion passant guardant of the same.* For crest *A sphere or globe celestial between two standards of St George*, and for supporters *Two sea lions gold and azure*. These very attractive arms tell the whole story and the allusions are obvious (Figure 40).[8]

The East India Company grew in size and wealth to such an extent that rival merchants, known as 'interlopers', flocked to India to make their fortunes, in despite of the Company's royal charters. The matter came before the House of Commons, and the upshot was that the Company and their principal rival were amalgamated by Act of Parliament in 1698. By Letters Patent dated October 7th, 1698 the Kings of Arms granted the new Company the following arms: *Argent a cross gules, on a shield in the dexter quarter the arms of France and England quarterly within a compartment adorned with an Imperial Crown proper*, and for supporters, *Two lions guardant gold and each of them holding a banner argent charged with a cross gules*.[9] These arms have the merit of simplicity and emphasise the close links which had grown up between the Company and the Crown (Figure 41).

The great trading companies of Elizabethan and Stuart times laid the foundations on which the British Empire was built in Victorian times, and

Figure 40   First arms of the East
India Company.

Figure 41   Second arms of the
East India Company.

the heraldry of these companies has reflected their aspirations, interests
and importance. There are, however, many more personal arms which
reflect some event of private or public interest.

Louis Caerlyon was probably born a little before 1450 and may well
have derived his name from the ancient village of Caerleon in Monmouth-
shire, for his life-long connection with the Tudors points to a Welsh origin.
He was a Master of Arts of Cambridge University in 1466 and a Doctor of
Medicine by 1481, about which time he was appointed physician to
Margaret, Countess of Richmond, the wife of Edmund Tudor, Earl of
Richmond, and to their son Henry, the second Earl who subsequently
became King Henry VII. In 1485 he was imprisoned in the Tower of
London by Richard III, obviously because of his Lancastrian connections,
but the defeat and death of Richard that year saved his life. He is reputed
to have acted as intermediary in the negotiations for the marriage of Henry
VII to Elizabeth, the daughter of Edward IV. Henry did not forget his
faithful physician and shortly after his accession he granted Caerlyon 40
marks a year for life out of the issues of Wiltshire, with a further pension
the following year, and in 1488 appointed him 'one of the Knights of the
King's alms in the free chapel or church of the College of St. Mary the
Virgin, and Saints George the Martyr and Edward the Confessor in
Windsor Castle' — what are now known as the Military Knights of
Windsor.[10]

In February 1494/5 he was paid £2 as physician to Queen Elizabeth, the

49

wife of Henry VII, but Louis Caerlyon was not only a notable physician but also achieved fame as an astronomer and mathematician, and was a great collector of astronomical manuscripts, which he transcribed and annotated himself. He presented copies of his astronomical tables to the Universities of Oxford and Cambridge. [11] He was knighted in October 1492. On July 25th, 1493 'Sir Louis Caerlyon, kt., Doctor of Medicine' had a grant of arms from John Wrythe, Garter King of Arms.[12] The Letters Patent open with the usual Tudor flourish, and go on to say in the curious Anglo-French of the period that by the report and testimony of several worthy men 'Messire Louis Caerlion, Chevalier et docteur en Medecine a longuement sursuy les faitz de vertu et de noblesse'. The arms were *Per pale argent and vert, on a chief azure three estoiles argent*. The Tudor livery colours were white and green so this was most appropriate for a faithful old servant of the crown, while the three stars in a blue sky testified to his fame as an astonomer. His crest was '*ung orynall dedem son cage en leurs propres couleurs*'. The urinal, of course, alludes to his considerable reputation as a physician. It is the only occasion on which this unexpected object appears as a charge in English armory or, indeed, anywhere, but here again the heralds have neatly encapsulated his career in his armorial bearings (Figure 42).

There is one early seventeenth-century grant of arms which has baffled all my brother heralds because so little is known about the grantee. In 1604 the 'learned' Master William Camden, Clarenceux King of Arms, granted to William Jordan, of Chilterne and Whitley, in Wiltshire, the following arms: '*Azure crusilly fitchy, a lion rampant and a chief or*', and for crest: '*a football or with Percussa resurgo*', on a ribbon encircling it.[13] At the Visitation of Wiltshire and Dorset in 1623 a pedigree of three generations was recorded for 'William Jordan, de Chilterne and Whitley, co. Wilts, miles', and this includes a finely drawn trick of the arms and crest (Figure 43).[14] William Jordan is known to have become an undergraduate of Merton College, Oxford, in 1581, aged fifteen, and he graduated B.A. in January 1582/3, proceeding the next year to the Middle Temple to study law, but he does not seem to have been called to the Bar.[15] Apart from this nothing is known about him and there is even some doubt about his knighthood. His motto can be broadly rendered as 'Having been smitten [or knocked down] I arise again'. The bouncing football obviously alludes to the motto, but one would dearly like to know what episode in his life made Camden feel the football to be an appropriate symbol to commemorate it. There is an additional point of interest in this crest because it shows the way in which footballs were sewn together in Tudor and Stuart times, quite differently from today.

This use of a football as an armorial charge remained unique until modern times. Then on March 30th, 1949 the Football Association were granted arms, *Argent, semée of Tudor roses, three lions passant guardant in pale azure.*[16] The Football Association was founded in 1863 and is the governing body for the game in England, administering the rules, discipline, control of referees and the like, as well as being responsible for representing England in international football. In 1978, at the request of the Council, the Kings of Arms agreed that, in view of its status, a crest and supporters might be granted as well as a badge. It was accordingly decided to grant them as crest: *On a cap of maintenance azure turned up argent a peregrine falcon rising, belled and jessed, holding in the beak an English wild rose slipped and leaved, all proper.* The cap of maintenance was felt to be appropriate in that the F.A. is the governing body for the game, while the peregrine, the fastest of all the falcons and regarded as the most sporting of all medieval birds used in falconry, speaks for itself. For supporters they were granted: *On each side a lion party per fess argent and azure, charged on the shoulder with a Tudor rose and with the interior hind foot*

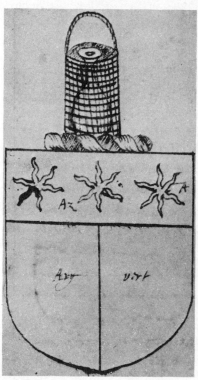

Figure 42
Arms and crest of Sir Louis Caerlyon.

Figure 43
Arms and crest of William Jordan.

resting on a football proper. The colours of the England international team are white shirts and blue shorts, so the colours of the supporters reflect these. For badge they were granted: *a representation of the Football Association Cup encircled by a chaplet of olive leaves proper*, the reward for the victor in ancient Greece.[17]

Meanwhile the Football League, to which are affiliated the ninety-two clubs in the four divisions, and which, while within the Football Association, is responsible for the principal domestic competitions within England, had petitioned for armorial bearings in 1973. On March 25th, 1974 the Football League were granted for arms: *Argent, on a cross gules a lion passant guardant between two lions' faces in pale or*. The St George's Cross and the lions allude to the fact that the Football League is responsible for organising the game in England. For crest they were granted, *On a grassy mount a football surmounted by a swift (Apus apus) volant, all proper*. The allusion here is self-evident. For a badge they were granted: *In front of a chain of twelve links in the form of an annulet argent a lion tricorporate the tails of the upper two bodies in chief or*. The twelve links represent the twelve clubs which originally formed the Football League, while a lion tricorporate, a pretty ancient charge in heraldry although very rare, is an appropriate allusion to a corporate body.[18] Football is, without any doubt, the most popular game in Britain and each week during the season attracts hundreds of thousands of spectators, and the banner of the Football League (twenty feet square) can be seen billowing in the breeze above Wembley Stadium. Thus we see heraldry playing its part in the modern world and fulfilling much the same functions as it did during the Wars of the Roses. Indeed, the parallel is sometimes a little too close for comfort. The Football League is also applying for badges on behalf of its affiliated clubs, which the League can then assign to particular clubs for their individual use. In most cases it has been possible to keep closely to designs which were already unofficially in use.

The arms of Admiral Nelson are frequently quoted in books on armory as the classic example of how to mess up a decent coat by piling one augmentation on top of another. Nevertheless, it is worth touching on these arms again because most writers have overlooked a strange coincidence. On October 28th, 1797, Rear Admiral Sir Horatio Nelson, Knight of the Bath, was granted for arms: *Or, a cross flory sable, a bend gules surmounted by another engrailed of the field, charged with three bombs fired proper;* and for crest: *The stern of a Spanish man of war proper thereon inscribed 'San Josef'.* On November 9th following he was granted armorial supporters of a sailor of the period, fully armed and holding a Commodore's flag and a Palm branch, and a Lion holding a broken flagstaff in its mouth with a Spanish flag.[19] On the same day Admiral Nelson signed the pedigree of his family, which had been recorded in the series of registers of pedigrees of Knights

Figure 44   (i) Arms granted to Rear Admiral Sir Horatio Nelson in October 1797.
(ii) Arms granted to Baron Nelson of the Nile in 1798. (iii) Augmentation granted
to Earl Nelson in 1805. (iv) Arms granted to Lady (Emma) Hamilton in 1806.

of the Bath.[20] This must be one of his earliest signatures with his left hand, after he lost his right arm during the abortive attack on Santa Cruz on the night of July 24th earlier that year. In 1798 he was created Baron Nelson of the Nile, and in reward for his services was granted an augmentation to his arms of *A chief undulated argent thereon waves of the sea from which a palm tree issuant between a disabled ship on the dexter and a ruinous battery on the sinister all proper.* He was also granted a second crest: *On a naval crown or the chelengk or plume of triumph presented to him by the Grand Signior,* while the supporters were given palm-branches to hold and the lion was also given a French tricolour flag to chew.[21]

After Horatio Nelson's death at the Battle of Trafalgar on October 21st, 1805, his brother William was created Earl Nelson of Trafalgar, and granted as a further augmentation to the arms *Over all a fess wavy azure thereon inscribed the word 'Trafalgar' or.*[22] This produced one of the messiest coats of arms conceivable. It certainly tells its story, but one feels it could have been said more subtly.

A year after Nelson's death Emma Hamilton, then residing at Clarges Street, off Piccadilly, in London, petitioned for a grant of arms to herself and her descendants, in consideration of the fact that during Sir William Hamilton's embassy to the King of the Two Sicilies she 'rendered great service at that Court during an important juncture as appears by the following clause in a codicil' attached to Nelson's last Will, as follows:

> Whereas the eminent services of Emma Hamilton, widow of the Right Honourable Sir William Hamilton, have been of the very greatest service to our King and Country to my knowledge, without her receiving any reward ... First that she obtained the King of Spain's letter in 1796 to his brother the King of Naples acquainting him of his intention to declare War against England ... Secondly, the British Fleet under my command could never have returned the second time to Egypt, had not Lady Hamilton's influence with the Queen of Naples caused letters to be wrote to the Governor of Syracuse that he was to encourage the Fleet being supplied with everything, should they put into any port in Sicily.

She was granted for arms: *Per pale or and argent, three lions rampant gules, on a chief sable a cross of eight points of the second*[23] a surprisingly simple coat compared to that of her adoring lover. The Maltese Cross is an allusion to the fact that she was a Dame Petite Cross of the Order of Malta (Figure 44).

Captain John Hanning Speke, the second son of William Speke of Jordans, near Ilminster, Somerset, who was born at Orleigh, near Bideford, in Devon, was descended from the ancient family of Speke of White

Lackington in Somerset, whose arms were *Argent two bars azure a double-headed eagle gules*; and for crest a *Porcupine statant proper*.[24] After Speke had discovered the source of the Nile he was granted, on October 28th, 1867, an honourable augmentation to his arms of *A chief azure thereon a representation of flowing water proper super-inscribed with the word 'Nile' in letters gold*;[25] he was also granted an additional crest of *A crocodile proper*. On the next day he was granted supporters to his arms to be borne 'for and during his life', in commemoration of his discovery, namely: *On the dexter side a crocodile and on the sinister side a hippopotamus both proper*.[26] Again, the design of the arms speaks for itself, and, apart from the chief, is not too bad a design. The interesting point about this last grant is that it is one of the very few occasions on which supporters have been granted as an honourable augmentation to one who was not a peer, K.G., or the like. There seems much to be said for reviving this practice.

There is one final example of *armes parlante* which merits a reference. In 1928 arms and crest were granted to Mr Noel McGrigor Phillips,[27] and the crest was *A representation of the dog that rescued William Phillips* [the great-grandfather of the said Noel McGrigor Phillips] *from the sea in Portsmouth Harbour on the fourth day of October 1789, sejant and reguardant resting the dexter fore paw on an escutcheon gules charged with a fleur de lys as in the arms*. It is an episode well worthy of immortality in a grant of arms and the gallant dog, whose name has, alas, eluded the pages of history, was stuffed after his (or her) death and admired by generations of visitors to the local museum. While a trifle the worse from the ravages of time it was, I am told, repaired not so long ago and is still to be seen.

SIX

ATTRIBUTED ARMS

 T AN EARLY STAGE in the development of heraldry we find arms being attributed to heavenly beings, or to mythological and historical persons who had existed well before armory was evolved in the western world. This was a logical development, because in the Middle Ages arms were invariably used by kings, princes and barons, so it followed that anyone in that position, however remote in time, would be expected to have borne arms. The designs for these arms were usually based on some Biblical, historical or literary reference or allusion, and never capricious.

Armory is a symbolic way of identifying an individual, so, when the Trinity, Christ, or even the Devil had to be identified in the illustration of a manuscript or, say, in a church, some kind of visual symbol had to be invented so that illiterate people (the bulk of the population) could readily recognise them. The fact that the well-known series of attributed arms was generally agreed throughout western Europe by the late twelfth century indicates that they must have evolved soon after armory itself came into use.

These attributed arms were probably invented by the twelfth-century minstrels and troubadours, who sang and wrote of 'the Matter of Britain', the cycle of Arthurian romances; 'the Matter of France', the *chansons de géste* which concerned the deeds of Charlemagne, Roland and the like; and of 'the Matter of Rome', which included the romances of Alexander the

Great. As many of the early heralds were recruited from the ranks of the troubadours, it is easy to see why these attributed arms are to be found in so many of the general rolls of arms throughout the Middle Ages.

The arms attributed to Christ, often called 'the Arms of Salvation', were made up of charges depicting the Instruments of the Passion – the Cross, the Nails, the Crown of Thorns, the Lance, the Sponge of Vinegar on the Reed, the Pillar of Flagellation and the Flagella. Often the medieval artist would try to squeeze them all on to one shield; at other times they were distributed among two or more shields. An interesting early example is the shield on the seal of the Vice-Custos of the Grey Friars at Cambridge, made about 1240 (Figure 45).[1]

Figure 45
Attributed arms of Christ.

Figure 46
Attributed arms of Satan.

Satan, as a former prince in the celestial hierarchy before his fall, was to the medieval mind a gentleman and, as commander-in-chief of the army of the damned, needed arms. The Book of Revelation was searched for a clue, and an attractive and interesting coat of arms attributed to the Devil: *Gules a fess gold between three frogs proper* (Figure 46).[2]

The Arms of the Nine Worthies of the World appear in many of the general rolls of arms compiled in all western European countries, as well as in contemporary romantic literature, so a keen armorist should be on nodding terms with them. William Caxton, in his preface to Sir Thomas Malory's *Le Morte d'Arthur*, printed in 1485, wrote:

It is notoriously known through the universal world that there be nine worthy and the best that ever were. That is to wit three paynims, three Jews, and three Christian men. As for the paynims they were tofore the Incarnation of Christ, which were named, the first Hector of Troy, of whom the history is come both in ballad and in prose; the second Alexander the Great; and the third Julius Caesar, Emperor of Rome, of whom the histories be well-known and had. And as for the three Jews which also were tofore the Incarnation of our Lord, of whom the first was Duke Joshua which brought the children of Israel in to the land of behest; the second David, King of Jerusalem; and the third Judas Maccabaeus, of these three the Bible rehearseth all their noble histories and acts. And Sith the Incarnation have been three noble Christian men stalled and admitted through the universal world into the number of the nine best and worthy, of whom the first was the noble Arthur, whose noble acts I purpose to write in this present book here following. The second was Charlemagne, or Charles the Great, of whom the history is had in many places both in French and English; and the third and last was Godfrey of Bouillon, of whose acts and life I made a book unto the excellent prince and king of noble memory, King Edward the Fourth.[3]

Many of the French and English treatises on heraldry, written in the fifteenth century, open with some statement to the following effect: 'As herodes [heralds] recorden, the beginninge and grownde of Armes was at the sege of Troy';[4] or that arms were originally ordained by 'le tres vaillant et victorieux Alixandre, roy de Macedoyne, le tres puissant troyan Hector, le tres prudent empereur Jules Cesar, et plusieurs aultres nobles princes'.[5] It would therefore have been assumed that these three worthy paynims would themselves have borne arms (Figure 47).

While there was general unanimity throughout Europe as to what these arms should be, one comes across variant forms. The commonest versions are these:

(i) HECTOR OF TROY

Sable, two lions combatant gold. These arms no doubt allude to the epic fight between Hector and Achilles in which the former was killed.

(ii) ALEXANDER THE GREAT

Gules, a lion gold, holding a battleaxe azure, and seated upon a throne argent. The lion, as the king of beasts, is an obvious choice, as is the throne, in allusion to the vast empire he ruled, but the significance of the battleaxe escapes me.

Figure 47 Attributed arms of the Nine Worthies of the World.

(iii) JULIUS CAESAR

Or, a double-headed eagle displayed sable armed gules. As the Holy Roman Emperors, who claimed to derive their authority as successors to the Roman emperors, bore these arms, it was natural for the medieval heralds to assume that Julius Caesar did so too.

(iv) KING DAVID

Azure, a harp gold. The field is sometimes gules. The arms allude, of course, to the well-known passage in the Bible, I Samuel, chapter xvi, verse 23.

(v) 'DUKE' JOSHUA

Lozengy argent and gules, a dragon sable. The tinctures of the lozengy field and of the dragon vary. Until the early fifteenth century, dragons had only two legs, but in English heraldry the four-legged variety gradually took over and the two-legged creature was called a wyvern, which is only another name for a flying serpent, as are all dragons. The significance of the arms is not known.

(vi) JUDAS MACCABAEUS

Gold, three ravens, wings elevated and addorsed proper. There is considerable variation in the arms attributed to him, the birds being sometimes two and sometimes three in number, and variously depicted as ravens or choughs, sometimes also with the wings closed. Here, too, the symbolism of the arms is obscure.

(vii) 'KING' ARTHUR

Two coats are attributed to Arthur, one being *Vert, a cross argent, in the first quarter the Virgin standing and holding the Child all gold*, the other being *Gules, three crowns in pale gold*, these being sometimes combined in a quarterly coat. The first coat alludes to the famous statement by Geoffrey of Monmouth in his *History of the Kings of Britain* written about 1138, that at the Battle of Mount Badon 'did he bear the shield that was named Pridwen, wherein, upon the inner side, was painted the image of holy Mary, Mother of God, that many a time and oft did call her back unto his memory'.[6]

(viii) CHARLEMAGNE

The Empire dimidiating France Ancient. Sometimes the coats are reversed. Although Charlemagne lived well before the time of heraldry, these attributed arms are quite logical.

(ix) GODFREY de BOUILLON

Jerusalem dimidiating gules an escarbuncle gold is often given for Godfrey in this context, but the well-known arms of the crusader

Kingdom of Jerusalem had not evolved by 1099 when Godfrey was elected King of Jerusalem, a title he declined, being styled *Advocatus Sancti Sepulchri* instead. He died there in 1100.

The well-known device of England, the red cross of St George, borne by English armies on many a hard fought field and famous the world over, is a bit of an armorial puzzle. The arms *Argent a cross gules* were attributed from a very early time to the Archangel Michael, commander-in-chief of the Heavenly Host (the only angel to be depicted wearing boots), who is painted in many a medieval manuscript with the red cross on a white field on his shield, surcoat and banner. He was also frequently depicted slaying a dragon. It would be interesting to know why a precisely similar device was attributed to St George, who was always a very minor saint.

One would have expected King Edward I, the foremost soldier of his day, to have selected the commander-in-chief of the army of God as the protector of England. However, during his Welsh wars in the last quarter of the thirteenth century, money was provided in the royal accounts to buy cloth to make arm-bands for the infantry, and these were to be marked with the Cross of St George.[7] A saint who brings mighty victories and wide territories is naturally regarded with affection, and from that time St George became one of the patron saints of England, and since Tudor times the only one. From the time of the First Crusade, St George had been held in great veneration by the Crusaders. At the siege of Antioch in 1098, during the First Crusade, he was believed to have intervened miraculously to aid the Crusaders, and a representation of the incident is to be seen above the south door of the Norman church at Fordington in Dorset, and the gonfanon at the head of his lance has a cross upon it. Richard Lion Heart, when on crusade in the Holy Land in 1191–2, is said to have had a dream that St George had assured him of his protection, which is why this saint was adopted as the patron of the English contingent. It is not clear why the provincial synod at Oxford presided over by Archbishop Stephen Langton, in 1222, ordered that the Feast of St George should be kept on April 23rd as a national holiday, although only as a lesser festival. One of the legends about St George, which obviously appealed to the chivalric notions of Edward I, who had gone on an abortive crusade in 1271–2, was that he had saved the life of a beautiful princess, who was about to be sacrificed to a dragon which was menacing her city. St George arrived in the nick of time and disabled the dragon with his spear, and it was led into captivity 'as it had been a meek beast and debonair' and its head was chopped off.[8] St George was chosen by Edward III as the patron saint of the Order of the Garter, whose first full meeting was held on St George's Day 1349. To this day The Queen impales the Royal Arms with those of St George, in her capacity as Sovereign of the Order (Figure 48).

61

Figure 48
The arms of H.M. The Queen as
Sovereign of the Garter.

Figure 49 (*right*)
The banners of the Trinity and the three
Patron Saints of England, as borne
at the Battle of Agincourt.

The patron saint of England had always been St Edward the Confessor, the last king in the direct male line of Alfred the Great, and he was much venerated, not only by the native English but also by their Anglo-Norman governors. Even after St George became the principal patron saint of England, St Edward the Confessor continued to be regarded, until the end of the Middle Ages, as almost equally important. The arms attributed to this saintly but ineffective king, beset by troubles and foes beyond his capacity to cope with, were *Azure, a cross flory between five doves or*. The gold doves are an appropriate emblem for this worthy king, who was buried in the great Abbey church of Westminster, rebuilt by Henry III in 1245, when the Confessor's arms were placed in it. It seems pretty clear that these attributed arms were inspired by a design on the reverse of St Edward's coinage, a cross between four doves.[9] English kings, in the later fourteenth and fifteenth centuries, were usually accompanied by several banners besides the Royal Arms when they went to war. At the Battle of Agincourt the King's command post was marked by the Royal Arms, St George, St Edward the Confessor, St Edmund King and Martyr and the Trinity (Figure 49).

Welsh attributed arms take us back to the laws and customs of Bronze Age Europe. The Celts emerge from the murk of pre-history about 2000 B.C., from their homelands in central Europe and, aided by their bronze weapons, this restless race soon spread throughout western Europe and the British Isles, as well as into Greece and Asia Minor. Strabo described them as 'madly fond of war, high-spirited and quick to battle, but otherwise

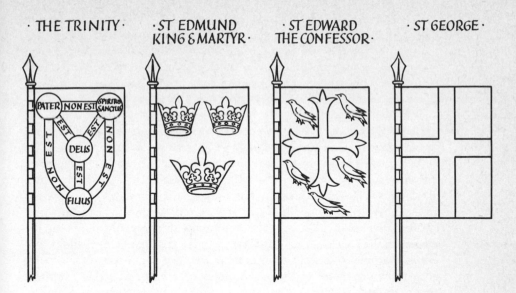

· THE TRINITY ·   · ST EDMUND KING & MARTYR ·   · ST EDWARD THE CONFESSOR ·   · ST GEORGE ·

straightforward and not of evil character'. This brave, bombastic, quick-witted people, with their two-horse chariots and better weapons, formed a warrior aristorcracy over the Neolithic peoples of the conquered lands, establishing their own laws and customs which were preserved, interpreted and adjudicated on by the Druids.[10]

Julius Caesar, writing of the Gaulish Celts, said that the Druids 'commit to memory immense amounts of poetry, and so some of them continue their studies for twenty years. They consider it improper to commit their studies to writing, although they use the Greek alphabet for almost everything else'. Among their feats of memory were of course the genealogies of the kings and chieftains. Until very recent years these traditional genealogies were regarded as unreliable, but when one pauses to reflect that a professional actor can commit to memory the plays, say, of Shakespeare, it is not unreasonable to expect a professional bard to commit to memory, with equal accuracy, a pedigree of anything up to thirty generations or more. In a barbaric and unlettered age memory is more tenacious, so that as the bard recited the deeds of his chieftain's ancestors, his audience would be quick to pull him up if he left out a generation or got the sequence wrong.

With the rise and expansion of the Teutonic tribes during the early years of the Christian era, the Celtic peoples were overrun or driven to distant corners of the wilder and more inaccessible parts of Europe. Of the remaining Celts the Welsh retained their ancient culture, organisation and system of land tenure more or less intact, and remnants of it still exist today. As Major Francis Jones, Wales Herald Extraordinary, says, the structure of Welsh society from very early times was essentially aristocratic, and it remained so until the destruction by Henry VIII of the legal concepts that buttressed it. The Welsh theory was that no one could be a freeman, inherit property, enjoy privileges, or be received into the community unless he could prove an agnatic ancestry for a certain number of generations.

He adds that certain legal processes demanded genealogy as a basic requirement, making it essential for Welshmen to know their pedigrees.[11]

At the same time, the petty principalities of Wales had an unexpected influence on Welsh heraldry. An aristocratic tribal society inevitably tends, in the early stages of its development, to be grouped in small self-contained areas. In Wales the basic unit was the 'commote', into which the whole country was subdivided, and the commotes undoubtedly represent the earliest area of Celtic tribal settlement under the rule of a chieftain. For example, in the county of Cardigan there were ten commotes. In the course of time two or more of these commotes became grouped in 'cantreds', either through dynastic marriages or through conquest, and several cantreds, for similar reasons, were grouped together into a traditional unit called a 'country' or *gwlad*. We are here talking about an heroic age, such as was described so excitingly by Homer, where the petty kinglet was larger than life. *The Cattle Raid of Cooley*, one of the greatest sagas of Iron Age Ireland, gives a vivid picture of this kind of society. Wales, throughout the Middle Ages, preserved much of this heroic pattern.

Until the Tudor steam-roller finally obliterated the ancient Celtic customs, the regality of the original Bronze Age conquerors continued to reside in the lordship of the commote, which was recognised in Welsh law as royal in character. The principal characteristics were the right to wage war and receive a third of the spoils, together with civil and criminal jurisdiction, both high and low. In Welsh law the terms lord, prince and king were synonymous. The lord of a commote was every inch a king, if only a very tiny one. When the Norman barons swept into the marches of Wales they took over the commotes along the march and therewith the regality of their former lands, where the English King's writ did not run, and the ancient right of waging local war was followed by the marcher barons with all the enthusiasm of their Welsh predecessors.[12]

The marcher lords were, however, also enfeoffed of vast estates in England and thus, as earls and barons of the Norman kingdom, were among the first to use armorial devices. When two different peoples with different cultural backgrounds impinge on one another, peacefully or forcefully, each is bound to influence the other. Intermarriage between families of the marcher lords and their Welsh neighbours was frequent; it is only in modern times that war inhibits social relationships between belligerents.

There is one fascinating example of uninhibited social intercourse across the lines at a very early period after the Conquest. A Norman marcher baron, Gerald of Windsor, was constable, for the King, of Pembroke Castle, which he defended valiantly against persistent Welsh attacks. During a truce about 1095, Gerald married Nest, the daughter of Rhys ap Tewdwr, Prince of Deheubarth (south-west Wales), no doubt in the hope of consolidating the peace with his powerful neighbour. They had three sons and two daughters. The elder sons, William and Maurice, were among the first of the Norman invaders of Ireland and founded famous families which became known by their patronymics, FitzGerald and FitzMaurice, with descendants existing to this day, while the third son, David, became Bishop of St Davids.[13] Their arms were *Argent, a saltire gules*, and these may have been in use as early as around 1100.

Gerald was subsequently granted the lordship of Pembroke and the castle, which he rebuilt in 1105 with a moat and a wall containing 'a gateway with a lock on it'. But love laughs at locksmiths, and a few months after its completion, Nest's cousin Owain ap Cadwgan stormed the castle one night and carried her off to his stronghold, together with her children. Gerald saved his life by hiding in a closet. By all accounts Nest was a pretty co-operative captive and her two illegitimate children with Welsh names, a son Howel and a daughter Gwladys, were probably the result of this escapade. Later Gerald got his own back, defeating and killing Owain and recovering his wife and family.

The chronology of Nest's amorous adventures is difficult to follow, owing to the lack of surviving contemporary records. At some stage she became the mistress of Henry I (who has the distinction of having sired a larger brood of bastards than Charles II), with whose co-operation she produced a son, known to his contemporaries as Henry the King's Son. It has been suggested that Nest had been Henry's mistress before marrying Gerald of Windsor, but it seems more likely that she came to Henry's libidinous attentions during one of Gerald's visits to the Court. Henry fitz Roy was later killed during an invasion of Anglesey in 1157, but left two sons, Meiler FitzHenry and Robert FitzHenry, who both achieved fame and fortune in the Norman conquest of Ireland.

Among Nest's other lovers was Stephen of Cemais (Kemys), constable for the Clares of Cardigan, by whom she produced Robert FitzStephen, who succeeded his father as lord of the cantred of Cemais. He also accompanied his half-brothers in the conquest of Ireland. He left three illegitimate sons who subsequently achieved some prominence.

Nest had two other bastards. One, William Hay or FitzHay, called in some documents William the Welshman, may have been the son of the lord of Hay on the River Wye, a Norman stronghold. The other, Walter, may have been by another father, but even less is

65

known about his antecedents.

The enthusiastic Nest must be a delight to the geneticists, because all those of her children and grandchildren whose histories are known turned out to be remarkably able, tough and successful – no doubt she fell in love only with able and successful men; or perhaps it was only tough characters who could handle her. On the other hand, those who believe that environment rather than genetics shapes the person can take some comfort from this instructive story: there is nothing like endemic border warfare for weeding out the weedy and teaching self-reliance.

Nests's grandson, Gerald of Barry, more usually known as Giraldus Cambrensis, the chronicler of his times, thought highly of his errant grandmother and was positively eulogistic about his cousins: 'Oh race! Oh family! sufficient of itself for the conquest of many kingdoms, but for the envy their energy excites.' He describes an occasion in Ireland in 1176 when some thirty related members of the family, mounted on splendid horses, displayed shields bearing the same arms.[14] This is a most interesting early example of the adoption of the same or similar arms by different members of related families, and evidence, too, that his Welsh cousins were by this time also using armorial devices.

It is reasonable to think that several of the Welsh princes and princelings, in the lands bordering the marches, probably adopted armorial devices during the twelfth century, and a few remaining seals from the later years of that century support this. Many more from the thirteenth century remain as evidence, and from the next century onwards armorial bearings were in general use throughout Wales. Later Welsh bards and heralds divided the armorial families of Wales into three distinct groups: the *advenae* or Norman and English adventurers who occupied the marcher lordships; the twenty-three Welsh royal dynasties and the many lords of commotes and cantreds, over 150 'heraldic ancestors'; and the lesser country gentry, as we should call them in England.

The striking feature of Welsh heraldry is, however, the remarkable number of attributed arms there are, and these evolved through the structure of Welsh society. As Major Francis Jones has explained,

A Welshman displayed arms because they proclaimed him to be the descendant of some particular ancestor – that was what really mattered. Accordingly Welsh heraldry acquired a dual purpose. In England a coat of arms was often entirely divorced from ancestry; in Wales it was the result of ancestry. The Welsh coat of arms is not merely a mark of gentility – it is the portrait of an ancestor.[15]

As it was generally thought in the Middle Ages that royal and tribal ancestors in Wales were armigerous, the bards assumed that they must have borne the arms which were currently being borne by their descendants. 'All ancestors were to have arms, and coats of many colours were bestowed upon Howel Dda who had lived in the tenth century, to Cadwaladr who had lived in the seventh, to Cunedda who had lived in the fifth, and to Beli Mawr who probably had never lived at all.' Major Jones adds that probably to distinguish between the different branches of a parent stock, we find the emergence of secondary 'heraldic ancestors'. A noted descendant of a primary 'heraldic ancestor' would have a particular coat attributed to him, sometimes based on the earlier coat, sometimes entirely different. The point that does arise from all this is that these traditional ancestors must have been of considerable importance in their day, for the memory of them to have persisted.

It is probable that the bards started to attribute arms to famous ancestors soon after arms began to be adopted by the Welsh princes and aristocracy, and that this process continued throughout the Middle Ages. By the fifteenth and sixteenth centuries, when these oral traditions and poems were being written down and heralds appointed in Wales, the opportunity was taken to bring some system and order to Welsh heraldry.

The most famous of these founding fathers was Cunedag, more usually known as Cunedda, who was indeed a genuine historic person. The crumbling Roman government of Britain was being threatened by foes on all sides, not least by Irish raiders and settlers at several places along the Welsh coast. At this time, it was Roman practice to transfer friendly tribes to threatened parts of their frontiers, granting them extensive lands and substantial privileges. Such a one was Cunedda who, with his eight sons and his tribesmen, was transferred by Stilicho, the last Roman Governor of Britain, from their ancestral lands beside the Firth of Forth to Anglesey and north Wales, about the year A.D. 400 (the exact date is uncertain, but it was before the last of the legions was withdrawn).[16]

Cunedda, who was a man of considerable ability, defeated and slew the leaders of the Irish settlers and their retinues, but no doubt enslaved their wives and families to work the captured farms. Before his death about the middle of the fifth century, Cunedda had established a kingdom covering Anglesey and north Wales, known as Gwynedd, stretching from the River Dee near Chester to the Teifi, at the mouth of which stands the present town of Cardigan. His descendants, who included many able and highly cultured kings, ruled this land, extending its frontiers from time to time, until for a period they exercised a hegemony over almost all Wales.

Very many Welsh families (and numerous English ones too) claimed descent from Cunedda, through either the male or the female lines, [17] so it is not surprising that the bards invented arms for him, and a very pretty, simple and dignified coat they produced: *Sable, three roses argent*, which is to be found illustrated in many a Welsh pedigree (Figure 50).

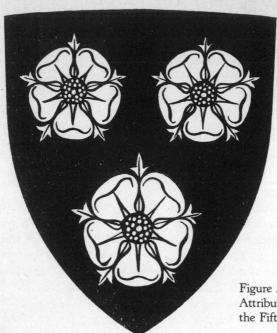

Figure 50
Attributed arms of
Cunedda, King in
Gwynedd about A.D. 400.

Figure 51 (*opposite*)
Attributed arms of the founders of
the Fifteen Noble Tribes of Wales.

So it was with the founders of the Fifteen Noble Tribes, as well as many another famous progenitor. The founders of the Fifteen Noble Tribes and their attributed arms were as follows (Figure 51):[18]

(i) HWFA ap CYNDDELW of Anglesey
Gules, a chevron between three lions rampant or. As he lived around 1100 to 1170, it is possible that these arms may in fact have been assumed by him. His family were hereditary stewards of the Princes of Gwynedd, having the right of placing the coronet on their heads at their investiture. There are several male line descendants living today.

(ii) LLYWARCH ap BRAN of Anglesey
Argent, a chevron between three crows statant close each holding in the bill an ermine spot. As Llywarch, too, lived in the twelfth century, these arms may well be actual. 'Bran' means a crow, and thus this is an example of typical medieval punning arms.

(iii) GWEIRYDD ap RHYS GOCH of Anglesey
Argent, on a bend sable three leopards' faces of the first. Here again we have a twelfth-century historic person, so these arms too may have been actually borne by him.

HWFA ap CYNDDELW

LLYWARCH ap BRAN

GWEIRYDD ap RHYS GOCH

CILMIN TROED-DDU

COLLWYN ap TANGNO

NEFYDD HARDD

MAELOC CRWM

MARCHUDD ap CYNAN

HEDD MOLWYNOG

BRAINT HIR

MARCHWEITHIAN

EDWIN of TEGAINGL

EDNYWAIN BENDEW

EUNYDD of GWERNGWY

EDNYWAIN ap BRADWEN

(iv) CILMIN TROED-DDU of Caernarvonshire
Quarterly, 1 & 4 argent, a double-headed eagle displayed sable; 2 & 3 argent, three brands enflamed gules; upon an inescutcheon argent a human leg sable. Troed-ddu means 'black foot'. As he flourished in the ninth century, these are attributed arms.

(v) COLLWYN ap TANGNO of Harlech
Sable, a chevron between three fleurs de lys argent. As he was a ninth-century chieftain, these are attributed arms.

(vi) NEFYDD HARDD of Nant Conway
Argent, a chevron sable between three spearheads also sable embrued with blood. This is another twelfth-century chieftain, so these arms may be actual.

(vii) MAELOC CRWM of Caernarvonshire
Argent, on a chevron sable three angels each kneeling on the sinister knee, the wings elevated and addorsed. He lived in the twelfth century, so that the same considerations apply.

(viii) MARCHUDD ap CYNAN of Caernarvonshire and Denbighshire
Gules, a man's head erased proper the brows bound round with a torse argent and azure. Marchudd was a tenth-century chieftain, ancestor of the Tudors. These are obviously attributed arms.

(ix) HEDD MOLWYNOG of Denbighshire
Sable, a stag trippant argent armed or. He lived in the late twelfth century, so here again these may be actual arms.

(x) BRAINT HIR of Denbighshire
Vert, a cross flory or. As he probably lived in the seventh century, these are attributed arms.

(xi) MARCHWEITHIAN of Denbighshire
Gules, a lion rampant argent. As an eleventh-century chieftain, his arms too are attributed.

(xii) EDWIN of TEGAINGL
Argent, a cross flory engrailed sable between four choughs proper. As he died in 1073, his arms are also attributed.

(xiii) EDNYWAIN BENDEW of Flintshire
Argent, a chevron between three boars' heads couped sable. Ednywain Bendew was another eleventh-century chieftain. The boars' heads allude to the legend that he killed three wild boars singlehanded.

(xiv) EUNYDD of GWERNGWY in Denbighshire
Azure, a lion rampant or. As an eleventh-century chieftain, his arms too are attributed.

(xv) EDNYWAIN ap BRADWEN of Merionethshire
Gules, three serpents interlaced argent. As a late twelfth-century chieftain, these may be his actual arms.

SEVEN

THE LOCOMOTIVE MERMAID

 HE MERMAIDS of the medieval bestiaries and of armory are creatures of the living world, sentient beings about whom one can speak in the present tense for, after all, heralds can claim to be on nodding terms with them. These strangely beautiful beings, the origin of whose pedigree is lost in the mists of mythology, are evidently born on the craggy coasts of distant lands, some say of the Mediterranean, within sound of the cicadas singing their cheerfully monotonous songs among the grey-green leaves of dusty olive groves. But the mysterious and forbidding world of 'the dragon green, the luminous, the serpent haunted sea' is their home, where they are 'gladde and merye in tempeste and sadde and hevye in fayre wether', where their siren songs are echoed by the wind playing its fatal tunes in the straining rigging of hard-pressed ships.

No proper biological study has been made of the life-cycle of the mermaid, let alone sociological or demographic studies. However, we have irrefutable evidence that they give birth to their young, like the generality of mammals, for there are pictures of them in two different medieval manuscripts. The Amesbury Psalter, written around 1250, has an excellent picture of a mermaid suckling her baby, while the Tenison Psalter, of slightly later date, has an even more charming illustration of a mermaid and her baby (Figure 52).[1] The Tenison Psalter was probably made for

Figure 52   Mermaid suckling child.

Alphonso, the elder son of Edward I, on his intended marriage with a daughter of Florent, Count of Holland in 1284.

The monkish illuminator, illustrating the manuscripts as they came from the hands of his brethren, murmuring to themselves in the abbey scriptorium like a hive of bees on a warm summer's day, would have had first-hand descriptions of mermaids from travellers from distant countries who stopped overnight in the abbey guest-house. 'I tell you, with these very eyes I saw it', and the traveller would then go on to recount how, on seeing the mermaids disporting themselves in the sea, the mariners in terror stopped their ears and threw an empty wine-barrel overboard for the mermaids to play with and thus, the mermaids' attention distracted, the ship escaped. One could not possibly disbelieve such stories, backed by such 'corroborative detail intended to give artistic verisimilitude to an otherwise bald and unconvincing narrative'.

But the mariners had good reason to be afraid of mermaids, because 'the Physiologus' himself, that great compiler of the earliest encyclopaedia, as quoted by Bartholomew the Englishman who himself wrote about 1230, said that 'with sweetness of song' they lulled 'shipmen' to sleep and then abducted them, bearing them away to a dry place to 'do the dede of lechery'. If the mariner refused or was too terrified to perform, the mermaid promptly ate him.[2] It is clear, therefore, that these alarmingly melodious creatures could not rely upon human beings to propagate their species. However, the mid-fourteenth-century illustrator of the *Roman de la Rose*, that immensely popular romance in verse of the triumph of erotic passion over sacred love, shows a merman and a mermaid embracing,[3] which seems to solve this problem.

Nevertheless, there were those who were not daunted by the more bizarre characteristics of mermaids, and many western European families

73

have harnessed them for armorial duties, including, most appropriately, the Byrons. One of the most enchanting portrayals of all is a rather jolly, fully locomotive mermaid, depicted in the margin of a very beautiful fifteenth-century copy of *Froissart's Chronicle*,[4] made for Philippe de Commynes, the French chronicler (1445–1509). Her upper, human, half is naked, as with all mermaids, and looking pertly adolescent, but she wears the tall 'steeple' hat much favoured by the fashionable Parisian ladies of the times. She is running along the ground on four short, furry brown legs which grow from beneath her pale blue fishy tail, and she is holding a banner of the arms of Philippe de Commynes, *Gules, a chevron or between three escallops argent, a bordure of the second*, quartering *Argent, on a chief gules three eagles displayed or* (Figure 53).

Figure 53   The Locomotive Mermaid.

EIGHT

THE HERALDRY OF HAITI

AITI, 'the mountainous country', was the name given by the original inhabitants to the whole island, of which the present state forms a part. These indolent and carefree people were brought with a jolt into the modern world by Christopher Columbus, who discovered the island in 1492 and named it Hispaniola. Within a generation the indigenous natives had been exterminated, and large numbers of slaves were imported from Africa to provide labour for the fruitful plantations and extensive mines of this lovely island. With the coming of Western civilisation the history of this once peaceful land has been bedevilled by murder, war and revolution.

By the eighteenth century the island had been partitioned between Spain and France, the latter holding the western end known as Saint Domingue. The fall of the Bastille in 1789 had echoes in the island, and the mulattos, descendants of French settlers and African women, who formed a substantial part of the population, demanded full civil rights, which were granted them. These were almost as quickly withdrawn by the National Convention in 1791, and the mulattos and slaves rose in revolt. After some years of chaos a Negro slave, François Domingue Toussaint, rose to prominence and restored order. He was an exceptional man by any standards, with military ability of a high order, and he was appointed Governor-General for life. In 1802 Napoleon decided to restore French rule and reintroduce slavery. He sent his brother-in-law, General Leclerc, with an army of 25,000 men to effect this, but failed to reduce the colony to submission and proposed terms which were accepted by Toussaint, who was then seized in spite of a guarantee of freedom, and sent to France where he died a few months after Leclerc had died of yellow fever.

Jean-Jacques Dessalines, another former slave, had been an active supporter of Toussaint, and took over leadership of the struggle against the French so successfully that they withdrew from the island in 1804 and never returned. Dessalines changed the name of the state to Haiti and had himself crowned as the Emperor Jean-Jacques I. Lacking the ability of Toussaint, his rule soon degenerated into tyranny of the most bloodthirsty kind, and his unhappy subjects rebelled and killed him.

The rebels had been led by another former Negro slave, Henry Christophe, who is believed to have been born in the British West Indian island of St Kitts (St Christopher). He was a man as remarkable as Toussaint, whose lieutenant he had been, but with boundless energy and outstanding administrative ability, to which he harnessed an ingenious and resourceful mind. This *coup d'état* was followed by a somewhat untidy period of civil war which was before long brought under control. A Council of State was convened and, on April 4th, 1811, it passed the *Loi Constitutionnelle*, which established Haiti as a kingdom. The President, Henry Christophe, was declared King of Haiti under the style of Henry I, and a stirring call on the loyalty of the people of Haiti was issued.[1]

Having ascended the throne of Haiti, King Henry I lost no time in buttressing it with a military establishement and a hereditary nobility. His first royal edict, dated April 5th, 1811, created a hereditary nobility. His next edict, dated April 8th, nominated this nobility, which consisted of four princes, seven dukes, twenty-one counts, thirty-five barons, and fourteen chevaliers or knights (also evidently hereditary). By other edicts he created an Archbishopric of Haiti; laid down what dress the various ranks of the nobility must wear; and created the Order of St Henry, which consisted of Knights Grand Cross, Commanders and Knights. He also reorganised the military commands of the kingdom, and the establishment of the Haitian army and navy.[2]

By another royal edict, undated but probably of May 12th, 1811, he appointed the Great Officers of State, including the Grand Almoner, Chancellor, governors of the palaces, chamberlains, secretaries and so on. Among these he established a College of Arms, under the general heading *Hérauts d'Armes*, consisting of one King of Arms and thirteen heralds, who took their titles from the principal towns of the kingdom.[3] These were:

Pierre Martin, King of Arms [of Haiti]
Germain, Cap Henry Herald
Baraquet, Sans Souci Herald

Jean Louis Narcisse, Fort Royal Herald
Simon Mancel, Port de Paix Herald
Louis Clement, Mole Herald
Jacques Thimotee, Gonaives Herald
Charles Chavanne, Saint Marc Herald
Leger, Port au Prince Herald
Hilaire Boisdore, Leogane Herald
Etienne Bastien, Jacmel Herald
Hyppolite Brangier, Dessalines Herald
Savary, Cayes Herald
Pierre Mouchet, Jeremie Herald.

Meanwhile, by a royal edict dated April 15th, 1811, King Henry had assumed armorial bearings to himself, and granted arms to the members of the royal family and to his newly created nobility. These are painted and also blazoned in the *Armorial Générale du Royaume d'Hayti*, which was acquired by James Pulman, Clarenceux King of Arms, who bequeathed it to the College of Arms on his death.[4] It is not known when or how he obtained it. Pulman was born in 1783 and worked as assistant to Sir Isaac Heard, Garter King of Arms, who had close interests in America. It is possible that he acquired the book after the *coup d'état* of 1820 which unseated King Henry. James Pulman was appointed Portcullis Pursuivant in 1822, Richmond Herald in 1838, Norroy King of Arms in 1846, and Clarenceux King of Arms in 1848. He died in 1859.

The *Armorial Générale du Royaume d'Hayti* is a manuscript book on paper, 7¼ by 10¼ inches. The drawings of the armorial bearings and the handwriting are of the early nineteenth century, and evidently were made soon after the royal edict of April 15th, 1811 granting arms to the new Haitian nobility. There is no indication of authorship, but it can probably be ascribed to one of the newly appointed heralds. The book begins with the arms of the King and the royal family, and proceeds through those of the princes, dukes, counts and barons to the chevaliers, and it may be of interest to describe some of the arms:

KING HENRY I OF HAITI

Arms: Azure semee of estoiles or, a phoenix crowned with the Royal Crown issuant from flames all of the second, in base on a ribbon [?or] the words 'Je renais de mes cendres'.

There is no crest, but the shield is surmounted by the Royal Crown of eight arches and encircled by the Collar of the Order of St Henry.

Supporters: Two lions guardant ermine each crowned with the Royal Crown.

Motto: Dieu, ma cause et mon epee (Figure 54).

Figure 54   Arms of King Henry Christophe of Haiti.

THE QUEEN
Arms: Azure semee of bees, but otherwise like those of the King, but
  without the Collar of the Order.
Supporters: As those of the King.
Motto: Dieu protege le Roi.

THE PRINCE ROYAL
Arms: As for the King, with a label of three points argent, and
  encircled by the Collar of the Order of St Henry and surmounted
  by a Royal Crown.
Supporters: As those of the King.
Motto: Les jeux de l'enfance annoncent les grands hommes.

THE CAPITAL CITY
Arms: Purpure, in base a warship with sails set upon the sea entering
  the port all proper.
There is no crest, and the shield is surmounted by a Royal Crown.
Supporters: Two figures of 'Hercules' sable clothed with lion-skins
  proper, and each holding in the exterior hand a club or.
Motto: Malgré les vents et les flots.

78

PRINCE NOËL
[Colonel of the Haitian Guards: Grand Butler]
Arms: Or, the Haitian flag upon a pikestaff, in chief three bees
   proper. There is no crest, but the shield is surmounted by a barred
   helm affrontee.
Supporters: Two ostriches argent each crowned with an 'antique
   coronet' gules.
No motto was given.

PRINCE JEAN [Grand Baker]
Arms: Or, the trunk of a tree [?erased] and broken off at the top with
   branches on either side vert, around the base of the tree the words
   'Ma souche fait ma gloire'.
There is no crest, but the shield is surmounted by a barred helm
   affrontee.
Supporters: Two buffaloes guardant gules collared argent the buckles
   azure.
No motto was given.

PRINCE EUGÈNE [not mentioned in the royal edict]
Arms: Azure a demi-lion rampant guardant and three estoiles in
   chief or.
   No crest was shown, but the shield is surmounted by a barred
   helm affrontee.
Supporters: Dexter a lion guardant proper, and sinister a horse
   argent.
Motto: Devouement au roi et à la patrie.

PRINCE DES GONAIVES [Lieutenant-General Andre Vernet, Grand
   Marshal of Haiti, Minister of Finance and of the Interior]
Arms: Or, a human eye proper between two sprigs of laurel crossed
   in base also proper.
No crest was shown, but a barred helm affrontee surmounts the
   shield.
Supporters: Two wild men proper each holding a club in the exterior
   hand also proper.
Motto: De la tête et du bras.

PRINCE DU LIMBÉ [Lieutenant-General Paul Romain, Grand Marshal
   of Haiti, Minister of War and Marine]
Arms: Or a crescent azure.
No crest was shown, but the shield is surmounted by a barred helm
   affrontee.
Supporters: The base of the shield rests upon two field-guns sable.
Motto: Les perils sont ses jeux.

PRINCE DE ST MARC [not mentioned in the royal edict]

Arms: Gules a comet the tail to the dexter or.

No crest was shown, but the shield is surmounted by a barred helm affrontee.

Supporters: The base of the shield rests upon the backs of two elephants argent.

Motto: Je seme la terreur.

Among the dukes, we find:

DUC DE L'ANSE [Apostolic Prefect Corneille Brelle, Archbishop of Haiti, Grand Almoner]

Arms: Purpure, a dove displayed argent billed or, the head towards the base, holding in the bill a phial azure, between in chief a mitre argent and in base a crozier or.

No crest was shown, but the shield is surmounted by an archbishop's hat vert.

Supporters: Two angels proper.

DUC DE LA MARMELADE [Maréchal de Camp Pierre Toussaint, Comte de la Marmelade]

[This entry differs from the royal edict of April 15th, 1811, where Toussaint is definitely described as Count. If he was subsequently elevated and we knew the date, this manuscript could be dated more precisely. On the other hand it may be a clerical error in the College of Arms copy. The arms in the College copy are totally different from those blazoned in the royal edict. Marmelade was a township in Haiti.]

Arms: Vert a sword argent in bend, the point upwards, hanging from the guard a key or.

No crest is shown, but the shield is surmounted by a barred helm affrontee.

Supporters: Two hyenas proper, collared gules with coronets vert.

Motto: Je ne la remets qu'a mon Roi.

Among the counts we find:

COMTE DE LIMONADE [Maréchal de Camp Julien Prevost, Secretary of the King]

[He was the author of the *Relation des Glorieux Evénemens Qui ont porté Leurs Majestés Royales sur le Trône d'Hayti.* Limonade was also a township in Haiti.]

Arms: Vert a sword argent, the point upwards, and a quill pen or, the nib downwards, in saltire.

No crest is shown, but the shield is surmounted by a barred helm affrontee.

Supporters: Two greyhounds argent, collared or the buckles gules.
Motto: Amour et fidelité.

Among the barons we find:

BARON DE BÉLIARD [Director and Steward of the Gardens, Waters
and Forests of the Royal Palaces]
[His marriage on August 20th, 1819 was witnessed by the King.]
Arms: Sable, a watering-can and a garden rake argent.
Crest: Upon a barred helm, a hat sable trimmed or, with a cockade
gules and two ostrich feathers argent.
Supporters: Two chameleons vert.
Motto: Utile en plus d'un genre.

The redoubtable and madly energetic King Henry proved too much of a
good thing for his countrymen, who increasingly resented his continual
calls upon their services and their purses. As his reign progressed, his
palaces and castles grew in grandeur and expense. King Henry's physique,
which was remarkable for any period, proved insufficient for the many
demands he made upon it, and in 1820 he had a stroke. His hold over his
subjects thus weakened, the Duc de la Marmelade, who had been
humiliated by the King, headed an insurrection. The army melted away
and, with the panache which had carried him forward to so many
triumphs, King Henry shot himself with a golden bullet.

Until recently the College of Arms copy of the *Armorial Générale du
Royaume d'Hayti* was thought to be unique, but in September 1976 my
attention was drawn to another, almost identical, copy of this book by Mr
Guy Beliard, the great-great-grandson of the first Baron de Beliard. Mr
Beliard tells me that his ancestor found the pages thrown away — and he
rescued them. The family tradition is that these pages, which are
incomplete through damage and lack the entries for the royal family,
formed part of the copy which was originally owned by King Henry. The
pages are a little larger than those of the College of Arms copy, but were
clearly drawn and written by the same man.

The discrepancy between the *Armorial Générale du Royaume d'Hayti* and
the royal edict of April 15th, 1811 raises one or two queries which have not
as yet been resolved. Either the *Armorial Générale* was compiled some
years after 1811, in which case it is possible that the Comte de la
Marmelade might have been raised to Duc and have changed his arms; or
the *Armorial Générale* was very hastily compiled at about the time of King
Henry's coronation by one or two obviously pretty amateur heralds.

81

II

HERALDRY
POLITICS AND LAW

THE TIME HAS COME to look at some examples of heraldry in action, how it was used to emphasise and assert sovereignty and dominion, its significance and implications during the turbulent years of our history, and its use by the warring factions in England during the dynastic struggles of the Wars of the Roses. Heraldry was and is a living thing, constantly being adapted to the purposes of its day and giving colour and panache to life. Any discussion of the realities of heraldry in a book of this length must naturally be selective, so the examples discussed here have been chosen to illustrate heraldry in the context of people.

Throughout the Middle Ages the use of armorial ensigns was no idle boast of ancient lineage, a nostalgic reminder of better and greater days, of empty pomp and flamboyant show. It gave point to the brutal reality of war and proclaimed the reality of power in peacetime. The start of a national or civil war or of a border foray was signalled by the sovereign or local lord unfurling his banner. The last occasion on which this occurred in England was when Charles I raised his banner at Nottingham on August 22nd, 1642, thus proclaiming the beginning of the Civil War and summoning his loyal adherents to join him.

NINE

THE ARMS OF THE KINGDOM OF JERUSALEM

HESE FAMOUS ARMS have been quoted in most of the heraldic treatises written since the thirteenth century as the classic exception to the armorial rule that metal may not be placed upon metal, nor colour upon colour. Much has been written at various times about their history and development, but not all writers are in agreement, and, moreover, much of what has been written is not readily available. It is therefore worth looking at the evidence again.

It is difficult to clarify developments in the early, formative years of heraldry owing to the absence of contemporary documentary evidence. We do not know, for example, if Godfrey de Bouillon and his immediate successors as Kings of Jerusalem used heraldic arms or not. If they did, what form did they take? It would also be interesting to know when the crusilly coat was adopted and when the crosslets were reduced to four, and when the simple principal cross became a cross potent.

The history and development of the arms of the Latin Kingdom of Jerusalem take us back to the dawn of heraldry and they are, of course, bound up with the turbulent history of that kingdom and its successor, the Kingdom of Cyprus and Jerusalem, as well as with that of the Kingdoms of Sicily and Naples. The heiresses of the different dynasties which succeeded the first King of Jerusalem have carried these arms to many of the royal and noble houses of western Europe, including that of the present Earl Marshal.

85

At the great council which Pope Urban II had convened at Clermont in France in November 1095, he urged his vast audience, gathered outside the cathedral, that military action be taken to open up the pilgrim routes to the Holy Sepulchre, which had been closed by the infidels.[1] The reaction in western Europe was immediate and enthusiastic. Pope Urban directed that all who took the vow to go on this crusade should sew cloth crosses on the shoulders of their tunics or surcoats, as a symbol of their profession of faith. Fulcher of Chartres, who was probably at Clermont at the time, wrote, 'How pleasing to us all to see these crosses, beautiful, whether of silk or woven gold, or of any kind of cloth, which these pilgrims, by order of Pope Urban, sewed on the shoulders of their mantles, or cassocks, or tunics, once they had made the vow to go.'[2] The anonymous knight who served under Bohemond of Taranto, afterwards Prince of Antioch, on the First Crusade, says the 'Franks' were so moved by Urban's eloquence that they 'straightway began to sew the cross on the right shoulders of their garments'. He does not describe the colour of the crosses.[3]

Hugh, Count of Vermandois, younger son of Henri I of France, and one of the senior commanders of the crusade, had been given a consecrated banner by the Pope. Hugh had intolerable pride in his high birth, and sent envoys to the Emperor of Byzantium demanding to be received at Constantinople with the dignity due to his royal rank. Anna Comnena, the Emperor's daughter, describes it as an absurd message, and adds that Hugh's envoy informed the Emperor that 'he brings with him from Rome the golden standard of St Peter'.[4] Although Anna wrote her memoirs some forty years later, she was generally accurate in her account of these stirring times which she witnessed as a girl, so we can take it that the field of the flag was gold, though unfortunately she does not describe the device on it.

Bishop Adhemar of Le Puy was appointed by Pope Urban leader of the crusading army and Papal Legate, and in 1098 he too was presented with a consecrated flag, to take on the First Crusade. Again we have no precise descriptions of it,[5] but it is not unreasonable to assume that it must have been similar to that given to Hugh of Vermandois. From what little is known of other consecrated banners given by Popes on other occasions during this period, it is likely that there would have been a cross upon both.

The Bayeux Tapestry depicts William the Conqueror holding a lance with a gonfanon at its head with a cross upon it, and during the Battle of Hastings Count Eustace of Boulogne is riding beside Duke William and holding a spear with a gonfanon at its head (Figure 2, p. 6). This is depicted in more detail and shows the field white with a yellow (gold) cross couped at the ends, which splay out very slightly, and four blue roundels between the arms of the cross, with a yellow bordure around the edge of the gonfanon. Two of the tails are green and one yellow. This has been taken to be a representation of the consecrated flag which Pope Alexander

II gave to Duke William in 1066, thus giving his expedition the character of a crusade.

I have argued elsewhere[6] that the flag depicted on the tapestry may not be the papal flag, but William's own battle flag, on the grounds that he was depicted earlier in the story, during his invasion of Brittany in 1064, with a standard bearer beside him holding a lance with a somewhat similar gonfanon at its head; in other words, some years before the Pope sent William the consecrated flag. I am now inclined to think that as the 'tapestry' was probably embroidered in England and possibly designed there as well, those who produced it may have assumed that William had always used a gonfanon similar to that which he used at Hastings. It is worth noting that the gonfanon depicted for his Brittany campaign is not precisely the same as the one shown at the Battle of Hastings, but this may be due to artistic licence. On the reverse of his Great Seal, King William is shown mounted and holding a spear with a gonfanon which has two tails, but no device can be seen upon it. So, after all, the flag depicted in the battle scene may well have been that blessed by the Pope and not William's personal gonfanon. This view is strengthened by the reflection that as William's expedition had papal blessing and approval, and was generally regarded in the rest of Western Europe as being in the nature of a crusade,[7] it is likely that Duke William would have displayed the papal flag as conspicuously as possible during the battle, to emphasise the legality of his invasion, hearten his troops and dismay the enemy. Finally it should be noted that this gonfanon bore a gold cross upon a silver field, the papal colours.

When the crusading army captured Jerusalem on July 15th, 1099, both Tancred and Gaston of Béarn had their personal banners placed on the Temple of Solomon to protect those who had taken refuge within it.[8] It can be assumed that one of the consecrated banners was placed above the Holy Sepulchre, the liberation of which had been the object of the crusade.

A week after the capture of Jerusalem the leaders of the expedition offered the crown to Godfrey de Bouillon, but partly from modesty and partly because of the objections of the clergy, who wished the election of a patriarch to precede that of a lay ruler, he took instead the title of *Advocatus Sancti Sepulchri*, the Defender of the Holy Sepulchre. It is probable that he either continued to use the device on the banner blessed by the Pope, or based the arms of the newly won kingdom on that device, which had brought such success to their endeavours. It is not without interest that it was Godfrey's father, Eustace II, Count of Boulogne, who had borne the consecrated gonfanon, charged with a gold cross, at the Battle of Hastings.

Godfrey died the next year leaving no heir, and his brother Baldwin, who had become Count of Edessa, had fewer scruples and was crowned on

Christmas Day 1100, thus founding the Latin Kingdom of Jerusalem. We have, alas, no direct evidence of the arms borne by Godfrey or Baldwin, any more than we have for Henry I of England, their contemporary. Matthew Paris, writing about 1250, gives the arms of both Godfrey and Baldwin as *Or, a cross argent*,[9] but this is not contemporary evidence. Baldwin died without an heir and the crown passed to the grandson of Ida, sister of Count Eustace II, who succeeded as Baldwin II. His daughter and heiress, Melisende, married Fulk, Count of Anjou, who became *jure uxoris* King of Jerusalem in 1131. He was succeeded by their eldest son Baldwin III, who died without an heir in 1162, and the crown passed to his brother Aimery (Amalric) I, and here we begin to come into the area of contemporary evidence. Aimery's seal shows a view of his capital city, with a tower from which flies a banner charged with a cross, but there is, of course, no means of telling what the colours were. He died in 1175 and his son, Baldwin IV, a leper, died without issue in 1185, being succeeded by his nephew Baldwin V, who also died without issue. Aimery's daughter Sybil, who had married Guy of Lusignan, thus succeeded, and they were both crowned. Guy's disastrous reign ended at the Battle of Hattin in 1187, where the Christian army was decisively beaten by Saladin and Guy was captured. This resulted in the permanent loss of Jerusalem and the conquest by the Turks of almost all the territory of the Latin Kingdom. Guy became Lord of Cyprus, which he bought from Richard Coeur de Lion in 1192. A denier of Guy's, evidently struck in Cyprus, bears a cross couped at the ends and with four roundels between the arms.[10]

On Guy's death in 1194, his brother Aimery de Lusignan succeeded to the Kingdom of Cyprus and in 1197, after marrying Queen Isabella, he was elected by the *Haute Cour* King of Jerusalem. He died in 1205. A silver *gros* of Aimery's reign bears a cross potent with four crosslets between the arms, impaling Lusignan of Cyprus.[11] Naturally it is not possible to determine the tinctures of the arms on the coin. Isabella died in 1208 and was succeeded by her very young daughter by Conrad of Montferrat, Maria. It was essential to have a King to rule the rump of this stricken kingdom, and the barons sent emissaries to King Philip Augustus of France to ask him to select a suitable husband for Maria. He chose John, Count of Brienne, a middle-aged, penniless minor baron from Champagne, descended from an ancestor who had seized Brienne in the tenth century. John turned out to be sagacious, able and courageous. The King of France gave him a very large endowment of money, which was matched by the Pope, who also provided three hundred knights. The family arms of John de Brienne were *Azure, semee of fleurs de lys, a lion or*.

John and Maria were married the day after his arrival at Acre in September 1210, and he became King of Jerusalem *jure uxoris*. Matthew Paris, writing about 1254, gave the arms of John, when King of Jerusalem, as *Or, crusilly argent, a cross argent (scutum aurem crux cum multis parvis crucibus albis)*.[12] Although Matthew was writing shortly after 1254, John had died only in 1237. Moreover Matthew had become a monk of the great Abbey of St Albans in 1217, and the abbey was frequently used as the first night's staging-post by English kings and magnates on their journeys north, so Matthew was well placed to hear the latest gossip, and probably spoke to people who had known John de Brienne and his children personally, for, as a monk, Matthew would naturally be interested in the arms associated with the Holy City. He is more likely to be right than wrong about the arms of Jerusalem.

Since Matthew Paris gives the arms of John of Brienne as King of Jerusalem in one place as *Or, a cross argent* and in another as *Or, crusilly a cross argent*, it looks as if the change may have been introduced during John's reign. The field of his personal arms was semée of fleurs de lys, and this may have prompted John to make the field of Jerusalem semée of crosslets. Those on whom Matthew Paris relied for his information could have been careless in their description of the arms.

Walford's Roll, compiled about 1273, gives the arms of the Kingdom of Jerusalem as '*Le roy d'Acre d'argent poudre a croysille d'or une croyz d'or bylette*' — as we should now blazon it, *Argent, crusilly a cross potent or*.[13] It is clear that the cross potent was introduced by John de Brienne's predecessor, Aimery de Lusignan, King of Jerusalem 1197–1205, for as we have seen, he used it on his coinage. After the loss of Jerusalem and most of his kingdom, the tattered remnants were ruled from the port of Acre and after 1191 its sovereign was often known as the King of Acre.

John de Brienne and Maria had a daughter who, on her mother's death in 1211, succeeded to the throne of Jerusalem as Queen Isabella II, although she was more usually known as Yolanda, and John stepped down to become Regent. She became of age in 1225 and was married to the Emperor Frederick II, of Hohenstaufen, who has the rare distinction of seducing Yolanda's cousin on their wedding night, and then keeping Yolanda in his harem at Palermo. Frederick claimed the throne *jure uxoris*, ousting John from the regency, much to his annoyance. Meanwhile, in 1214, John had married Stephanie, otherwise known as Rita, one of the co-heiresses of King Leo II of Armenia. She died in 1219, it was thought as a result of a severe beating given to her by John for trying to poison her step-daughter, Yolanda. In 1224, while John was still Regent of Jerusalem, he married Berengaria, sister of King Ferdinand of Castile.

Yolanda died the year after her marriage to the Emperor Frederick, giving birth to their son Conrad, who succeeded to the throne of Jerusalem and later to that of Sicily. Conrad does not appear to have used the traditional arms of Jerusalem, and Matthew Paris, his contemporary, gives his arms as *Or, a double-eagle sable, and in chief a crescent gules enclosing a*

Figure 55
The seal of Louis de Beaumont, Bishop of Durham (1318–33), grandson of John
de Brienne, King of Jerusalem. On his vestments the arms of Brienne, to his
right (dexter) side a shield of England, to his left a shield of Jerusalem.

small roundel gules.[14] He died in 1254. His son Conradin succeeded to the
Kingdom of Jerusalem, but his tenure of the throne was uncertain, and in
1258 he was displaced by his bastard half-brother, Manfred. Finally,
Conradin was executed in 1266 by Charles of Anjou. The Kingdom of

90

Jerusalem then devolved upon the Kings of Cyprus, as being next heirs after the Brienne family had waived their rights.

That remarkable and indefatigable man, John de Brienne, being disappointed of acquiring the Kingdom of Armenia, of which he had had hopes through his marriage to Stephanie, took service under Pope Gregory IX, commanding his forces in southern Italy fighting Frederick II. In 1228 the barons of Constantinople offered the hand of Baldwin II of Constantinople, then a minor, to Mary, the daughter of John de Brienne and Berengaria, on condition that he became Emperor and would serve for life, thus ensuring reasonable prospects for young Baldwin. John, then nearly eighty, accepted and was crowned Emperor of Constantinople. He died in 1237. It is not without interest that the arms borne by the Latin Emperors of Constantinople were *Crusilly a cross overall*, the crosslets varying from sixteen to twenty.[15]

It has been necessary to traverse the tangled history of the Latin Kingdom of Jerusalem during its last chaotic years, in order to get some kind of background against which to relate the shadowy and equally tangled history of the arms of that brilliant but unhappy kingdom. What is still not clear is when the tinctures of the arms were reversed from the argent crosses on gold. New dynasties followed hot-foot after one another, and it is more than likely that a new dynasty effected some change in tincture or design in order to emphasise that a new management had taken over.

There are, however, a few pointers. John de Brienne and Berengaria had several children and their third son, Louis of Acre, became Vicomte of Beaumont in Maine, France, on marrying the heiress. Two of their sons went to England. One, Louis de Beaumont, became Bishop of Durham (1318–33), and his beautifully engraved seal shows the Bishop standing in his vestments, with the arms of Brienne on his breast, on his dexter side a shield of the arms of England, and on the sinister side a shield of Jerusalem, here depicted as semée of twelve crosslets arranged in threes between the arms of a cross potent.[16] Naturally, on the seal there is no indication of tinctures (Figure 55).

Louis' brother, Henry de Beaumont, took service under Edward I in the Scottish war of 1302, being rewarded with large grants of lands in England. He was also created Baron Beaumont and Earl of Buchan, thus founding the English branch of the family, the two principal lines being represented today by Miles, Duke of Norfolk and Earl Marshal (who inherited the ancient barony of Beaumont through his mother) and by the Beaumont baronets. Henry de Beaumont would almost certainly have used the same version of Jerusalem as his brother. It is not unreasonable to infer that John de Brienne also used this version of the arms of Jerusalem.

TEN

THE LEOPARDS AND THE LILIES

HE FAMOUS ROYAL ARMS OF ENGLAND probably go back to the earliest days of heraldry, and the Lion is one of the oldest of all armorial charges. The early writers of the encyclopaedias and bestiaries invested him with a remarkable range of symbolism, equally appropriate to the battlefield or the cloister. Bartholomew the Englishman, writing around 1230, emphasised the Lion's qualities of boldness and magnanimity, saying that when in peril he accounted it 'vile shame to lurke and to hyde himself', but always attacked his enemies. On the other hand the Lion was noted for his mercy to the fallen and to those who had been prisoners of war 'and comen out of thraldom', and allowed them to proceed on their way homeward. These princely qualities of courage and magnanimity naturally appealed to the warrior aristocracy of the Middle Ages. Apart from this, the Church regarded the beast as allegorical of Christ, the Lion of Judah. It is understandable therefore that the Lion was the most widely used of all heraldic charges, other than the ordinaries.

It is clear from the medieval armorial treatises that the heraldic Lion was always depicted as rampant. Indeed, Bartolo di Sassoferrato, writing about 1354, said that 'the Lion, Bear and other similar creatures are painted erect, rampant, and with gnashing teeth and clawing feet'. He also said that 'animals, whenever represented, must be depicted in their most noble act, and furthermore must exhibit their greatest vigour'. What nobler and more vigorous act can one depict than the king of beasts striking out with his forefeet at his foes? The couchant Lion would have had no symbolic meaning to the knights or heralds of the Middle Ages, and would have had no place in a medieval battle line.

The evidence of the earliest French seals, between 1127 and 1300, produces 220 Lions rampant, and only forty passant.[1] The writers of the bestiaries were uncertain of the origin of the Leopard, believing it to be the offspring of a Lion and a Pard, 'lyke unto a Catt of the mountaine', as Nicholas Upton described it, and it was drawn like a Lion, but walking with its right forepaw outstretched as if to maul a foe, and looking sideways out of the shield towards its enemies. The Lion and the Leopard are always male. The real Leopard of the wilds became in later heraldry the Panther Incensed, itself a bit of a muddle. The heraldic Leopard is nowadays blazoned as a Lion passant guardant, but it seems a pity to abandon its original name, and we use it here.

The earliest documentary heraldic evidence is in the contemporary chronicle of John of Marmoutier, who described the knighting of Geoffrey of Anjou by Henry I in 1128, just before Geoffrey's marriage to Henry's daughter the Empress Matilda.[2] The ceremony included the investiture of Geoffrey with a shield painted with six Lioncels (as they were called when there were more than three on a shield or banner). The enamelled brass plate which was placed on Geoffrey's tomb in 1151 is still in the museum at Le Mans, and shows him holding his long, tapering blue shield with six golden Lioncels painted on it. This marriage had a particular dynastic, political and strategic importance for Henry, as King of England and Duke of Normandy. Matilda was twenty-five at the time, while Geoffrey was aged only fifteen. It was most important to bind the interests of Anjou, which included Touraine and Maine, closely to those of Normandy. What more natural, therefore, to mark this important event than that Henry should give Geoffrey a shield of arms which would symbolise it, and this indicates that Henry must have borne for his own arms one or more Lions.

The arms borne by the descendants of Henry I of England, where these are known, give some pointers to the arms probably borne by Henry himself. His only legitimate son and heir, William, was drowned when the *White Ship* foundered, and it is not known what arms he used. Henry I had, however, at least nine illegitimate sons and twelve illegitimate daughters. The most famous of these bastards was Robert, the King's son, otherwise known as Robert le Fitz Roy and Robert of Caen, from his place of birth, and also sometimes called Robert the Consul. Born about 1090, he was created Earl of Gloucester in 1122 and was an active supporter of his half-sister, the Empress Matilda, and her son Henry, in the politics and civil war of Stephen's reign. There is much doubt about Robert's arms.

Henry's third bastard son, Reginald de Dunstanville, created Earl of

93

Cornwall by Matilda in 1141, is said to have borne *Gules, two leopards or*, but this is doubtful.[3] Reginald's daughter and co-heiress, Denise, married Richard de Reviers, Earl of Devon. The Reviers family bore *Or, a lion azure*; Matthew Paris blazons it as *Scutum aureum leo de azure*.[4] The Reviers Lion was rampant, but Matthew Paris who was writing about 1244–59 does not use the word, because a Lion was always rampant. Glover's Roll, *c.* 1253–8, similarly blazons the arms as *d'or ove un leon d'asur*.[5] It is not impossible that the Reviers family may have adopted a Lion in allusion to their connection with Henry I, but this is conjecture.

With the children of the Empress Matilda and Geoffrey of Anjou, we are on firmer ground. Their eldest son, Henry Fitz Empress, succeeded to England and Normandy as Henry II, but we have no direct evidence of his arms. However, the seal still exists of Geoffrey's younger son, William Fitz Empress, Count of Poitou (died 1164). The seal engraver has depicted him mounted, with his shield on his left arm, but the wretched man has drawn the shield in such a way that only the dexter half is visible. This shows a Lion rampant facing towards the sinister, actually to the middle of the shield.[6] Two Lions rampant are depicted on his horse-trapper, both facing to the sinister, that is, towards the horse's head (Figure 56). Bartolo di Sassoferrato, regarded in his own day and ever since as a most authoritative writer on armory, wrote that 'when arms are depicted on the caparisons of horses, the nobler parts should face the horse's head'. Thus the two Lions on the other, invisible side of the horse would be facing to the dexter, so that their faces would also be towards the horse's head. By the same token one would, therefore, expect another rampant Lion to be on the invisible half of the shield facing to the dexter, so that William Fitz Empress may have borne *two lions combatant*. While Bartolo was writing some two hundred years later, when heraldry was becoming more strictly systematised, one cannot say that he was not reflecting earlier doctrine.

There is no contemporary evidence for the arms of most of Henry's children, but what we have got is interesting. Henry's eldest son died during his father's lifetime, so he was succeeded by the second son, Richard Lion Heart. The first Great Seal of Richard I still exists and, like that of his uncle, William Fitz Empress, the seal engraver shows him mounted, but with only the dexter half of the shield visible. Here, too, there is a Lion rampant facing to the sinister,[7] and the inference is that he bore *two lions combatant*. Such contemporary evidence as there is seems to support this theory. Richard I was described during the Third Crusade as having a red saddle decorated with 'a pair of small golden Lions gazing ferociously at one another, each with one of his forefeet stretched out towards the other as though to claw him'.[8] This is a description of two Lions combatant, and it is improbable that Richard would have used them thus on his saddle if they were not so depicted on his shield (Figure 56).

Figure 56   (*top*) First Great Seal of Richard I (before 1195).
(*centre*) Seal of William Fitz Empress.
(*bottom*) Seal of Gilbert Fitz Gilbert, Earl of Pembroke (created 1138, d. 1148).

King Richard's ship was wrecked in the Adriatic on the way home, so he tried to travel through Europe in disguise, but was discovered and imprisoned by Duke Leopold of Austria. The story is well known, so it need not be repeated here. When King Richard had been ransomed and returned to England, he had a new Great Seal made about 1195, and completely altered his arms to *Gules, three leopards or*, and these have remained the Royal Arms of England ever since (although from time to time quartered with other arms).

In 1185, when Count of Mortain and Lord of Ireland, John, Richard's younger brother, bore two Leopards in pale,[9] but on succeeding to the throne in 1199 he assumed the three Leopards of his brother. John's elder son, Henry, succeeded to the throne in 1216, and used the three Leopards, as did his successors. What is more interesting and significant are the arms borne by John's illegitimate issue, of which there were five sons and one daughter. Of these, Richard de Douvres, also known as Fitz Roy, and de Warenne, Lord of Chilham Castle in Kent, bore 'de gules a deux leopardz d'or' in Glover's Roll, (Figure 57).[10] His sister Joan married Llywelyn ap Iorwerth, Prince of North Wales (died 1240). Their son, Dafydd ap Llywelyn, bore *Quarterly or and gules, four leopards counterchanged*, and these arms are clearly derived from those of his grandfather, King John. When Owain Glyndwr became Prince of Wales (he died in 1416), he changed this quarterly coat to four Lions (rampant) counterchanged.

King John's bastard half-brother, William Longespée, son of Henry II and the 'Fair Rosamond', used a single Lion on his seal when created Earl

Figure 57
Seal of Richard de Douvres, Lord of Chilham.

of Salisbury on his marriage to Ela, daughter and heiress of William Fitz Patrick, Earl of Salisbury (died 1168). This may have been in allusion to the Lions borne by his father, or possibly great-grandfather, but more probably he continued to use the arms believed to have been borne by Earl William, his father-in-law.[11] Before long, however, William Longespée adopted the arms with which King Henry I had invested his grandfather, Geoffrey of Anjou, *'d'azur vi Leonceux d'or'*, which can be seen today on his tomb in Salisbury Cathedral (see Figure 33, pp. 38–9).

In view of the fact that William Fitz Empress probably bore two Lions combatant, and that Richard I probably bore the same before 1195, it seems not unreasonable to assume that Henry II possibly bore a similar coat. Two Lions (rampant) don't go snugly into one shield unless one depicts them as combatant. One, three or six, yes, but two, no. This brings us to Henry I. It has been suggested that he bore two Lions for his arms, and if this were so they must have been combatant, for I can find no early examples of two Lions walking erect across a shield, one behind the other. If Henry I bore anything it was probably one Lion, or two Lions combatant, or possibly two Leopards. It seems most unlikely that he would have invested Geoffrey of Anjou, on such an important political occasion, with a shield of Lioncels if he did not himself bear a Lion or Lions rampant for his arms.

In the countries which formerly comprised the Holy Roman Empire it is still allowable to depict lions, or other rampant creatures, as facing to the sinister, but this seems to be guided as much by artistic considerations as by armorial convention. In the very early days of heraldry usage was much more flexible, so it may not have been of any particular significance which way round you painted your lions, but a shield carried on your left arm would show the lion as retreating from the enemy. It doesn't make sense.[12]

There are however two other, almost contemporary, examples which, I feel, support the *two lions combatant* view. No one would seriously adduce the seal of Gilbert fitz Gilbert, Earl of Pembroke (1138–48) as evidence that the original arms of the Clares were *Six bendlets sinister*, just because the seal engraver depicted him holding his shield on his left arm, with only the dexter half of it visible (Figure 56). The shield of his nephew, Gilbert de Clare, Earl of Hertford (1141–6) is similarly depicted. Fortunately we have the seal (between 1156 and 1167) of the former's sister Rohese (Rose), Countess of Lincoln, which shows her Clare arms frontally, and there they are *Six chevronels* (it was soon after this time that the chevrons were reduced to three). Why then should the first seal of Richard I follow a different convention from that of his contemporaries, particularly when his rampant lion is facing to the sinister from the dexter side of the shield boss?

While the Lions and the Leopards achieved fame in England,

Normandy and Aquitaine, the Fleur de Lys became equally illustrious in France. It is one of the most beautiful of all heraldic emblems, and can be rendered in a wide variety of forms. It goes back to a very early period, being found in ancient Egypt, where it was a symbol of life and resurrection. It was used by the Byzantine emperors and by the Romans, but this was, of course, well before the days of heraldry. In western Europe, several of the Carolingian kings used it as a decorative motif on sceptres and coins. We find it associated with subsequent French kings; for instance, the Great Seals of Henry I (1031–60) and of Louis VII show them holding a Fleur de Lys. The famous arms of the Kings of France, *Azure semée of fleurs de lys or*, make their appearance on the Great Seal of Louis VIII in 1211 (Figure 58). In western Europe this beautiful, highly stylised historic flower was originally regarded as a kind of yellow iris and, indeed, was blazoned as a 'Fleur de Glaieul' before 1300, while the White Lily, the 'Lis' proper, was regarded as the special flower of the Virgin Mary.[13]

The royal emblem of France was occasionally still called the 'French Flower' by the English as late as the early fifteenth century. The reason for this was probably due to the legend which arose in the early Middle Ages, that King Clovis was given a Fleur de Lys at his baptism by an angel sent to him from God. It would, therefore, be natural in the later Middle Ages to suppose that the 'French Flower' and the Virgin's Flower were similar, and to call both the Fleur de Lys.

There is another famous coat containing Fleurs de Lys, that granted by King Charles VII to Joan of Arc, *Azure, between two fleurs de lys of France a sword erect the hilt gold and the blade proper, the point enfiled by a coronet also gold*, which is a beautiful example of heraldic symbolism, apt, concise and simple (Figure 59).

Apart from royal heraldry the French also had a national flag, the Oriflamme, the scarlet battle-flag of the French, possibly in use from the time of Charlemagne until almost the end of the Middle Ages, which is the most famous of historic flags. In peace time it was put up in the great Abbey of St Denis near Paris, but during the Hundred Years War it would have been frequently unfurled, and would have been a well-known sight to the men of the English armies as the French battle line was formed opposite them and the advance began. Before King Charles VI of France set out from Paris to intercept the English army under King Henry V on its way to Calais, he went to offer prayers in the Cathedral of Notre-Dame, and received with great ceremony from the Abbot and Convent of St Denis the Oriflamme. He appointed Guillaume Martel, Sire de Bacqueville, to bear it and, on unfurling and displaying the sacred emblem, open war was declared. The Battle of Agincourt, fought on October 25th, 1415, in which Guillaume Martel was killed, was the last occasion on which the Oriflamme was displayed in battle. It seems a pity that so famous a flag

Figure 58   France Ancient.   Figure 59   Arms of Joan of Arc.

should be forgotten, so it is interesting to see how Matthew Paris depicted it in the *Chronica Majora*, written between 1245 and 1253. It was common during the early Middle Ages to have small streamers from the fly of flags, and in this case Matthew Paris, who can be expected to know what he was talking about, gave it eight streamers (Figure 30 (iii), p. 30).[14]

When King Charles IV died in 1328, there was no direct male heir to the throne of France, and the heraldry of England and France played a most important part in the political history of those countries. Contemporary feudal practice and the prevailing uncertainty about the law of succession made it almost inevitable that a claim should be preferred on behalf of Edward III, as failure to do so would have allowed any potential rights to go by default. However, Edward was not then in a position to take any positive action. Charles's cousin Philip of Valois promptly got himself crowned as Philip VI. The position of the claimants is more clearly shown in the pedigree overleaf.

Relations between France and England steadily deteriorated until, in 1337, Philip declared Gascony confiscate. This brought matters to a head, and in October that year Edward formally claimed the French crown. At Ghent in January 1340, for political reasons, Edward assumed the title of King of France and quartered those arms with his, thus heralding the beginning of the Hundred Years War. As France was regarded as the more ancient and illustrious kingdom, the Lilies, known as *France Ancient*, were marshalled first and fourth, and the Leopards second and third (Figure 60), thereby demonstrating Edward's claim to the French throne.

99

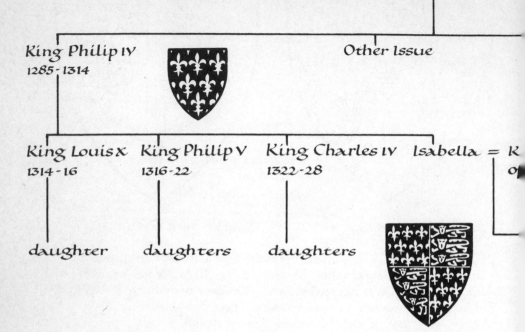

Pedigree: Claimants to the throne of France, 1328.

King Philip III o
1270-1285

King Philip IV
1285-1314

Other Issue

King Louis X
1314-16

King Philip V
1316-22

King Charles IV
1322-28

Isabella = K
o

daughter

daughters

daughters

It is generally thought that it was Charles V of France who changed the semée coat to three Fleurs de Lys, known as *France Modern*, in 1376, but it has been suggested that the change did not occur until about 1394. It was not until after Henry IV ascended the throne of England in 1399 that the Royal Arms were changed in conformity. The date of this change is generally thought to be 1405, but it was possibly earlier. For his first Great Seal Henry used that of his predecessor, merely having the name altered. Henry's second Great Seal, cut about 1406, shows *France Modern and England quarterly* (Figure 60).

In 1399 Anne, daughter and heiress of Thomas of Woodstock, Duke of Gloucester, married secondly Edmund (Stafford), fifth Earl of Stafford, and to mark this occasion richly embroidered vestments were made. One, known as the Butler-Bowden Burse after the owners, and now on loan to the Victoria and Albert Museum, shows the arms of Stafford, *Or, a chevron gules*, impaling those of Woodstock, *France Ancient quartering England within a bordure argent*. The Butler-Bowden Chasuble, which was presumably made for the obsequies in 1403 when Edmund Stafford was killed at the Battle of Shrewsbury, shows Woodstock as *France Modern quartering*

e

Charles of Valois
died 1325

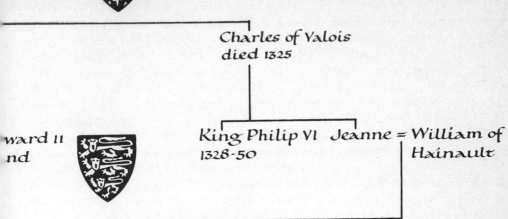

ward II   King Philip VI   Jeanne = William of
nd   1328-50   Hainault

Edward III = Philippa of Hainault

Figure 60
(*left*) France Ancient and England quarterly and
(*right*) France Modern and England quarterly.

England (with the Fleurs de Lys the wrong way round, which may indicate that the change in France had been fairly recent and the embroiderer was unsure of it). It is a most beautiful vestment, with the arms of Stafford, Woodstock, Clare and Stafford again down the front, and on the back the arms of Bohun, Woodstock, between Clare and Stafford, and below Clare again, Bohun again, and the arms of the Constable of England, with Woodstock again at the bottom.

There is another little-known pointer to the date of the change in the Royal Arms of England, and this comes from Turkey. The Knights of the Hospital of St John of Jerusalem had seized the island of Rhodes in 1308, and some years later they captured Smyrna, where they built a castle; but in December 1402, Timur the Lame, in the course of a brilliant campaign which left a trail of devastation and massacre all over the Middle East, drove the Knights of the Hospital out of Smyrna. The Order then decided about 1404 to erect a castle at Bodrum, the ancient Halicarnassus, opposite the island of Kos where they already had a castle. This was known as the Castle of St Peter Liberator which, apart from its strategic importance, was intended as a place of refuge for escaping Christian slaves.

Money for building the castle was solicited from all over Europe, and indulgences were widely sold. The Grand Master, Philibert de Naillac, visited Henry IV, staying at the Priory of the Order at Clerkenwell. The King and the magnates contributed large sums of money, and this was used for building the fortifications of the south-east corner of the castle, still known as the English Tower.

The arms of the principal contributors were carved on slabs of white marble which were let into the north wall, above the doorway opening on to the ramparts, and the Royal Arms were repeated alone on the west wall. In the centre are the arms of Henry IV surmounted by a sideways-facing helm with Leopard Crest upon a Cap of Maintenance, with a simple mantling. On each side of the Crest is a shield of the Order. On each side of the Royal Arms are eleven shields (twenty-two in all) in a horizontal line, and below the Royal Arms are three shields (Figure 61). This is not the place to describe these in detail, but all of them were famous men, and seventeen were Knights of the Garter.

The arms of Henry IV are there marshalled with *England first and fourth, and France Modern second and third.* The interesting thing is that the three nearest shields on each side of the Royal Arms are those of members of the royal family or closely related; namely the King's sons, Henry of Monmouth, Prince of Wales (later Henry V); Thomas, Duke of Clarence; John, Duke of Bedford; and Humphrey, Duke of Gloucester; the other two being John Beaufort, Duke of Somerset; and Edward, Duke of York: and that all these six shields show the arms correctly marshalled, with France Modern first and fourth, and England second and third. It cannot be, therefore, as one might at first assume, that this arrangement of the Royal Arms was a mistake by a Levantine stonemason, because if so, all the arms would have had England in the first and fourth quarters. It seems reasonable to assume that the alteration of the Royal Arms must have been effected before 1406, but that there may have been an experimental period during which Henry IV had not quite made up his mind in which sequence he wanted to marshal the Royal Arms, and communications between England and Rhodes were slow.[15]

The Lilies won, and remained in the first and fourth quarters of the Royal Arms, with the Leopards in the second and third quarters, until the death of Elizabeth I, when further changes became necessary with the accession of the Stuarts and later with the accession of the Hanoverians, and it was not until 1801 that the Lilies of France were finally abandoned, and today the Leopards hold pride of place.

Figure 61
Arms of Henry IV on the English Tower of Bodrum Castle.

ELEVEN

RICHARD II AND HERALDRY

HE REIGN OF RICHARD II saw some remarkable developments in English armory which were to have important and tragic political consequences more than a century later. To see these in context, we must glance briefly backwards. The romantic revival during the reign of Edward I got its inspiration from 'the Matter of Britain', the body of Arthurian romances, as well as from the legend of the Swan Knight.[1] Inspired by this, Edward I was a keen patron of jousts and tournaments, and a promoter of the great festive occasions in which the age delighted, such as the Feast of the Swans in 1306. Indeed, Edward nearly founded an Order of the Swan.

Edward III carried the concept of romantic chivalry to greater heights and actively encouraged the holding of 'Round Tables' based on the legend of Arthur and the Knights of the Round Table. These were social gatherings where the rules of precedence were waived, and they were the occasions for jousts and other sports, ending with feasts and dancing; jolly, informal parties where, some said, there was a certain amount of promiscuity.[2] By January 1348, Edward III had founded the Order of the Garter, soon to become the most illustrious order of chivalry in the world. Edward of Woodstock, known to later generations as the Black Prince, was one of the founder members of the Order and was regarded by his contemporaries as the model of knightly chivalry. His son, Richard of Bordeaux, was deeply influenced by his romantic world.

The almost continuous warfare during the fourteenth century gave the heralds much employment as military staff-officers and as ambassadors, while the frequent tournaments and ceremonies which were organised by them led to the growth in importance of the heralds. When Richard succeeded his grandfather as Richard II, the heralds were much about the Court and enjoyed the patronage and friendship of the King and the magnates. It is not to be wondered at, therefore, that Richard himself showed such a close interest in heraldry.

Richard II intervened personally on several occasions in armorial matters. An English man-at-arms, John de Kyngeston, had been challenged to a duel by a French knight, but was unable to accept the challenge as he was not of the armigerous noblesse. So the King, by Letters Patent dated 1st July 1389,

> in order that our said liege may be received honourably and may be able to perform the said deeds, have received him into the estate of Gentleman, and have made him Esquire [*et luy fait Esquier*] and will that he be known by Arms and bear them henceforth as follows, *Argent a chapeau azure with an ostrich feather gules.*[3]

On August 13th, 1385 began the famous lawsuit in the Court of Chivalry between Sir Richard le Scrope and Sir Robert Grosvenor, as to the right to the arms *Azure a bend or*. The Court found in favour of Sir Richard le Scrope, and ruled that Grosvenor must difference his arms by a *Bordure argent*. Grosvenor appealed to the King, and Richard disallowed the bordure as being a mark of cadency more suitable as a difference between cousins in blood, but not sufficient to difference the arms of two strangers

Figure 62   Arms of Scrope and Grosvenor (modern).

in blood in the same kingdom. Grosvenor then adopted the coat *Azure, a garb or* (Figure 62).

One of the most popular heraldic treatises in the Middle Ages, the *Tractatus de Armis*, was finished by John de Bado Aureo shortly after 1394. He stated in the Introduction that it was written at the special request of Queen Anne, the first wife of Richard II. This is clear evidence that heraldry was of considerable interest in Court circles.

We now come to some rather strange heraldic practices instituted by Richard II. One assumes that it must have been Richard who thought them up, in consultation with his heralds, because there is no evidence that they were armorial doctrine or practice at an earlier time. The best known was Richard's adoption of the attributed arms of Edward the Confessor, impaling them with the Royal Arms of England: France Ancient and England quarterly (Figure 63). Sir John Froissart, the historian, says this was done about 1394, and he recounts the story of Richard's expedition to Ireland, as told him by an English squire who had accompanied the King as an interpreter, and the inference is that the account of the Royal Arms came from the same source. After extolling the real and fictional virtues of Edward the Confessor, Froissart says that Irishmen held the Confessor in greater esteem than any other English King:

> And therefore our soverayne lorde kyng Richarde this yere past, whan he was in Ireland in all his armories and devyses, he lefte the beryng of the armes of Englande, as the lybards [leopards] and flour delyces [fleurs de lys] quarterly, and bare the armes of this saynt Edwarde . . . whereof, it was said, the yrisshmen were well pleased.[4]

As Froissart heard this story during his visit to King Richard in England and spoke, so he tells us, to many members of the Court, we must, I think, give it some credence, odd though the reason may seem. Whatever the cause the fact is that he apparently started using these arms about this time, and may at first have substituted the Confessor's arms for the Royal Arms.

Trokelowe, in the *Annals of Richard II*, says that Richard adopted the arms of Edward the Confessor, and added them to the Royal Arms (which must surely mean impalement) at the time he created the new dukes in 1397. There is no mention of Ireland.[5] However, there is one significant piece of evidence which supports Froissart's story. Edward (Plantagenet) of Norwich, Earl of Rutland, accompanied Richard on his Irish expedition of 1394, and was appointed Captain of Ireland from 1394 to 1395. He was already Admiral of England. On March 9th, 1395 he concluded a truce with France, and his seal appended to this document shows a square-rigged ship, the sail of which bears his arms, St Edward the Confessor impaling

King Richard II

Henry of Bolingbroke
Earl of Derby
cr. Duke of Hereford

Edward of Norwich
Earl of Rutland
cr. Duke of Aumale

Thomas Holland
Earl of Kent
cr. Duke of Surrey

John Holland
Earl of Huntingdon
cr. Duke of Exeter

Thomas de Mowbray
Earl of Norfolk
cr. Duke of Norfolk

Figure 63
Arms of Richard II and the five dukes created by him in 1397.

the Royal Arms with a label of five points.[6]

By Letters Patent dated January 12th, 1393/4, Richard II ruled that while Thomas de Mowbray, Earl of Nottingham and Earl Marshal (who later inherited the Earldom of Norfolk), had the hereditary right to bear as his crest a gold leopard with a white label around its neck, it was rightly the crest of the King's first-born son, if he had any, and that therefore Mowbray's leopard should be differenced with a crown argent instead of the label.[7] The interesting thing is that the King recognised that Mowbray had a 'hereditary right' to bear Thomas of Brotherton's crest, from which it followed that the King also recognised Mowbray's hereditary right to the Brotherton arms alone. From the wording of the Letters Patent, this would seem to have been settled heraldic doctrine, recognising that the arms of younger children of the Sovereign could be transmitted entire and alone through their female heirs by many removes.

Margaret, later created Duchess of Norfolk, was the eldest daughter and eventual heiress of Thomas of Brotherton, Earl of Norfolk and Earl Marshal (died 1338), second surviving son of King Edward I. His arms were *England with a label of three points argent*. It is when we come to her daughter that the new doctrine seems to take shape. Her elder daughter Elizabeth Segrave married John de Mowbray, Earl of Nottingham (died 1382), and their son Thomas de Mowbray, Earl of Nottingham and Norfolk and later Duke of Norfolk and Earl Marshal (died 1399), was the grantee named in the patent of January 12th, 1393/4. It will be seen, therefore, that the Brotherton arms went entire and alone through two heiresses.

Thomas Mowbray was succeeded by his second son John in the Earldoms of Nottingham and Norfolk, and as Earl Marshal (died 1432). His seal, appended to a document of 1414, shows him using the Brotherton arms alone.[8] He was created a Knight of the Garter in 1421 and his stall-plate shows him using Brotherton alone, and for crest a gold Leopard crowned argent, without the label.[9] His son, another John, succeeded as Duke of Norfolk, Earl of Nottingham, Warenne and Surrey, and Earl Marshal. He was created a Knight of the Garter in 1472, but his stall-plate, while continuing the use of the Brotherton arms alone, has the white label around the neck of the crowned Leopard crest.[10] He died in January 1475/6, without male issue, when his titles became extinct. The eventual heiress of the Mowbrays thus became Margaret, daughter of Thomas Mowbray, first Duke of Norfolk, who married Sir Robert Howard (died 1436), and their son, John Howard, was created Duke of Norfolk and Earl Marshal. It is from them that the present Dukes of Norfolk are descended.

The parallel case of the Staffords is even more interesting. Thomas of Woodstock (the name was derived from the royal manor near Oxford), youngest son of Edward III, whose arms were *France Ancient and England quarterly with a bordure argent*, married Eleanor, elder daughter and co-heir of Humphrey de Bohun, through whom he acquired the Earldom of Essex and the hereditary Constableship. He was also created Earl of Buckingham and Duke of Gloucester. He was murdered in 1397 on the orders of Richard II, apparently being smothered with a feather mattress. He left no male issue, and his elder daughter Anne married Edmund Stafford, Earl of Stafford. Their son Humphrey Stafford succeeded to the Earldoms of Stafford and Buckingham, and as Constable of England, and was created Duke of Buckingham in 1444. When Humphrey was created a Knight of the Garter in 1429, his stall-plate showed the Stafford arms alone. It was after he was appointed Captain of Calais in 1442 that the change occurred. His seal then showed his quarterly arms with Woodstock in the first quarter, Bohun of Hereford second, Bohun of Northampton third, and Stafford last (Figure 64).

Figure 64   Arms of Humphrey Stafford, Duke of Buckingham.

The first Duke was succeeded by his grandson, Henry Stafford, as 2nd Duke of Buckingham and Earl of Stafford. In 1483 he was acknowledged to be hereditary Lord High Constable. Some ten years earlier, possibly when it had been intimated to him that he was about to be created a Knight of the Garter, he had consulted the Kings of Arms about his armorial position. A chapter of the heralds was convened to look into it, and their ruling echoed the doctrine expressed in the reign of Richard II almost 100 years earlier. The ruling of the chapter is so important for the political history of the succeeding years that it is worth quoting in full:

An order made for Henry, Duke of Buckingham, to beare the Armes of Thomas of Woodstock alone without any other Armes to be quartered therewith, Ano. 13 E.4

Memorandum That in the yeare of the Reigne of our Soveraingne Lord King Edward the iiijth the thirtein [year of his reign] in the xviijth Day of Feverir [February 18th, 1473/4] it was concluded in a Chapter of the Office of Armes that where a Nobleman is descended lenyallie Inheritable to iij or iiij Cotes, and afterwardes is ascended to a Coate neere to the Kinge, and of his Royall blood, may for his most honour beare the same Coate alone: And non lower Coates of Dignetie to be quartered therewith. As my lord Henry, Duke of Buckingham, Earl of Harford [Hereford], Northampton and Stafford, Lord of Brecknoke and of Holderness, is assended to the Cootes and ayer [heir] to Thomas of Woodstocke, Duke of Gloucester, and sonne to King Edward the third, hee may beare his Coate allone. And it was soe concluded: by Clarencieux King of Armes; March Kinge of Armes; Guyenne Kinge of Armes; Windesor Herauld; Fawcon Herauld; Harford [Hereford] Herald.[11]

This is one of the most interesting armorial rulings ever made, so let us look at the men who came to this conclusion. William Hawkeslowe, an active herald with many years' experience, was appointed Clarenceux in 1460 and during his tenure of office made many grants of arms, of which some dozen survive. He was drowned in the Spanish Seas in 1476, leaving his widow penniless so that Edward IV had to make provision for her. March King of Arms at this time has not been definitely identified, but may have been John Ferrant or Richard Stanton, both of whom were active heralds. Guyenne King of Arms was probably William Brereton, of whom little is known. Windsor Herald was John More, another distinguished herald, much employed on diplomatic missions to several countries. Falcon Herald was John Wrythe, the most experienced of all the group who met that day. Many important armorial manuscripts still in the College of Arms were made by him or under his direction. He was subsequently appointed Norroy and later Garter King of Arms. He died in 1504 after an exceptionally long career as a herald. Hereford Herald was originally the private herald of the Bohun Earls of Hereford, and presumably at this time Buckingham's private herald, but the identity of this one is not known.[12]

It will be seen that the group of heralds who met in the chapter of 1474 included several of weight and experience, so their conclusions cannot be brushed aside and we must take it that this was established doctrine by that time, echoing the statement made by Richard II in January 1393/4. One wonders, therefore, whether, after all, this might not have been armorial doctrine as early as, say, the time of Edward III, because Thomas of Brotherton was a son of Edward I, and Thomas of Woodstock a son of Edward III. I cannot find any record that the ruling of 1474 was ever officially rescinded or overruled by some subsequent decision.

Henry Stafford, 2nd Duke of Buckingham, on his creation as a Knight of the Garter in 1474 put up his stall-plate in St George's Chapel showing the arms of Woodstock 'without any other arms quartered therewith'; his crest was a gold leopard with a gold crown on his head and a plain silver collar about his neck. As King Edward IV and the magnates were very interested in heraldry, Buckingham's action would have been noticed immediately if it had been off-side. Garter King of Arms at this time was John Smert (himself the son-in-law of a famous herald, William Bruges, the first Garter King of Arms) who was appointed Chester Herald by Richard II in 1398. Smert was much employed about the Court and on diplomatic missions, so we can take it that he too agreed with the chapter ruling, for Garter has always had a special responsibility for ensuring the correctness of the arms of the Knights of the Order.

But we have not yet finished with the armorial tangles of the later Plantagenets. Edmund of Woodstock, Earl of Kent, was the youngest son of Edward I (and thus younger brother of Thomas of Brotherton) and he bore *England alone within a bordure argent*. He had two sons who died without issue, and they were eventually succeeded by their sister Joan, the 'Fair Maid of Kent'. She married, first, Sir Thomas Holand, who obtained through her the Earldom of Kent; second, the Earl of Salisbury; and, third, Edward the Black Prince, and so was the mother of Richard II.

By Thomas Holand she had two sons: Thomas Holand, Earl of Kent, and John Holand, Earl of Huntingdon. No doubt with the precedent of the Mowbrays before him, Richard II allowed his half-brother Thomas Holand to use the arms of Edmund of Woodstock alone and undifferenced,[13] while John Holand used *England with a bordure of France*.[14]

The last years of Richard's reign became increasingly troubled, but by 1397 he had turned the tables on his enemies, and cemented his victory by executing or exiling his opponents. Rewards for his adherents and friends followed. At a parliament on September 25th, 1397 he created five new dukes, one marquess and four earls.[15] At the same time he evidently allowed the new dukes to use the attributed arms of Edward the Confessor, either alone or impaled, as he himself did. It was presumably done verbally, because there is no official record of it. Let us glance at these new dukes to see if anything of heraldic significance can be squeezed out of them.

Thomas Holand, Earl of Kent, K.G., the King's half-brother, became Duke of Surrey. After his creation he bore the arms of *the Confessor within a bordure argent impaling Edmund of Woodstock* (Figure 63).[16]

John Holand, Earl of Huntingdon, K.G., the King's other half-brother, became Duke of Exeter. He bore *the Confessor with a label of three points impaling Woodstock with the bordure flory* (Figure 63).[17]

Thomas Mowbray, Earl of Norfolk and Nottingham and Earl Marshal, K.G., became Duke of Norfolk. He bore *the Confessor (undifferenced) impaling Brotherton* (Figure 63).[18] He was exiled by Richard II and died at Venice in 1399. His second son John was restored to the Dukedom in 1425, had been created a Knight of the Garter in 1421, and his stall-plate shows Brotherton alone,[19] as did that of his son[20] and his grandson, John Mowbray, K.G., in 1472.[21]

Edward of Norwich, sometimes called Plantagenet, Earl of Rutland, K.G., was created Duke of Aumale; later succeeding to the Dukedom of York. His paternal arms were *France Ancient and England quarterly, a label of three points gules each charged with three castles or.* He had been appointed Lord High Admiral in 1392, and in 1395 he was using a seal with his arms depicted on the sail of a ship as, *the Confessor with a label of three points, impaling France Ancient and England quarterly with a Label of five points argent each charged with three torteaux* (Figure 63),[22] some two years before he was created duke.

Henry of Bolingbroke (eldest surviving son of John of Gaunt, Duke of Lancaster) was Earl of Derby and K.G., and became Duke of Hereford in 1397. His arms had been the Royal Arms, France Ancient and England quarterly, with a blue label of five points each charged with three gold fleurs de lys.[23] The next year he paid his goldsmith 36s. 9d. for making a silver matrix 'with arms of St. Edward, England and Hereford, and name Duke of Hereford'.[24] He succeeded his father as Duke of Lancaster in 1399, and his seal as such shows *the Confessor with a label of three points impaling the Royal Arms with a label of five points in turn impaling Bohun of Hereford* (Figure 63).[25] An interesting reference to the use of the Confessor's arms by Henry is in 1397, when Peter Swan was paid 13s. 4d. for 'embroidering 9 labels with feathers on a cotearm with arms of St. Edward'.[26]

It is significant that when he succeeded to the throne as Henry IV, he abandoned the Confessor's impalement and seems to have discouraged the other recipients of this dangerous honour from continuing to use it. But this time-bomb which Richard II had planted was to explode with unhappy consequences over a century later.

It now appears that the second half of the fourteenth century was a much more important period in the development of armory than one had thought. Bartolo di Sassoferrato had produced his classic work on armory, *De Insigniis et Armis*, about 1355, and it achieved immediate popularity, being extensively copied over the next couple of centuries. Honoré Bouvet (Bonet) had written *L'Arbre des Batailles* about 1385, and Christine de Pisan's *Le Livre de Faits d'Armes et de Chevalerie* appeared about 1400; both dealt mainly with the conventions and tactics of war, but both also contained important sections on armory, and were widely read. Francois de Foveis (or des Fosses) wrote *De Picturis Armorum* about this time and was, apparently, lecturing on armory in France, and he had a considerable influence on heraldic thought on both sides of the Channel. In about 1395 John de Bado Aureo, whose identity still eludes us, produced his great work *Tractatus de Armis* which was extensively copied during the next two centuries. Heraldic lawsuits like those of Scrope v. Grosvenor are also evidence of the importance of armory in the times of Richard II. This aspect of his reign may well repay further study.

TWELVE

THE WARS OF THE ROSES AND THE TUDORS

ATER GENERATIONS tend to romanticise the past, and the 'Wars of the Roses' are no exception. Not only did those who took part in them never think of them by that name, but the red rose was only one of the badges of the house of Lancaster and the white rose only one of the badges of the house of York, and not their most important badge. The Wars of the Roses were invented by Sir Walter Scott. It was only after Henry VII married Princess Elizabeth, daughter and heiress of Edward IV, that he sought to create an appropriate badge to symbolise the union of the houses of Lancaster and York, and thus create a suitable mythology to bolster the new dynasty. The two rose badges lent themselves more readily than the other badges of the rival factions to some form of amalgamation. The badge adopted by Henry VII consisted of half a red rose impaled with half a white rose, surmounted by a royal crown. It was the heralds of Henry VIII who created the lovely badge of the 'Tudor Rose', the crowned red rose of Lancaster with the white rose of York superimposed on its centre.

Remarkable as the fifteenth century was for recurring private as well as public war, we must not think of it as influencing all levels of society. It certainly affected the great magnates and their household retainers, and those of the more substantial country gentry and the lawyers who actively supported these magnates naturally shared in their fortunes and misfortunes, but war only occasionally impinged upon the ordinary country gentry, yeomen and labourers, and touched the townsmen hardly at all. Indeed, in the whole thirty-two years between the First Battle of St Albans in 1455 and the Battle of Stoke in 1487, there were no more than thirteen weeks of active campaigning. Most of the loveliest of our parish churches were built or added to during the fifteenth century, while the more well-to-do country gentry were building manor houses rather than castles for themselves. The strange thing is that the leaders and adherents of the opposing factions often lived only a few miles from each other, and this led to many little local difficulties, some only tiresome, though others were alarming and sometimes calamitous.

Philippe de Commynes, whose memoirs were completed in 1498, brings home to us the destruction of the Plantagenets. Discussing the end of the Wars of the Roses, he mentioned that the Earl of Richmond,

At present king [Henry VII had] defeated and killed in battle the cruel King Richard, who shortly before had had his nephews murdered. Thus, within my memory, more than eighty members of the English royal family, some of whom I knew, were killed in these disturbances in England. The English who were living [as refugees] with the Duke of Burgundy, when I was there, told me about the rest.[1]

Commynes also made an interesting observation that

England enjoyed this peculiar mercy above all other kingdoms, that neither the country nor the people, nor the houses were wasted, destroyed or demolished, but the calamities and misfortunes of the war fell only upon the soldiers and especially the nobility.

Chivalry died during the fifteenth century amid a blaze of heraldry, a glorious sunset of ideals and a way of life which were even then outdated. The most extensive use was made of banners and surcoats, painted with the bright colours of armory. Gregory's Chronicle[2] gives us a vivid picture of the scene just before the Second Battle of St Albans on February 17th, 1460/1:

And the 17 day next following King Harry [VI] rode to St Albans, and the Duke of Norfolk with him, the Earl of Warwick, the Earl of Arundel, the Lord Bourchier, the Lord Bonville, with many great lords, knights and squires, and commons of an 100,000 men [a wild exaggeration]. And there they had a great battle with the Queen [Margaret], for she come ever on from the journey [Battle] of Wakefield till she come to St. Albans, with all the lords aforesaid; and her meinie and every lord's men bare their lord's livery, that every man might know his own fellowship by his livery. And beside that every man and lord bare the Prince's livery, that was a bend [? band, i.e., armband] of crimson and black with ostrich's feathers.

The Wars of the Roses had opened in 1455 with the First Battle of St Albans which was won by the Yorkist faction who seized power. King Henry VI managed, with the help of his Queen, to reconcile the two parties, but by 1459 the situation had deteriorated and both sides prepared for war. Queen Margaret actively solicited support in those parts of England sympathetic to the Lancastrian cause, 'and made her son [Prince Edward] give a livery blazoned with a swan to all gentlemen of the country, trusting through their strength to make her son king.' The swan was originally the badge of the Bohun family, but through the marriage of Henry IV to Mary, the daughter and heiress of Humphrey de Bohun, Earl of Hereford and Essex, it became a royal badge and it is interesting to see it being used in this way.[3] The Lancastrian army, bedecked with the swan badge, marched to their bloody defeat at the Battle of Blore Heath by a more experienced Yorkist army. Perhaps this discouraging experience led to the Lancastrian army using the Prince's ostrich feather badge at the Second Battle of St Albans a couple of years later, when they temporarily turned the tables.

The leaders of the opposing factions made extensive use of heraldry to illustrate their power and emphasise their claims. The case of Richard Nevile, Earl of Warwick and Salisbury (born 1428, died 1471), known as the 'Kingmaker', the most powerful man in England for many years during the Wars of the Roses, is an example of this. The sequence of quarterings on his seal, made about 1465, would make a modern King of Arms shudder.[4]

Richard Nevile is conventionally depicted on the obverse of his seal as if armed for a tournament, because shields were no longer used in battle after about 1360,[5] and crests were used only in tournaments. The shield he is holding depicts his Nevile family arms only, *Gules a saltire argent, a label gobony argent and azure*. The Nevile arms are very ancient. The gobony label, by which he differenced his arms from other branches of the family, was evidently an allusion to the gobony border round the Royal Arms borne by his grandmother Joan, daughter of John of Gaunt, Duke of Lancaster, after her legitimation.

The arms on his horse-trapper are marshalled in a most interesting way, in two separate portions. The first, on the horse's neck, represents his Earldom of Salisbury, *Quarterly 1 and 4, Or an eagle displayed vert; 2 and 3, Argent three fusils in fess gules*. According to modern practice these are marshalled back to front, because the eagle of Monthermer came to the Montacutes through an heiress.

Behind the saddle the arms are marshalled in four grand-quarters as follows: *1st and 4th Grand-quarters: 1 and 4, Gules a fess between six cross-crosslets or* (Beauchamp), *2 and 3, Chequy or and azure a chevron ermine* (Newburgh). *2nd and 3rd Grand-quarters: 1 and 4, or three chevrons gules* (Clare), *2 and 3, Quarterly argent and gules fretty or, overall a bend sable* (Despencer). These represented the immense lordships brought to the Kingmaker by his wife Ann, daughter of Richard Beauchamp, Earl of Warwick and his wife Isabella, daughter of Thomas Despencer, Earl of Gloucester. Again, the quarterings are marshalled in order of importance.

On the reverse of the seal, the quarterings are even more unusually re-shuffled to emphasise the Kingmaker's territorial power. Here again the arms are marshalled in four grand-quarters. The first shows Beauchamp quartering Clare, the second Montacute quartering Monthermer, the third Nevile, which he must therefore have regarded as of less importance than the others, and the fourth Newburgh quartering Despencer, a very odd arrangement, but presumably lumped together in the last quarter as being not so important.

The Hundred Years War produced thousands of experienced, battle-seasoned soldiers, who found return to civilian life in England boring and unremunerative. As the ambitions and rivalries of the great nobles grew, they began to recruit these restless mercenaries into their private retinues. They also enlarged their military power by the device of 'livery and maintenance', by which the great lords offered to protect and maintain their lesser neighbours and champion them in their quarrels and lawsuits, in return for wearing the lord's livery and supporting him with arms when summoned. Thus many thousands of Englishmen, from substantial country gentry down to village layabouts, could spring to arms at very short notice, wearing the Bear and Ragged Staff badge of the Neviles, the Stafford knot, or many another famous badge. The Bear and Ragged Staff badge of Richard Nevile, Earl of Warwick and Salisbury (see Figure 29, p. 27), was originally two separate badges of his wife's Beauchamp ancestors, which the Kingmaker united, although he also used them separately. His retainers usually wore red coats embroidered with white ragged staves.[6]

It was the Tudors who made a thoroughly unscrupulous use of heraldry, bending the rules to bolster their political ends and debasing the coinage of armory. The heralds of the sixteenth century interpreted their masters' wishes with a subservience which was only redeemed by the colourful flamboyance of their productions.

That ancient Welsh family of country gentry, of modest estate and no particular note, the Tudors, were to found a remarkable dynasty which finally brought Wales fully within the English administrative, legal and social system. Meredith Tudor, a cousin through his mother of Owen

Glyndwr (known to Englishmen as Glendower), had been a minor royal official in Anglesey. His penniless but good-looking son, Owen, made his way to England to seek his fortune. He was appointed squire of the body by Henry V, and after Henry's death in 1422, Owen obtained a secretarial job in the household of Henry's young widow, Queen Catherine of Valois. He charmed his way into her bed and she produced three sons, Jasper, Edmund and Owen, and two daughters. There is considerable doubt about the validity of their marriage, no evidence having ever been found for it, even by the Tudor Kings. The Privy Council heard of this union about 1425 and was scandalised and furious, and in 1428 Parliament passed an Act making it a grave offence to marry the Queen Dowager without the Privy Council's consent. Owen Tudor was thrown into Newgate goal, but was later released, possibly owing to the protection of the great Duke of Bedford. In 1436 he was again imprisoned, Queen Catherine was sent to Bermondsey Abbey and her children were taken from her. She died there the following year. Owen escaped to Wales in 1438. Henry VI, Catherine's son by Henry V, recognised the legitimacy of his half-brothers in 1453, and created Jasper Earl of Pembroke and Edmund Earl of Richmond, and knighted their father. The youngest son, Owen, had already become a monk.

The ancestor of the Tudors, Edynfed Fychan (died 1246), Steward of Llywelyn the Great, had originally borne for his arms, *Gules, a chevron argent between three Englishmen's heads couped proper*, in commemoration of a successful border foray of long ago, but Owen, possibly on coming to live in England, prudently altered his arms to *Gules, a chevron between three helms argent* (Figure 65). When the brothers were ennobled by Henry VI in 1453, they were granted totally new arms in lieu of their old ones: namely, for Jasper, *Quarterly France Modern and England, the whole within a bordure charged with martlets or*, while for Edmund the bordure was charged with martlets and fleurs de lys alternately (Figure 65).

Now this is most interesting to modern heralds, because John de Bado Aureo, who wrote his famous treatise on armory in 1394 at the behest of Queen Anne, wife of Richard II, stated that martlets borne in arms indicated that the first bearer of them had acquired nobility by his own exertions, or by the patronage of lords or kings; since the martlet is painted without feet, it was held that this showed he had lacked foundations of his own to begin with. Nicholas Upton, whose equally famous treatise on heraldry was written in 1466, and who was thus a contemporary of the brothers, also subscribed to this view. The heralds had neatly commented on the origins of the Tudors.

The Wars of the Roses were being fought with increasing bitterness and brutality, and the Tudor family, through their relationship to Henry VI, were naturally firm partisans of the Lancastrian cause. A Lancastrian army

Sir Owen Tudor

Edmund Tudor
Earl of Richmond

Jasper Tudor
Earl of Pembroke

Henry Tudor
Earl of Richmond
King Henry VII

Figure 65   Arms of the Tudors.

under the command of the Earls of Pembroke and Wiltshire was defeated in 1461 at the Battle of Mortimer's Cross, on the Welsh border. Pembroke escaped but his father, Sir Owen Tudor, was captured and taken to Hereford for execution. Ever the incurable optimist, he thought until the very last moment that he would be reprieved but, when the executioner ripped off the collar of his red velvet doublet, he met his fate with fortitude, remarking that the head that would lie upon the block was wont to lie upon Queen Catherine's lap. His severed head was placed upon the market cross, and a 'mad woman' came and combed his hair, washed the blood off his face and set 'more that a hundred' lighted candles about his body.[7] As candles were then pretty expensive she could hardly have been some poor vagabond, and one wonders whether she may have been a heartbroken and distraught mistress. So ended the colourful and romantic life of the most likable of all the Tudors.

Owen Tudor's son Edmund, the 1st Earl of Richmond, who died in 1456, married Margaret, daughter of John Beaufort, Duke of Somerset and Earl of Kendal, the grandson of John of Gaunt, Duke of Lancaster. The legitimation of Gaunt's son John in February 1396/7 was confirmed by Henry IV in 1406/7, but a clause in the confirmation specifically excluded the family from succession to the throne. This was generally accepted at the time, but it has been argued since that the King alone cannot limit an Act of Parliament.

Edmund Tudor's son Henry, 2nd Earl of Richmond, won the throne at the Battle of Bosworth from the last of the undoubtedly legitimate Plantagenets, Richard III, and Henry VII executed Edward (Plantagenet), Earl of Warwick in 1499. It can be seen that the Tudor claim to the throne was remarkably shadowy, really resting on the arbitrament battle, for the Tudors had no English royal blood before Henry VII, and his was pretty diluted and questionable. The acceptance of Henry was influenced mainly by war-weariness, by the absence of any immediately obvious alternative, particularly of Lancastrian blood, and partly by the accident of his father having been granted a differenced version of the Royal Arms, which gave some colour to his royal claims.

Henry promptly took the precaution of marrying Elizabeth of York, eldest daughter of Edward IV. Her antecendents were, however, as questionable as those of the Beauforts. The principal ground for Richard III's claim to succeed his brother as King was that Edward's marriage to Elizabeth Woodville was not valid. Edward had previously been allegedly betrothed to Lady Eleanor Butler, daughter of the renowned John Talbot, Earl of Shrewsbury, and widow of Sir Thomas Butler. In the eyes of the Church such a contract was a sacred obligation (Henry VIII himself used this as an excuse for the annulment of his marriage to Anne Boleyn, since she had previously been engaged to marry the Earl of Northumberland). It

Figure 66   Standard of Henry VII.

followed that many at the time supported Richard's contention that Edward IV's children were illegitimate.[8]

It is, therefore, not surprising that the early Tudors were very conscious of the fact that their title to the throne was, like the martlets in Edmund Tudor's arms, based on flimsy foundations. This uncertainty suggests, too, why all the Tudor sovereigns made such an extensive use of heraldry, for they employed it to demonstrate in a graphic and dramatic way their claim to be in line of succession to the ancient Kings of England.

At the same time, it made them uncommonly quick to see a threat to their positon in any armorial display which might indicate the remotest pretension to be of ancient blood royal, and thus a potential threat to themselves. Henry VII, therefore, did away with the son of the Duke of Clarence, and Henry VIII executed Clarence's daughter, as well as the Duke of Buckingham, the Earl of Suffolk, the Marquess of Exeter, and others. As a result of these Tudor preoccupations, the heralds were actively involved in building up the country gentry as a counterwieght to the pretensions of the old aristocracy, and benefited enormously from royal employments under the new regime.

In Tudor times, a creature called a male griffin makes his appearance, and has been a puzzle to us all ever since. In medieval heraldry all creatures, except mermaids and harpies, were always male and so drawn, including griffins, so it seems very odd to find a creature definitely labelled as male, with the implication that an ordinary griffin must be female, which it is not, for it is always drawn with the appropriate male equipment.

The so-called male griffin of heraldry is depicted like an ordinary griffin, but without wings and also differing by having tusks, and curious spikes in bunches of three sticking out haphazardly from different parts of its body. Queen Anne (Boleyn) of unhappy memory, the second wife of Henry VIII,

121

had a male griffin as the sinister supporter of her arms. It will be recalled that Henry's divorce from his first wife, and his marriage to Anne, led to the downfall and ruin of Cardinal Wolsey, and the fact that both had griffins of a sort as supporters is a strange coincidence — or was it a neat heraldic way of recording the supplanting of Wolsey by Anne?

Anne Boleyn's own arms as Queen are a splendid heraldic example of cooking the books. Her father, Sir Thomas Boleyn, or Bullen as it was then more often spelt and always pronounced, had a simple and ancient family coat of arms, *Argent, a chevron gules between three bulls heads couped sable*, clearly a play on the name. Anne, being an ambitious and unscrupulous woman, persuaded her doting husband to instruct the Kings of Arms to devise for her something infinitely grander. After much scratching of heads, the Kings of Arms, obviously terrified of Henry and badgered by Anne, came up with a quarterly coat including the arms of families from whom she could, in fact, claim only the slightest and most distantly tenuous of descents. It is quarterly of six: first *England with a label of France* (that is, a blue label with gold fleurs de lys on the tags), for Lancaster; second *France Ancient with a label gules*, for Angoulême; third *Gules, a lion passant guardant gold*, for Guienne; fourth *Quarterly 1 and 4, Gold a chief indented azure*, for Butler, *and 2 and 3, Argent, a lion rampant sable crowned gules*, for Rochfort; fifth *England with a label argent*, for Brotherton; and sixth *Chequy gold and azure*, for Warrenne (Figure 67). The sheer effrontery of it takes one's breath away.

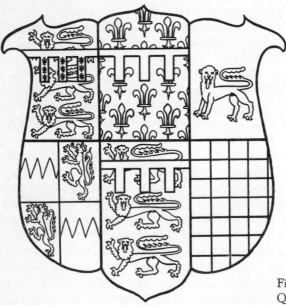

Figure 67 Arms of
Queen Anne Boleyn.

THIRTEEN

THE HERALDIC CONSEQUENCES OF RICHARD II

HE ARMORIAL PRECEDENTS set in the reign of Richard II encouraged the ambitions of the great magnates, with the most tenuous claims to royal descent, and aroused the deepest suspicions of one king after another. It was, however, not only the use of the Royal Arms which made successive kings uneasy, but the ostentatious use by the Staffords of one of the most important Royal Badges, the Antelope, during the fifteenth and early sixteenth centuries (Figure 68).

The angry Antelope of heraldry, fierce and fell, was believed to be one of the most ferocious of beasts, wild and untamable. With his serrated horns he could saw down large trees, but his horns often proved his undoing, because they were apt to become entangled in bushes when he went down to the river to drink, and so he was caught by the hunters; a moral which the Staffords failed to heed.

Probably because of the Antelope's reputation for fierceness, he was adopted as a badge by Humphrey de Bohun, Earl of Hereford, Essex and Northampton, K.G., and Constable of England (died 1372/3), an active and successful soldier. He had no sons, and his younger daughter and co-heiress Mary married Henry of Bolingbroke, afterwards Henry IV, and the famous Bohun badges of the Antelope and the Swan descended to Henry V and Henry VI, and were subsequently adopted by the Tudors.

The elder daughter Eleanor married Thomas of Woodstock, Duke of

123

Figure 68
Antelope badge of the
later Staffords, Dukes of
Buckingham.

Gloucester, who became Constable of England and also inherited the Swan badge, which alluded to the Bohun descent from the Swan Knight. It was their daughter and heiress who married Edmund (Stafford), Earl of Stafford, who inherited through her the Earldom of Buckingham and the Constableship. He then also assumed the Antelope badge.

Their son Humphrey (Stafford) was created first Duke of Buckingham, and was killed at the Battle of Northampton in 1460. His quarterly shield showed 1 Woodstock, 2 Bohun of Hereford and Essex, 3 Bohun of Northampton, and 4 Stafford, with two Antelopes as Supporters. This is a clear indication that the Staffords had one eye on the throne during these turbulent years and were prepared to throw their hat into the ring if opportunity offered. It was Duke Humphrey's grandson, Henry, Duke of Buckingham, who got that Chapter of the Kings and Heralds of Arms in February 1473/4 to agree that he could properly bear the arms of Thomas of Woodstock 'alone without any other Armes to be quartered therewith'. Although Duke Henry had been an active supporter of Edward IV and Richard III, by 1483 he was beginning to see himself in the part of kingmaker, and raised a rebellion in favour of Henry (Tudor), Earl of

Richmond, but was easily defeated and was executed in the market-place at Salisbury. All his honours were forfeited and the hereditary office of High Constable of England came to an end for ever, to be revived for one day only, on the day of the Coronation of the Sovereign.

After Henry VII gained the throne in 1485, he restored Buckingham's dignities and lands, except for the Constableship, to his son, Edward Stafford, who became one of the wealthiest of the nobility, with family connections and territorial power in many counties. His magnificence was truly regal. At his Epiphany feast on January 6th, 1507/8, he had 519 persons to dinner and 400 to supper, attended by yeomen and grooms, with minstrels, trumpeters and players, and it took 521 quarts of ale to wash down the sumptuous banquets.[1] With vast financial resources, strategically based castles, and well-equipped retainers, the Duke of Buckingham was almost as powerful as the King himself, and the wary Tudors watched him with growing unease. He was a man of considerable presence, with a reputation as a jouster. The Venetian Ambassador reported in 1519 that he was extremely popular, and that it was commonly thought he might easily obtain the Crown if the King died without heirs.[2]

Although Buckingham avoided his father's too ostentatious flaunting of his Plantagenet blood, by reverting to the earlier practice of his ancestors in using the quarterly coat, 1 Woodstock, 2 Bohun of Hereford, 3 Stafford, and 4 Bohun of Northampton, he still placed Woodstock first. Coupled with this, his use of the royal Antelope badge, together with the motto 'Dorsanavant' (Henceforward), convinced Henry VIII that he was too much of a potential danger. At the same time, he had been rash enough to incur the enmity of Cardinal Wolsey. A few months after the King and Buckingham had returned from the Field of Cloth of Gold, Buckingham was arrested, to the amazement of all Europe. He was accused of high treason on the flimsiest of trumped-up charges and a rigged court was hastily appointed, over which the Duke of Norfolk was forced to preside and, weeping, pronounce the sentence of death against his own father-in-law. Buckingham was executed on Tower Hill in 1521, and his arms were deleted from the records of the College of Arms.

This subservience to Henry VIII was not, however, to save the Duke of Norfolk or his son, when they got into trouble through reliance on the armorial rulings of Richard II. One of the most famous trials in which heraldry was the main and only ostensible ground for prosecution was that of Henry Howard, the poet Earl of Surrey and his father, the old Duke of Norfolk. Henry Howard was a headstrong young man, intensely proud of his descent from Edward I, through Thomas of Brotherton, and from Thomas (Mowbray), 1st Duke of Norfolk of the early creation. It will be recalled that in January 1393/4, Richard II had recognised the right of Thomas Mowbray to use the arms and crest of Brotherton alone, and that in September 1397 he had authorised Thomas Mowbray to impale the Brotherton arms with those of Edward the Confessor undifferenced. There is no evidence that this was rescinded, but Henry IV evidently discouraged the practice, and Thomas Mowbray's son John, who was restored to the Dukedom in 1425, used Brotherton alone on his Garter stall-plate.

In 1546 Henry VIII was dying, and the fight for power between the rival factions increased in ruthlessness and intensity, the prize being control of the heir to the throne. Henry Howard, who felt that his father had a right to the regency, made a series of breathtakingly silly and rash remarks. Everyone about the Court must have known how the great but extraordinarily suspicious King reacted to political pretensions demonstrated in a heraldic way. The Earl of Surrey had several examples very close to home to teach him caution, apart from that of his Stafford grandfather. His indiscretions enabled his enemies the Seymours to pounce.[3]

The Duke of Norfolk and his son were arrested on December 8th, 1546 and thrown into the Tower of London. Norfolk himself had been indiscreet in criticising the King's advisers and, by implication, the King himself. Surrey was one of those people whom no one can save from themselves. Headstrong and violent, he had been several times arrested by the authorities; proud and arrogant, he had continually attracted the attention of his coldly calculating Sovereign. Surrey, too, had spoken disparagingly of many of the King's councillors and, as always happens, this got back to them. It was said that he was so proud of his descent from Edward I through Thomas of Brotherton that he put on almost regal airs, persuading his entourage to pay him the kind of respect normally due only to royalty. They called him 'prince', and discussed the possibility of his succeeding to the throne, and this was too much for Henry VIII.

Even Norfolk had confided to his mistress, Elizabeth Holland, who was interrogated by the royal officials, that Surrey had 'placed the Norfolk arms wrong', and that he had found fault with his son over it. Apart from being lumbered with a dangerous heir, the Howard family was deeply divided against itself and Surrey's sister Mary, who had married Henry Fitzroy, Duke of Richmond and Somerset, the bastard son of Henry VIII, who had died in 1536, was prepared to give evidence against her brother. It is a sordid and sorry tale.

Surrey would, of course, have known of the ruling of the Chapter of the Kings and Heralds of Arms in 1473/4, that his great-grandfather, Henry (Stafford), Duke of Buckingham, might bear the arms of Thomas of Woodstock 'alone without any other Armes to be quartered therewith', and would have seen his great-grandfather's armorial stall-plate in the Garter Chapel at Windsor. Surrey would also have known of Richard II's ruling in favour of his ancestor Thomas de Mowbray, Earl of Norfolk, that he could bear the arms of Brotherton alone, although the story might well have become garbled in the course of time.

In August 1546 Surrey had shown Sir Christopher Barker, Garter King of Arms, a 'scutcheon of the arms [of] Brotherton and St. Edward and Anjou and Mowbray quartered, and said he would bear it'. Garter says he protested that this would be improper, but that Surrey had been determined to do so.[4] As well as placing the arms of Brotherton in the first quarter, Surrey also proposed to remove the label from them, thus turning them into the old Royal Arms of England, which was certainly asking for trouble, while to quarter the arms of Edward the Confessor, which the dying King said 'appertain only to the King of this realm', added to the offence.

Surrey's passionate interest in his illustrious ancestry, coupled with an imperfect grasp of armory, led him into yet deeper heraldic bogs. His sister deposed that

> instead of the Duke's Coronet was put to his Arms a Cap of maintenance purple, with powdered Furr [i.e., ermine] and with a Crown, to her judgement much like to a close Crown [i.e., with arches, like a royal crown], and underneath the Arms was a cipher, which she took to be the King's cipher, H.R.[5]

It is quite possible that this spiteful woman misread 'H.H.' (Henry Howard).

There is a manuscript, possibly contemporary, which depicts a quarterly shield in trick, over which is written 'Howard Earle of Surry, for which he was attainted'. This shows the quarterings marshalled in a strange way. Howard is in the first quarter, but with the augmentation for Flodden as a crowned inescutcheon instead of on the bend without a crown. The second quartering is for Brotherton but without the label, and the arms of St Edward the Confessor in the fifth quarter have a label.[6] If this scheme of quarterings was, in fact, drawn up by him, it looks very much like amateur heraldic doodling, and it is certainly nothing like the arms entered for him when he was created a Knight of the Garter.

Father and son were tried at the Guildhall of the City of London and both were condemned. The Earl of Surrey was executed on Tower Hill on January 19th, 1546/7 aged about twenty-nine or thirty (his date of birth is not known). The old Duke of Norfolk escaped by the skin of his teeth, as Henry VIII, in the last stages of his disease, died before he could sign the death warrant, and Norfolk remained in prison until Queen Mary ascended the throne, when he was released and reinstated in his honours and properties. Surrey was buried at Allhallows, Barking, but in 1614 his second son Henry, Earl of Northampton, removed his remains to Framlingham Church, where he erected to his memory the splendid tomb which the present Duke of Norfolk and others of his descendants restored in 1977.

There is, alas, no Garter stall-plate for Henry Howard in St George's Chapel at Windsor Castle. No doubt it was removed when he was executed. Neither can any record be found in the official registers of the College of Arms. However, there are relevant entries in two manuscripts in the College library. One, which depicts the arms of contemporary Knights of the Garter, has the following reference: 'Henry Howard Earle of Surrey sonne to Thomas Duke of Norfolke. A.° 1541, 33 H.8'. This gives his arms as the normal Howard coat, *Quarterly, 1 Howard with the augmentation for Flodden on the bend, 2 Brotherton (correctly), 3 Warenne, 4 Mowbray*, but without the label for the son and heir. It was in 1541 that Henry Howard was created a Knight of the Garter.

The other manuscript is even more interesting. It is also contemporary, entitled 'Coats of Arms of Noblemen and Knights temp. Hen. 8 and Edw. 6', which is in colour, and it gives the arms of 'The yerle of Surrey ...' (the rest is difficult to read). The arms are shown with the correct quarterings, but with a gold label over all, as one might expect for the eldest son and heir of the Duke of Norfolk. The arms are scored through in ink, so were presumably painted before Henry Howard's execution.[7] Against these two manuscripts must be set the fact that there is at Arundel Castle a seal matrix with the quartered arms of the Howard Dukes of Norfolk, but showing Brotherton without the label. One wonders whether this might have been the seal of Henry Howard. If so, he certainly was 'the most foolish proud boy that is in England'.

In the painting of Henry Howard, Earl of Surrey, which is now at Arundel Castle, the identity of the artist and the date of the painting have remained a puzzle. For a long time it was believed to be by, or after, the Court painter Guillim Strete, and thought to have been painted about 1551, but it is not known for whom, as the Howards were then in eclipse. There is a remarkably similar picture at Knole House, which is similarly attributed. Both show the poet Earl of Surrey standing, with his right elbow resting on a broken pillar, but the Knole portrait omits the elaborately sculptured arch and has only the Brotherton arms. Dr Roy Strong has recently suggested that the picture at Arundel may not have been painted until 1615–20, possibly for the 'collecting' Earl of Arundel (1586–1646), who was Surrey's great-grandson.

If the original portrait of the poet Earl of Surrey was first painted by Guillim (or William) Strete (see the *Dictionary of National Biography*) in March 1551/2, then it was done at a time when Edward VI was on the throne and the old Duke of Norfolk was still in prison, stripped of all his wealth, and his enemies in power. It was not until after Mary had been proclaimed Queen on July 16th, 1553 that Norfolk was released and his honours and property restored on August 29th, 1553, dying on August 25th, 1554.

If the portrait, of which that at Arundel is thought to be a copy, was in fact painted in 1551/2, it seems very odd indeed that it should contain, in the most flamboyant way, two shields of arms which had, only recently, brought so much pain and grief to so many people. In the picture at Arundel the Earl of Surrey is flanked on his right side (on the left as one looks at it) by a man supporting with his exterior hand a shield of *Brotherton* (correctly shown), and he is flanked on his left side (the right of the picture) by a woman supporting with her exterior hand a shield of *Woodstock*. Both are depicted 'alone without any other Armes quartered therewith'. The picture appears to be an allegory emphasising Henry Howard's male descent through the Mowbrays and Thomas of Brotherton from Edward I, and his female descent through his mother and the Staffords through Thomas of Woodstock from Edward III.

As Henry Howard had been executed only four years before the original is thought to have been painted, and the principal ground for his conviction had been his flaunting of his royal descent, it is most unlikely that the picture at Arundel can be based on an original of 1551/2. The imprisoned old Duke of Norfolk was not then in a position to commission a major painting and would certainly not have stuck his neck out in this way even if he were. He had learnt his lesson. Dr Roy Strong has argued, very persuasively, that the Arundel picture shows influences of the period around 1615–20.[8] Now the political climate had by that time changed to such an extent that Henry (Howard), Earl of Northampton, Surrey's second son, could pluck up the courage to move his father's remains to Framlingham and give Surrey a magnificent tomb. The picture could not have been commissioned by the Earl of Northampton, because he had the correct arms of the Howards placed on the side of the tomb, with the quarterings in the normal sequence. The poet Earl's great-grandson Thomas, Earl of Arundel, the 'collecting Earl', could have commissioned the picture around 1615–20. The shape of the shields is definitely not normal for Tudor times, and smacks more of the antiquarianism of Stuart times, because shields of the shape shown in the picture were used at the time of the Battle of Hastings, whereas by about 1100 and afterwards, shields had flat tops (Plate I).

This is a fascinating example of the way in which heraldry becomes inextricably tangled with the lives of people long dead, poses problems for people now living, and can assist in the dating of important pictures.

FOURTEEN

THE ARMS OF THE CONSTABLE AND THE MARSHAL

BOTH THE Constable and the Marshal were important military officers, the former being roughly equivalent to a commander-in-chief and the latter roughly to a modern adjutant-general. In Norman and Plantagenet times these two great officers of state were also two of the most powerful of the marcher barons.

The constable was originally the *comes stabuli*, the Count of the Stables, who was one of the chief officers of the Byzantine emperors. Charlemagne followed their example and instituted the office at his own court, and thence it was adopted throughout western Europe. After a time the name was applied fairly widely to officials exercising disciplinary powers. Thus we find not only the King's Constable, or Constable of England, but also constables of castles (an important military command), and constables of hundreds (administrative districts within a county), responsible for keeping the peace.

King Henry I had four royal Constables, who took it in turn to serve at Court for three months at a time, and these offices appear to have been hereditary in the families of Montfort, d'Oilli, d'Abitot and Gloucester, and the castles of Dover, Oxford, Worcester and Gloucester respectively went with the office.

The first three constableships seem to have fizzled out around the middle of the twelfth century. Walter of Gloucester, the son of Roger de Pitres, the Domesday tenant-in-chief, who was hereditary Sheriff of

Gloucester and constable of the castle under Henry I and thus one of the four King's Constables, was succeeded in these offices by his son, Miles of Gloucester. Miles was already an important marcher baron and lord of Abergavenny, and through his wife Sybil, the daughter and heiress of Bernard de Neufmarché, he acquired the lordship of Brecknock, the former Welsh kingdom of Brycheiniog, with all its regalities, and many other lands on the March. He was created Earl of Hereford in 1141 and died in 1143. His four sons succeeded him as King's Constables but all died without issue, and his elder daughter Margaret carried the constableship to her husband, Humphrey de Bohun, whose grandson, another Humphrey de Bohun, was created Earl of Hereford in 1200 and recognised as hereditary Constable of England.

Miles of Gloucester had borne for his arms *Gules, two bends the upper or and the lower argent.* Until the time of the last-mentioned Humphrey de Bohun their family arms had been *Azure, a bend argent between six lioncels or*, but about this time they placed the silver bend within two gold cotises, which clearly formed an allusion to their inheritance of the constableship from Miles of Gloucester (Figure 69).

But that is not the end of the story. This remarkable family continued to flourish for some centuries, playing an important part in the centre of the stage of English politics and producing a succession of able soldiers. With the death of the last Humphrey de Bohun in 1373, the main line died out. His elder daughter and heiress, Eleanor, carried the hereditary con-

Figure 69
Arms of Miles of Gloucester (d. 1143) and Humphrey de Bohun, created Earl of Hereford in 1200.

131

stableship of England and the Earldom of Essex to her husband, Thomas of Woodstock, who was created Earl of Buckingham and Duke of Gloucester. His seal, attached to a letter of attorney dated January 8th 1390/1, shows a leafless tree (or wood stock) from which is suspended his shield of arms, and hanging from the branches on either side two shields of the arms of Miles of Gloucester. This is pretty clear evidence that those arms were regarded as the arms of office of the Constable.

Another seal of Thomas of Woodstock has, on the counterseal, three circles in triangle, the uppermost containing his crest, that to the bottom left his arms, and that to the bottom right a shield of Bohun quartering Miles of Gloucester.[1] Anne, the daughter and eventual heiress of Thomas of Woodstock and Eleanor, married Edmund Stafford, Earl of Stafford, who thus acquired the Earldoms of Essex and Buckingham.

In a roll of arms complied about 1480, depicting the banners of English princes, dukes, earls and lords of the reign of Edward IV and earlier, we find the ancient arms of Miles of Gloucester, the gold and silver bends on a red field, but the origin of the arms had evidently been forgotten by Garter Wrythe, for they are described as 'The Armys of Essex'. The fact that they are shown separately from the arms of the Duke of Buckingham indicates that they were probably borne and used separately as the arms of office of the Lord High Constable.[2]

Like those of the Constable, the origins of the Marshal go back to Carolingian times and, like him, the Marshal was an officer of the royal household mainly responsible for the King's horses and for the payment of the wages of the soldiers, huntsmen and falconers in the King's service, and was originally subordinate to the Constable. The Master Marshal was paid 2s. a day (the same as the assistant constables) and there were four marshals under him. He was also responsible for the Fleet prison, in which insolvent debtors languished.

Gilbert the Marshal was King's Marshal, or Master Marshal, in the court of Henry I and a minor tenant-in-chief holding lands in Wiltshire and Somerset, but the origins of his family have not yet been discovered. The fact that they were already hereditary Marshals of the Conqueror's son suggests that they may have been Master Marshals of the Dukes of Normandy before the Conquest. They were certainly well-connected there, being related to the powerful Tancarville family, hereditary Chamberlains of Normandy, and the fact that Gilbert's son John married the sister of the Earl of Salisbury indicates that the family was regarded as of considerable feudal and social standing.[3]

John Fitz Gilbert, more often styled John the Marshal, succeeded his father in 1130, paying a moderate relief for his lands and an additional relief for the office of Marshal of the Court. He married first the daughter and heiress of Walter Pipard, another minor tenant-in-chief, thus extending his lands, and second Sybil, a sister of Patrick, Constable of Salisbury Castle, a great tenant-in-chief in Wiltshire, who was soon afterwards created Earl of Salisbury. John was a redoubtable soldier, described by a contemporary as 'a man illustrious as a Knight', and an enterprising and daring commander, who early in the civil war threw in his lot with the Empress Matilda. A story of the war illustrates his ruthless toughness. His son William had been handed to King Stephen as a hostage during the siege of one of John's castles. John broke the terms of the truce and took the opportunity of reinforcing the garrison. William's life was forfeit, as John refused to surrender the castle and told Stephen's messenger that he was unmoved at the threat to kill his son, as he had the anvil and hammers with which to forge still better sons. Little William was thereupon taken out to be hanged from a tree, but seeing the Earl of Arundel holding a spear and about to slay him, he innocently asked for the weapon. Stephen, who was a chivalrous soldier, was so taken by this that he countermanded the order.

When William was about thirteen years old he was sent as a squire to be educated in the household of his cousin William de Tancarville, whose great castle on the Seine would be full of the comings and goings of a busy baron, with the service of ninety-four knights at his command. William was knighted in 1167, during the war between Normandy and France, when he greatly distinguished himself. After the war he became a knight-errant, taking part in one tournament after another, to his great financial advantage.

In the early tournaments, the defeated knight forfeited his horse and armour to the victor, while the heralds received as their perquisite the broken armour. In view of the fact that the Earl Marshal still today has control over the heralds, it is interesting that the earliest surviving references to heralds occur in connection with William Marshal, the first concerning the rebellion in Anjou of Prince Henry against his father, Henry II, in which William Marshal, at that time tutor to the Prince, was assisted by 'Hirauz de armes'.[4] William Marshal succeeded his father and elder brother as Master Marshal. His loyalty to successive kings was rewarded with extensive lands in England, Ireland and Normandy. Through his marriage to Isabel, daughter and heiress of Richard de Clare, William acquired the Earldom of Pembroke and Striguil and extensive lands there and elsewhere. After the death of King John, he was appointed Regent of England. 'The best knight who ever lived' died in 1219.

It has been suggested that the original arms of this family were *Gules, a bend fusilly or*, but there is insufficient evidence either way. The Marshals of Ireland, who were of the same family, bore these arms.[5] There is some possible support for this in the *History of William the Marshal*.[6] William was taking part in a tournament shortly after he had been knighted when,

Figure 70
Arms of William Marshal,
Earl of Pembroke and Striguil.

Figure 71
Arms of Fitz-Alan Howard,
Dukes of Norfolk and Earls Marshal.

during a mêlée, his helm was knocked back to front. As he was putting it straight two knights rode past. 'Sir John,' said one, 'who is that knight who is so capable with his weapons?' 'That is William Marshal,' the other replied. 'There is no man more true. The device on his shield shows that he hails from Tancarville.' We know that William was closely related to the powerful Tancarville family. They never bore for their arms a rampant lion, so it would be interesting to know if they bore, at that time, a bend of some kind. The arms which William Marshal made famous were *Party per pale or and vert, a lion rampant gules*,[7] sometimes depicted as *queue fourchée* (Figure 70).

William Marshal's five sons succeeded him in turn as Master Marshal and Earls of Pembroke and Striguil, but all died without issue by 1245, and the extensive family possessions were divided between his five daughters. The oldest, Maud (Matilda), married Hugh Bigod, Earl of Norfolk, and carried the office of Master Marshal and her paternal arms to that family, who appear to have borne these arms separately from their own, *Or, a cross gules*, as arms of office as hereditary Marshals.[8] The Bigods continued as hereditary Master Marshals until the death of Roger, 5th Earl of Norfolk, in 1306, when the office lapsed to the Crown. In 1316 the office was granted by Edward II to his younger brother, Thomas of Brotherton, who was created Earl of Norfolk. By this period the office was becoming known as that of 'Earl Marshal'. The office again reverted to the Crown and was then granted to Thomas Mowbray, Earl of Nottingham, as representative in blood of Thomas of Brotherton, and the style of 'Earl Marshal' was confirmed to him in 1386, and he was subsequently created Duke of Norfolk.

Thomas Mowbray's daughter married Sir Robert Howard and, with the extinction of the male line of the Mowbrays in 1475, his son, John Howard, was created Duke of Norfolk and Earl Marshal by Richard III in 1483, but he was killed at the Battle of Bosworth and his titles suffered attainder. John Howard's son, Thomas, was restored to the Earldom but not to the Dukedom of Norfolk. He commanded the army which defeated the Scots at Flodden in 1513 and was created Duke of Norfolk. It was this battle which brought the 'Flodden Augmentation' to their arms. With a few hiccoughs, the title of Earl Marshal has continued in the Howard family to this day (Figure 71).

Like the arms of Miles of Gloucester, which became associated with the hereditary office of Constable of England, so did the arms of William Marshal become associated with the hereditary office of Earl Marshal, for we find in an early Tudor book of arms compiled for Garter Wriothesley, the ancient arms *Party per pale or and vert, a lion rampant gules*, described as 'Bygod, Erll Marischall'.[9]

FIFTEEN

THE EARL MARSHAL AND THE COURT OF CHIVALRY

HE HEREDITARY CONSTABLESHIP was abolished in 1483 when the Duke of Buckingham was executed. Although Henry VII restored his titles, honours and lands to Buckingham's son, the Constableship was retained in the hands of the Crown, only to be conjured up from the past, like an insubstantial ghost, for the one day of the Sovereign's Coronation. On the other hand the Marshalcy, after many vicissitudes, continues to flourish to this day. The joint responsibilities of the Constable and the Marshal over the heralds of England, and their joint presidency of the High Court of Chivalry, are now exercised by the Earl Marshal alone. The Earl Marshal is thus much more than just a gilded Great Officer of State: he is a constitutionally appointed judge of a High Court, and has as well wide powers over the English Officers of Arms.[1]

Lord Goddard, Lord Chief Justice, sitting in the High Court of Chivalry as the Earl Marshal's Surrogate (or deputy) in December 1954, in his judgment at the end of the Manchester Corporation Case in which the City of Manchester sued a firm for pirating its arms, said that 'as Surrogate to the Earl Marshal I declare that the Court has jurisdiction in this matter and I give judgment for the Plaintiffs for the agreed amount of costs'. In his written reasons for this judgment, he stated that 'in view of the opinions which I have cited of authors whose words are recognised as of the highest authority, I have no hesitation in holding that this Court has jurisdiction to deal with complaints relating to the usurpation of armorial bearings'.[2] The Court of Chivalry still exists and can grant an injunction and award damages. 'Should it be necessary to commit for contempt of the Court of Chivalry at the present time, the inherent jurisdiction of the High Court to punish contempts of inferior courts could be invoked.'[3]

The Court of Chivalry is a civil-law court and can proceed only in accordance with that law, and in accordance with the customs and usages of the Court. In the past it was empowered to deal with three classes of action: (a) causes of instance, (b) causes of office, and (c) appeals of treason and murder; but the court no longer has jurisdiction in the third class. Causes of instance were cases brought by one party against another, alleging defamation of character and the like, or alleging misuse or appropriation of the plaintiff's armorial bearings by the defendant. Remedies for defamation can now be sought in the common law courts, but the latter type of case is still actionable in the High Court of Chivalry, as was decided in the Manchester Corporation Case in 1954. Causes of office were the correction of faults by the judge in virtue of his office. They would be promoted by the King's Advocate, or by one or more Kings of Arms, or by a private individual, not necessarily himself damaged by the act of the defendant. There has been no recent case of this kind, but it is considered that the Court is still capable of being seized of such a case. An appeal from a judgment of the Court of Chivalry would be made by way of a petition of appeal addressed to The Sovereign and lodged with the Clerk of the Privy Council, and would proceed in the same manner as any other appeal to the Privy Council.

It has been the custom for the Earl Marshal to appoint a distinguished lawyer as his Lieutenant, Assessor or Surrogate, to act as judge. In earlier times these lawyers were usually appointed as and when required, and often only for a particular occasion. In more recent times the Surrogate has been appointed as permanent judge in the High Court of Chivalry.

The Earl Marshal's position as regards the Officers of Arms individually and collectively as the College of Arms has evolved over the centuries, and like most ancient institutions lacks precise definition, which has sometimes led individual Earl Marshals and individual Kings of Arms to try to extend the frontiers of their powers. There seems little doubt that throughout the Middle Ages the Kings of Arms, Heralds and Pursuivants of Arms, whether on the pay-roll of the King or of one of the greater nobles, came under the command of the Constable and Marshal when on active service in time of war or rebellion, while they had a general responsibility for the royal heralds in time of peace.

From the time of Henry VIII to that of Charles II there had been continual controversy between the three Kings of Arms over the right of the two Provincial Kings of Arms (Clarenceux and Norroy) to grant arms separately from Garter or each other, whilst Garter claimed that he and his predecessors had the right to grant arms anywhere in England, with or without a Provincial King.

By Letters Patent of Charles II dated October 19th, 1672, Henry Howard was created Earl of Norwich and hereditary Earl Marshal. This confirmed that the Earl Marshal could preside over the Court of Chivalry alone, in the absence of the Constable, with extended limitations to include, in the event of Henry's death without male issue, the other descendants of his grandfather Thomas, Earl or Arundel, from whom the present Earl Marshal is descended. These Letters Patent were read out at the start of the Manchester Corporation Case, as evidence of the authority by which Duke Bernard was presiding over the cause in the Court of Chivalry.

Henry Howard promptly asserted his authority over the disputatious Kings of Arms and introduced reforms in the conduct of their duties. His directions were challenged by Sir Edward Walker, Garter King of Arms (Plate II). The Earl appealed to Charles II for a ruling on the scope of his jurisdiction and authority, and the King referred it to the Earl of Aylesbury, the Lord Privy Seal, for an opinion.

As a result the King promulgated a Declaration, dated June 16th, 1673, in which he described the Earl Marshal as

> the next and immediate Officer under Us for determining and Ordering all matters touching Armes, Ensigns of Nobility, Honour and Chivalry ... the rule, Government and Ordering of them [the Officers of Arms] in all things belonging to their Faculty and Employment being an Indubitable Right belonging to and naturally consistent with the Office of Earl Marshal

and stated that it appertained to the office of Earl Marshal of England to order, judge and determine all matters touching arms, ensigns of nobility, honour and chivalry, according to the law of arms, and to make and prescribe, from time to time, rules, ordinances and decrees for the due regulation and settlement thereof, including the good government of the Kings, Heralds and Pursuivants of Arms, 'in all things touching their Faculty and Imployment'. The Declaration also confirmed the Earl Marshal's right to nominate officers for appointment, as well as his powers of correction and punishment of such Officers of Arms as shall not conform themselves to the orders made by him, or misbehave themselves in the execution of their duties.[4]

This was pretty sweeping, and the Officers, and particularly the Kings of Arms were horrified. Garter Walker immediately appealed to the King, on the grounds that this ruling made him a 'Subordinated Minister to the

Earl Marshal in all things belonging to his Faculty and Employment', and requested that it be reviewed. The King submitted the matter to the Privy Council who, on January 22nd, 1673/4, 'having accordingly met, and both parties being again heard, their Lordships did this day Report to his Majesty in Council that they found no cause to alter anything in the said Declaration', whereupon the King confirmed the Declaration. This established the Earl Marshal's authority over the Kings, Heralds and Pursuivants of Arms 'in all things touching their Faculty and Imployment', and effectively clipped the wings of the Kings of Arms. Sir Peter Lely has immortalised Garter Walker and several of these heralds and pursuivants in a series of lively drawings.

III

THE HERALDS
IN THE MODERN WORLD

ANY PEOPLE are very hazy about what heralds do, and find our heraldic titles too strange to be true. All of us in the College of Arms are constantly being reminded of this, and the misapprehensions are sometimes hilarious and sometimes bizarre. In the modern world, where the urban guerrilla is part of the social scene and 'arms' has only one connotation, we occasionally find foreigners expecting to buy guns from us. Many people ask if the job is hereditary. Others assume that we are highly paid civil servants, working in one of the idler backwaters of government, or they presume that as the place in which we work is called a college, it must be some kind of educational establishment. In fact, the College of Arms is not supported from public funds, neither is it part of any United Kingdom government department. The Officers of Arms are members of the Royal Household, and are responsible through the Earl Marshal to the Sovereign in those countries of which she is Queen and Head of the Commonwealth, with the exception of Scotland within which Lord Lyon King of Arms has jurisdiction.

The earlier parts of this book have been designed to show how heraldry grew and was adapted to the developing needs of its time, with the active assistance of the heralds. We have seen heraldry and the heralds in action at different times in the past. What follows is an attempt to show how the heralds have adapted to the modern world, and avoided becoming social fossils.

In discussing the heralds and the College of Arms as they are today, and writing about activities in which we are currently engaged – for this is one's life – I shall describe our duties in a personal, indeed almost autobiographical way, when this helps to bring them to life.

For reasons of space it is not possible to discuss every one of the remarkably varied activities of a modern herald, so this account must be selective. Naturally, there are some chapters where one needs to cover the ground in some detail because, as in 'The Heralds and the College of Arms', this is basic to any understanding of this unusual body and the activities which flow from its constitutional position. Because so many people are interested in the subject, grants of armorial bearings are discussed at some length, and so it is with ancient arms and genealogical records. In a different category are the activities described in Chapters 19 to 21 of which few people have had more than a glimpse; and to many they are practically unknown.

The ceremonial duties of the heralds are better known to the public, because they have been given considerable coverage in the press and on television and radio, but very few indeed have any idea of the work involved in producing a Ceremony of State which looks effortless. Here again space makes it impossible to deal with all these activities in detail, so I have taken the first, the Proclamation of the Accession of The Sovereign, as being of interest because so little has been written about it, and the last the State Funeral of Sir Winston Churchill, because I was personally much involved in it and can therefore speak with some authority about it. Moreover, it may well turn out to be the last great ceremony of its kind.

SIXTEEN

THE HERALDS AND THE COLLEGE OF ARMS

HOMAS FULLER, whose *History of the Worthies of England* was published in 1662, has a chapter on 'The Good Herald', who is 'a Warden of the Temple of Honour', being 'grave and faithfull in discharging the service he is imployed in '. After touching on the military duties of heralds, our author then passes 'from his use in warre to his imployment in peace', and discusses the good herald's skill 'in the pedigrees and descents of all ancient Gentry'. Here he makes a very shrewd observation that 'to be able onely to blazon a Coat doth no more make an Herald, than the reading the titles of Galley-pots makes a physician'.

Richard III, when Duke of Gloucester, had been Constable of England and thus much concerned with the Officers of Arms. On March 2nd, 1483/4 he granted to Garter, Clarenceux, Norroy, and Gloucester Kings of Arms, and all other Heralds and Pursuivants then in existence, a charter constituting them a body corporate with perpetual succession and a common seal, and also granted them a great house called Coldharbour beside the Thames in the City of London.[1] The next year the King was killed at the Battle of Bosworth, and the Act of Resumption by which Henry VII annulled grants made by Edward IV and Richard III enabled him to seize Coldharbour and give it to his mother.

The Officers of Arms were obviously in a most unsatisfactory position after this, and without a house where they could meet, transact their business and keep their rapidly growing library, they were anxious to put matters on a better footing. The chance came soon after Edward VI ascended the throne, and they obtained a charter dated June 4th, 1549 confirming to the three Kings of Arms, six Heralds, and seven Pursuivants named in the charter, and to 'all other Kings, Heralds and Pursuivants of Arms that hereafter shall be', their ancient privileges and liberties, which included exemption from the payment of all subsidies, reliefs and other forms of taxation, both in war and peace, and also exemption from tolls and customs, and freedom from jury service, watch and ward, and service in any public office.[2]

The modern history of the English heralds begins with the charter of King Philip and Queen Mary (Tudor), dated July 18th, 1555, creating Garter, Clarenceux and Norroy Kings of Arms, Windsor, Chester, Richmond, Somerset, York, and Lancaster Heralds, and 'all other heralds and officers or pursuivants of arms, who shall be so at that time' (i.e., 1555), a body corporate with perpetual succession and a common seal. The Pursuivants at that time were Portcullis, Bluemantle, Rouge Croix and Rouge Dragon. The wording follows closely that of the charter of Richard III. The Officers of Arms mentioned in this charter, together with the four Pursuivants, have from that time been regarded as the Officers of Arms in Ordinary, that is to say, on the establishment, whilst Officers of Arms created additionally, and thus extra to the establishment of 1555, are known as Officers of Arms Extraordinary.

This charter of 1555 granted the Corporation of the Kings, Heralds and Pursuivants of Arms, as they became known in law, the normal powers of a corporate body. It also granted them the 'house called Derby Place' in the City of London (burnt down in the Great Fire of 1666 and rebuilt shortly after 1672, which remains to this day the house of the College of Arms), where they could

> at their pleasure turn by turn sojourn there, and be able to meet at suitable and convenient days, places and times, as often and when it shall be pleasing to them, to do business, communicate, confer and agree among themselves, together with others, deliberately and with due heed for the good state, learning and government of their faculty.

The other object of giving them a house was to provide them with a place where they could keep records and library.[3] A college is an organised society of persons performing certain functions and possessing in common certain rights and privileges. The corporation thus became known to the public as the Heralds' College or College of Arms, although not so described in the charter of 1555, and this name is loosely applied to their house as well, which is one of the architectural jewels of the City of London.

Here again there was no mention of the Earl Marshal, and it seems to have been taken by the Kings of Arms as confirming the autonomous position they believed themselves to hold. This led to the contentions which caused an exasperated Earl Marshal to seek royal support for bringing his tiresome Kings of Arms to heel by the Declaration of 1673. In fact the functions of the Corporation are limited to those set out in the charter of 1555, and it has been held on good authority that all Officers of Arms dealing with matters unconnected with the Corporation are clearly subject to the ancient authority of the Earl Marshal, while the Corporation is not. This has led to confusion of thought from time to time, but as there would be no Corporation without the Officers, the Earl Marshal manifestly has indirect control over it.

A 'Chapter' was originally a meeting of the canons of a collegiate or cathedral church or monastic order, which was opened by the reading of a lesson, or chapter from the Epistles, and thus the meeting itself became so known. Soon the term was applied to the meeting of any order or recognised body, such as an order of knighthood or group of heralds. As early as January 5th, 1419/20, a chapter of the English Kings of Arms and Heralds was held at Rouen, evidently for the purpose of forming themselves into a corporate body, with rules for admission and conduct and a common seal.[4] Thereafter there are increasing references to chapters of the English Officers of Arms. What led to the confusion in later times was the fact that after the charter of 1555 the Officers of Arms dealt with Corporation business at the Chapter meetings, as well as heraldic and armorial matters.

One of the objects of the royal charter of 1555 was to provide the heralds with a place where they could 'keep the records, enrolments and other benefits touching and concerning the said faculty', and ever since the College of Arms has been regarded as an office of record. As time went on it became necessary to define what actually constituted the 'records' or official registers of the College. Lord Hardwicke, Lord Chancellor (died 1764), in a judgment quoted in 1767 by Lord Mansfield, Lord Chief Justice, ruled 'that Office books made by Heralds in the execution of their offices were evidence, but that books collected by the Heralds and coming into the Office by purchase or gift were not, but might be admitted as ancient books'. The former became known as the Records of the College of Arms, while the latter became known as the Collections.[5]

The Official Records of the College of Arms fall into the following classes, some of which sub-divide into particular groups:

I   THE VISITATION BOOKS

By Letters Patent in 1530 Henry VIII instructed all sheriffs, mayors, bailiffs and other officials concerned to give all aid and assistance to Clarenceux King of Arms on his forthcoming visit to each of the counties within his province of Southern England and South Wales, for the purpose of confirming and registering the arms of those who claimed to be gentry, where evidence could be shown that they were legally borne, and to 'reform all false armory and arms devised without authority', and grant new arms to such as qualified for them.[6] The last Visitation was that of London between 1687 and 1700.[7] Nothing as comprehensive as these Visitation records exists in any other European country. They are of outstanding importance to genealogists and armorists, and are of growing value for other academic studies. Although many contemporary and later copies were made, and are now to be found in such famous collections as the Harleian manuscripts in the British Library, the College Visitation Books are the only ones which can be accepted as record evidence for proof of descent. Naturally there is a continual requirement from all the English-speaking countries for recourse to them.

II   MODERN PEDIGREES

Some years before the Visitations fizzled out the voluntary recording of pedigrees began, and the College of Arms was the only office of record where the evidences in support of these pedigrees could be professionally and officially checked before they were accepted for registration.

(a) The earliest of the series of voluntary pedigree registers, which is known as *D.14*, ran until about 1885. Pedigrees were also entered in a volume known as *Howard* from about 1766 until superseded by the *Norfolk* series, with the *Surrey* series for shorter pedigrees since 1885, and these last two series are still current. The *Arundel* series, mainly used for royal descents, seize quartiers, documents certified under the Common Seal of the College and the like, is also still continuing.

(b) The series of *Peers' Pedigrees* began in 1767, when peers were required to prove their descent before their succession was recognised, but after 1802 this became voluntary.

(c) *Baronets' Pedigrees* began in 1783, when proof of arms and descent became obligatory, but later this was not insisted on. Today proof of descent certified by Garter King of Arms is still required by the Home Office if more than a father-to-son succession is involved.

III THE EARL MARSHAL'S BOOKS

This designation is loosely applied to the whole of the *I Series*, which began in the reign of Henry VIII and has now reached I.84, but strictly speaking the Earl Marshal's Books begin with I.25-7, and are continuous from I.32 until the present. I.1 is a book of designs by Maximilian Colt for important tombs, while I.2 is a magnificent book containing paintings and line drawings in trick of armorial banners and standards, compiled about 1520. The volumes from I.3, with some exceptions, down to I.31 contain Funeral Certificates, which give much valuable information on the deceased, his immediate family, and the armorial ensigns carried at his funeral, as approved by the officiating Herald.

IV GRANTS OF ARMS

Before 1673 the three Kings of Arms confirmed existing arms and made grants of new arms on their individual authority, but the records of these were retained by them. In consequence the records varied greatly in completeness, sometimes giving no more than a roughly drawn trick of the arms and crest with the name of the owner beside them, in other cases preserving the complete draft of the Letters Patent. Nevertheless these are invaluable records of arms granted mainly during the sixteenth and seventeenth centuries, and the series is known as *Old Grants*. The volumes of modern grants begin in 1673, though they include some of earlier date, and continue to the present day. The series now consists of over 140 volumes. These are the only authentic records, anywhere in the world, of arms granted by the English Kings of Arms.

The thirteen officers who comprise the Corporation of the Kings, Heralds and Pursuivants of Arms, more commonly known as the College of Arms, consist of Garter Principal King of Arms, Clarenceux King of Arms and Norroy & Ulster King of Arms; six Heralds: Richmond, Somerset, York, Lancaster, Chester and Windsor; and four Pursuivants: Portcullis, Bluemantle, Rouge Croix and Rouge Dragon. The Declaration of 1673 confirmed the right of the Earl Marshal to nominate suitable persons for appointment by the Sovereign as Officers of Arms.

The question we are frequently asked is how one becomes a herald, what the qualifications are, and how heralds are created. From the earliest times the heralds had to be literate and thus many of them were recruited from the troubadours and minstrels. However, the anonymous author of the *Sloane Tract*, written about 1470, believed that comely girls were once upon a time employed as heralds. One of their functions was to carry messages between the commanders of opposing armies, but as they often became pregnant through these arduous duties, retired knights were appointed instead, but they could not stand the pace and as a result of this discouraging experience, young men of good family were thereafter employed as heralds.[8] By the later Middle Ages it became customary to appoint young men of good education as pursuivants, who had to serve an apprenticeship for seven years before being eligible for promotion to Herald, and during this time they should be diligent in learning their profession. If, at the end of his apprenticeship, the pursuivant was found to have no aptitude for the work he would be dismissed.

Today much the same considerations apply, but the requirements are stricter. A suitable university degree is usually needed, and a legal qualification, either as a barrister or solicitor, is extremely helpful. These requirements can be waived if the candidate for an appointment has had appropriate experience in, say, the foreign service or the armed services. A candidate must be prepared to work as a clerk to one of the Kings of Arms or heralds for a few years, to give him experience of all sides of the work of the College. As Officers of Arms are required to act on occasion as staff-officers to the Earl Marshal in the planning and organisation of the Great Ceremonies of State, they also need the right temperament to be able to take responsibility and act decisively. With an establishment of only thirteen officers, whose patents of appointment have no retiring age written into them, so that they are, in effect, for life, vacancies occur infrequently and promotion is consequently slow.

At a Chapter held on June 26th, 1539, attended by Garter, Clarenceux and Norroy Kings of Arms, and Chester, Carlisle, Windsor, Richmond, Somerset, York and Lancaster Heralds, it was resolved

> that at all tymes hereafter when any officer of Armys shall dye and the roome be voyde, that none of the office shall goo alone to the Kinge or th'Eerle Marshall to able or disable any man to any souch roome, but that the Kinges of Armes shall call a councell or chapter, wher souch a man that shalbe recreatyd into the roome, ther shalbe before all the hole company approved, and if they find him able by his witte, learninge and auncientrye to be admytted to the same roome than all the hole company to go together and present and able hym to th'erle Marshall accordinge to the dew order thereof. Provided alwaye that if any that is auncyent being in any place in the Kinges business if he be Knowen and able by the said Companye, to have then hys roome.[9]

This ruling of Chapter has never been rescinded.

When, normally, the senior of the heralds is promoted to King of Arms, all the other heralds move up one place in seniority but retain their titles, thus causing the vacated appointment to go to the bottom of the Heralds' list. Normally the senior pursuivant is then promoted to the vacancy, thus causing his lately vacated title to go to the bottom of the pursuivants' list.

When a suitable candidate for the vacancy comes forward and is acceptable either on his own merits or after having served a probationary period in the College, Garter King of Arms (mindful no doubt of the Chapter ruling of 1539) discusses the candidate with the Officers of Arms in Chapter. If no adverse comments are made Garter then submits that candidate's name to the Earl Marshal, who by that time will usually have got to know him personally. The Earl Marshal then writes to The Queen's Private Secretary to ascertain whether The Sovereign would be pleased to approve the appointment of the person proposed. On receipt of notification from The Queen's Private Secretary that Her Majesty approves, the Earl Marshal instructs the Earl Marshal's Secretary (always a very senior Officer of Arms) to prepare the necessary Warrants for his signature. One is addressed to the Clerk of the Crown in Chancery (part of the Lord Chancellor's Office), informing him that The Queen is pleased to appoint so-and-so to the vacancy caused by the promotion, resignation or death of the former holder of that appointment, and requesting him to prepare the necessary Royal Warrant for The Queen's signature to cause Letters Patent of Appointment under the Great Seal to be prepared. This Royal Warrant is submitted to The Queen through the Secretary of State for Home Affairs. The Queen signs it at the top and the Home Secretary signs it at the foot on the right, and it is passed to the Lord Chancellor, who signs it at the foot on the left, after the clause noting its receipt. The Crown Office then prepares the Letters Patent, a copy of which is entered on the Patent Rolls, and the original is conveyed to the new Officer of Arms, and the Crown Office arranges for the appointment to be published in the *London Gazette*. At the next meeting of Chapter, the Letters Patent are read out by the new Officer, and Chapter then instructs that a copy be entered in the official register of the College entitled 'Patents of Officers of Arms'. The second Earl Marshal's Warrant is addressed to the Lord Chamberlain, requesting him to provide the new Officer of Arms with a tabard of the Royal Arms and a wand, and, in the case of Kings of Arms and Heralds, with the appropriate Collar of SS. Originating in the time of Henry IV, Collars of SS were given by the Lancastrian kings to their loyal adherents. Today they are worn only by the Lord Chief Justice, the Kings of Arms, Heralds, the Lord Mayor of London and the Serjeants-at-Arms.

In medieval times the creation of Heralds and Kings of Arms was attended by much ceremony, which became more elaborate as the centuries rolled on. The new officer was baptised with wine from his lord's vineyard as his new heraldic name was given to him, and invested with a tabard of his lord's arms, while the Kings of Arms were crowned with their special crowns. Newly appointed officers took an oath appropriate to their office, which included, for Heralds, an undertaking to forsake all vices and follow the path of virtue, avoiding taverns, dice, playing of hazard and the company of loose women.

Our heraldic names are still legally our alternative surnames, and it is equally correct to address a herald by his family name or his heraldic name. During the eighteenth century, the elaborate ceremonial creations of heralds died out, and we are now only created by Letters Patent under the Great Seal. In the time of James I the annual salaries were £50 for Garter, £40 each for the Provincial Kings, £26 13s. 4d., for each Herald, and £20 for each Pursuivant. William IV, in a fit of economy, reduced Garter to £49 1s. 4d., the Provincial Kings to £20 5s. 0d., the Heralds to £17 16s. 0d., and the Pursuivants to £13 19s. 0d., and these have remained unchanged to this day — the longest pay pause ever.

The College of Arms is not supported from public funds, neither does it come under the control of any government department, but still remains a part of the Royal Household. We would not wish it otherwise. Because the heralds' salaries have been insufficient to support them, they have been allowed a small percentage of the fees of those grants of arms they themselves handle, the major portion going to the maintenance of the fabric of the building and the payment of the salaries of the few permanent staff they employ. They have also been allowed for centuries to undertake genealogical research and armorial work, and act generally as high-level consultants on connected matters, and to charge fees for this work.

The most important routine duty of the heralds and pursuivants is to act as duty officer, what we call Officer in Waiting. The system of waiting was initiated by the Earl Marshal, Thomas Howard, 9th Duke of Norfolk, on July 18th, 1568, under which a Herald and a Pursuivant together were in waiting for a month at a time. This was changed in 1912 so that the Heralds and the Pursuivants thenceforth waited singly, by rotation, for a week at a time. The Waiting Officer is responsible for general control of the College building and for the security of its records and contents. He has to deal with all enquiries which are not addressed to a particular officer by name, to receive visitors to the College who do not have an appointment with another Officer, and to try to answer their queries and resolve their genealogical and armorial problems, for which service he charges a consultation fee.

SEVENTEEN

GRANTS OF ARMORIAL BEARINGS

S THE LATE Sir George Sitwell pointed out, the basic social division in England, as in the mainland European countries, was originally between the free and the unfree.[1] The earls and great magnates holding their extensive lands of the King by barony, down through the ranks of the substantial feudal barons and bannerets, the knights and lords of manors, and even smaller fractions of knight's fees, to the franklins (who, as the name implies, were the lowest rank of free men – in the later Middle Ages called yeomen), were all to be found on one side of the social fence; in short, all these were equally gentlemen, whatever their rank and however small their means and rugged their life. The English gentry were, therefore, roughly equivalent to the *noblesse* of the mainland European countries and were, like them, entitled to bear and use arms should they wish or need to do so. On the other side were all those who held their little farms and cottages by the various forms of bond or servile tenure, and on this side of the fence were also lumped the merchants, tradesmen, artisans and craftsmen of the towns and villages.

This tidy categorisation of society persisted on the European mainland more or less until modern times, and continued to have some residual effect on social attitudes. In most of these countries, burgher or bourgeois arms are still not officially recognised. This ancient concept of society continued in its purest form in Poland until the Second World War. In

England developments took a different turn, for reasons which we need not go into here, and this resulted in much greater social mobility and a different attitude to the bearing and use of arms. By the end of the fourteenth century the wealthy merchants were buying manors and estates in the country, marrying into county families and being accepted as gentry. The most remarkable example is Michael de la Pole, who was created Earl of Suffolk in 1385 and was one of the most powerful men in England before his fall. He was the first merchant to be created an earl. His father was a prosperous wool merchant of Hull in Yorkshire, of which he was mayor, and money-lender to the King.[2] By a series of judicious marriages and capable royal service the family rose steadily; Michael's grandson was created Duke of Suffolk, and his descendant in Tudor times entertained a claim to the throne and was beheaded in 1513. The English have always been pragmatists and the heralds have reflected this, and tidied up the armorial position of the self-made gentleman.

While the gentry were entitled to bear arms, by no means all of them did. The barons, bannerets and 'strenuous knights', the commanders of feudal contingents and later the commanders of indentured troops, would need to use armorial ensigns, as would most of the knights. The men-at-arms, who in the fourteenth century included esquires and pretty well everyone except archers and infantry,[3] would not normally use individual armorial ensigns as that might cause confusion, unless they were, for example, esquires holding a junior command, or franklins or yeomen on staff duties.

Henry de Berkhamsted, who appears regularly in the records as 'the Prince's yeoman', is buried in a splendid tomb in Berkhamsted parish church, shown in full armour and wearing a jupon, or surcoat, of his arms. He rose from humble beginnings and served on the staff of the Black Prince at the Battle of Poitiers, for which he was rewarded with lands and appointed Constable of Berkhamsted Castle. As a staff officer of the Black Prince he would need to wear a heraldic jupon of his personal arms on active service so that he could be readily identified when needed. His armorial seal, which is now in the Aylesbury Museum, would no doubt have been used when he was Constable of Berkhamsted Castle, a most important command, during which he would certainly need to bear arms, but he remained a yeoman until his dying day about 1400.

An English man-at-arms, John de Kyngeston, had been challenged in 1389 to a joust by a French knight, but could not accept as he was not armigerous. King Richard II acknowledged that he was a gentleman 'and have made him Esquire and will that he be known by Arms and bear them henceforth'.[4] Clearly John de Kyngeston had happily set out on the wars without any personal arms and no one had thought any the worse of him for that.

Throughout the fourteenth and fifteenth centuries in England social divisions were being steadily eroded and the labels attached to the various ranks and grades of society were acquiring somewhat different connotations. With the advent of professional armies in the sixteenth and seventeenth centuries, the man-at-arms died out and 'esquires', in England, were regarded as ranking just below knights, while 'gentleman' became a term for those who were accepted as being somewhere between the esquires and yeomen, and the latter tended to become downgraded, though the dividing lines between all of them were fluid. The abolition of villein and bond tenures in England in late Tudor times made the whole population technically free, although some were obviously more free than others. The neat social division of the early Middle Ages was replaced by an untidy categorisation of 'classes', which was bedevilled by the Industrial Revolution and the social upheaval which accompanied it. There are today in England very many who have the 'port, charge and countenance of a gentleman', and who are regarded as entrenched 'Establishment' figures, but whose origins, no more than two or three generations ago, were very humble. Now that England is rapidly becoming a meritocracy we are entering a more easily identifiable social scene.

It has been maintained by many writers on armory, until recent times, that any man may adopt arms of his own volition. This proposition is based partly on the fact that in the earliest days of armory the sovereigns and greater barons undoubtedly did so, and partly on certain statements of some medieval writers on heraldry. In the case of the rulers and greater barons their numbers were small and they all knew each other, at any rate within their own kingdoms, so that they would choose designs for their arms which were sufficiently distinguishable from one another, and no particular organisation or control would be needed to achieve this. The same would be true of the minor 'feudal barons' holding their lands of the great tenants-in-chief, and regularly visiting the court at the castle which was the administrative centre of the 'honour' of which they were members. It was only when arms began to be used by the knights and later the esquires and yeomen that duplication and confusion was likely to arise, and greater control became necessary.

The two medieval writers on armory on whom people mainly rely for support for the voluntary adoption theory are Bartolo di Sassoferrato and Nicholas Upton. Bartolo's treatise, *De Insigniis et Armis*, was written about 1354 and became immediately popular and widely copied during the next two or three centuries.[5] His statements on the subject are ambiguous and contradictory and a really scholarly edition of his work is long overdue. In his third chapter he states that only those who have been granted insignia and arms may use them, adding that he and his descendants were granted arms by the Emperor. In the next chapter he says that anyone may assume

153

arms and insignia, which may be borne and displayed in his own property. This is fine for a greater baron but not much use to the esquire holding a manor of a few hundred acres. Possibly his most important statement is in the ninth chapter: 'It is useful to have a grant of arms from a prince, because they are thereby publicised and cannot be prohibited by another. They are also of greater dignity and, if two men bear the same arms, the preference is given to him who had them from a prince.' One may ask why John de Kyngeston, who was living only a generation after Bartolo wrote his book, did not adopt arms of his own volition. The answer lies in Bartolo's ninth chapter and not in his fourth, and so Kyngeston petitioned for a grant from Richard II.

The other passage often quoted is from Nicholas Upton's treatise, *De Studio Militari*, which was written about 1446, and immediately became essential reading and was much copied and widely distributed.[6] There he says:

> In these days we openly see how many poor men, labouring in the French wars, are become noble ... of whom many of their own authority have assumed Arms to be borne by themselves and their heirs ... I say, however, that Arms so assumed, though they are borne freely and lawfully, yet cannot be of such dignity or authority as those which are daily bestowed by the authority of Princes or lords.

He goes on to say that he does not consider heralds can grant arms. Earlier in his book Nicholas Upton, who was on the staff of the Earl of Salisbury, tells us that he himself designed and granted arms to one of the personal squires of the Earl after the Battle of Verneuil, to commemorate his distinguished service. He also quotes another occasion on which the Earl of Salisbury rewarded a man-at-arms for valour by granting him a coat of arms. If anyone could assume arms of his own volition, of what value is a grant of arms for valiant service? How does one distinguish one from the other?

I suspect that arms assumed of their own volition by the lower ranks of the gentry were rapidly becoming discredited. In the first place few of them would be sufficiently well versed in the rules and technicalities of armory to produce a satisfactory coat. In the second place even fewer of them would have ready access, or the necessary knowledge, to consult the rolls of arms and ordinaries of arms regularly maintained by the heralds as part of their duties. They could not therefore check that the design they wished to use was not already in use by someone else. As is always the case, the man sitting on the records has a head start on anyone else.

The matter was finally settled by Henry VII in 1492, and the armorial authority of the English Kings of Arms firmly established. A Gentleman

Usher of Henry VII, Hugh Vaughan (who later had a distinguished career), wished at that time to take part in a joust, but the other participants declared that they would not compete with him as his gentility had not been established by the possession of armorial bearings. Vaughan then produced Letters Patent of John Wrythe, Garter King of Arms, demonstrating that he had recently been granted arms and crest. The original is now in the Victoria and Albert Museum. Accounts by two contemporary heralds, although differing slightly, agree that the King accepted and supported this grant by his properly authorised King of Arms.[7] This was a most important declaration and established the position of the English Kings of Arms as granting authorities. To this day English heralds on promotion to King of Arms are individually authorised, by Letters Patent under the Great Seal, to grant arms on behalf of the Crown 'to eminent men subject to the approval of the Earl Marshal first obtained'. Whatever may have happened during the Middle Ages is only of historical and antiquarian interest; it is the legal position today that matters.

The difference between a mainland European grant of arms and an English grant of arms is that the former normally forms part of and is inseparable from a grant of nobility. In short, the grantee, who must necessarily be of the non-armigerous part of society, is elevated into the ranks of the *noblesse* (our gentry) and granted a title, often only the equivalent of esquire, and simultaneously arms, to demonstrate the fact. In England, as we have seen, all gentlemen are eligible to petition for a grant of arms. The problem, in modern conditions, is to decide who, now that all men are free, qualifies for a grant of arms. Obviously, the Kings of Arms have a responsibility to see that those petitioning for a grant of arms are of sufficient excellence and merit to qualify.

In 1530 Henry VIII issued Letters Patent instructing all royal and county officials to assist Clarenceux King of Arms during his forthcoming visitation of his province, for the purpose of confirming the authenticity of arms being then borne by those who made claim to them and 'to reforme all false armory and Arms devised without authority'. At the same time Clarenceux was authorised to grant arms to those, not yet armigerous, who had done good service to the Crown, or had risen to possessions and riches which enabled them to maintain the position of an armigerous gentleman, providing they were not of 'vyle blood', that is to say of villein or unfree descent, rebels or heretics, but were men of good, honest reputation. Further documents of this period show that there was also a pretty stiff means test.[8] At a rather later date we find the phrases used that one had to have 'the port, charge and countenance of a gentleman', or be a 'worthy man of good repute and adequate substance', before one could be recognised as a gentleman and so granted arms. In short, the Crown authorised the Kings of Arms, later subject to the approval of the Earl

Marshal, to decide whether someone had made the grade and become a gentleman, in the post-Tudor meaning of the term.

The English Kings of Arms, as we have seen, are authorised by The Sovereign, in their Letters Patent of Appointment under the Great Seal, to grant arms to 'eminent men subject to the approval of the Earl Marshal first obtained'. This includes, of course, women and corporate bodies. 'Eminence' is not defined because the discretion in these matters has lain for centuries with the Earl Marshal. While it can be taken that the considerations which moved our Tudor predecessors still hold good, petitions for arms, while never being automatically approved, are considered in a sympathetic and common-sense way. In any event, the Earl Marshal's decision is final and he never gives his reasons. In fact, the kind of people or corporations who wish to petition for a grant of arms are usually those who qualify.

If a potential petitioner knows an Officer of Arms personally or by introduction, then it would be sensible to consult him; otherwise the Officer in Waiting should be consulted. After the Officer of Arms has satisfied himself that the petitioner would probably be acceptable to the Earl Marshal, the petition or Memorial, as it is called is drawn up and addressed to the Earl Marshal. This describes the petitioner's status so that there can be no doubt as to his or her identity, and requests the Earl Marshal, if he approves, to issue his Warrant to the Kings of Arms, authorising them to grant arms to the petitioner.

When the Memorial, accompanied by a cheque for the grant fees, goes forward, the Officer of Arms handling the application (known as the Agent), then discusses with the petitioner the design for his or her arms. Legally the Kings of Arms can grant whatever arms they consider appropriate, but as a matter of courtesy the wishes of the petitioner are always consulted. Some have no ideas and ask for suggestions; others have clear and simple wishes; while others again want everything put in the shield including the deep-freeze. The Kings of Arms are likely to be sympathetic so long as the new design is sufficiently different from any which has been recorded before, is as simple as possible, and aesthetically pleasing and well balanced. Sometimes agreement is reached quickly, sometimes only after much correspondence and several discussions.

When a design for the armorial bearings has been agreed with the petitioner, the Agent then checks it against Garter's Ordinaries, to ensure that it is not too similar to a coat or crest which is already on record. If it clears this hurdle, the design is submitted to Garter King of Arms who either agrees it, on behalf of himself and the Provincial King of Arms involved, or makes suggestions for improving the design.

The approved sketch is then passed to one of the Herald Painters of the College of Arms for him to paint the armorial bearings and the heading of the Letters Patent. With so many grants going through, each must take its place in the queue. When the Letters Patent have been painted the Agent checks them and, if he approves, they are passed to the Clerk of the Records for engrossing with the text. After that the Letters Patent are submitted to the Kings of Arms for signing. For individual grants, Garter and one of the Provincial Kings sign; for grants to people domiciled north of the River Trent, Norroy signs, and south of the Trent, Clarenceux signs; grants to corporate bodies and individuals resident overseas are signed by all three Kings. Grants of supporters, whether to individuals or corporate bodies, are the prerogative of Garter alone, as are grants to Knights of the Garter.

The Letters Patent are then returned to the Clerk of the Records, who sees to it that an exact copy of the text and the painting of the armorial bearings is entered in the official registers of grants of arms, and the Registrar endorses the fact on the back. Thereafter the seals of office of the granting Kings of Arms are affixed to the Letters Patent, which are then ready to be presented to the grantee. Some think that the period of gestation of a grant of arms is unconscionably long, but Letters Patent are an official instrument conveying a right to certain arms to the grantee and to his descendants or successors for all time. Care must, therefore, be taken to ensure that everything is incontrovertibly correct (Plate III).

For many centuries sovereigns have granted arms to foreigners permanently or temporarily resident in their territories. These have often been in the nature of rewards for meritorious service. There are several examples of this. In the case of Englishmen so honoured they appear, at any rate from Tudor times onwards, to have had the grant confirmed and re-granted by the English Kings of Arms, usually fairly soon after they returned home, thus giving the arms protection within the English heraldic jurisdiction. The foreign sovereign could, of course, only protect the arms he had granted within his own dominions.

While it is clear that when legitimate bearers of arms feel aggrieved by the infringement of their arms by others, in England and Wales, recourse can be had to the Court of Chivalry, and in Scotland to Lyon Court, the position in the Commonwealth is uncertain and liable to different interpretations. In the early days of overseas colonial expansion the settled colonies were deemed to have carried with them such of English law as was applicable to their new circumstances. When these colonies became independent Commonwealth countries, kingdoms or republics, the position became obscure. In some, such as British Columbia, it seems that the successor courts inherited English jurisdiction, including the functions of the Court of Chivalry. In others the functions of the Court of Chivalry seem to have been lost.

In the case of Lyon Court it seems pretty clear that none of the settled colonies of the British Empire were governed under Scottish law, and that the successor states which grew out of them took with them a framework of English law, which included, in some cases at any rate, the powers and procedures of the Court of Chivalry.

For example, the French settlement of Acadie was seized by the English colonists of Virginia in 1613, and in 1621 James I granted the territory to Sir William Alexander, and it was renamed Nova Scotia. It was regarded as a Scottish settlement, as its arms demonstrate, and to raise money for the establishment of the colony, the order of Baronets of Nova Scotia was instituted. In 1632 it was returned to France, but was captured by a Cromwellian force in 1654, being restored to France in 1667. In 1710 the province was taken by a British force and finally ceded to the United Kingdom in 1713, and it was thenceforward governed under English law. It was therefore only under direct Scottish control and law between 1621 and 1632.

As far as Lyon Court and the Court of Chivalry are concerned, 'no court can operate effectively without proper machinery for initiating its process and, in the last resort, for enforcing its judgment against a recalcitrant unsuccessful party.' Mr G. D. Squibb, Norfolk Herald Extraordinary, also expressed the view that 'outside Great Britain heraldic jurisdiction, if exercisable at all, belongs to the ordinary courts of the several countries of the Commonwealth.[9] He subsequently expressed the view that 'while the Court [of Chivalry] has jurisdiction only over persons in England, it could, like other English Courts, have before it cases which have to be decided in accordance with private international law.'[10] The same considerations apply, *mutatis mutandis*, to Lyon Court.

It might be thought that this is an academic question of interest only to pedants. Not so. In the last decade or so there has been a remarkable surge of interest in the countries of the Old Commonwealth, as well as in America, in the acquisition of armorial bearings. In a world where the accepted foundations of life are crumbling, people naturally seek to strengthen their bonds with more permanent values and become interested in some of the more outward and visible manifestations of them. Armory provides a minor, but not negligible, contribution.

So, we are brought back to the problem of how to protect the grants of arms made by the Kings of Arms. Within England and Wales the Court of Chivalry can provide this protection, and within Scotland Lyon Court can do so. In other words, if a defendant is subject to either jurisdiction and cannot wriggle away before a case is brought, he can be clobbered if the case goes against him. Clearly, the position overseas is more obscure and will only be clarified when a case is brought in some appropriate Court, administering such English heraldic law as may have devolved to that Commonwealth country or state. Such law would have flowed from

I Henry Howard, Earl of Surrey, the 'Poet Earl'. Possibly painted about 1615–20;
the artist has not been identified. Now in Arundel Castle.

II   Sir Edward Walker, Garter King of Arms, born 1611, died 1677. Painted by
William Dobson.

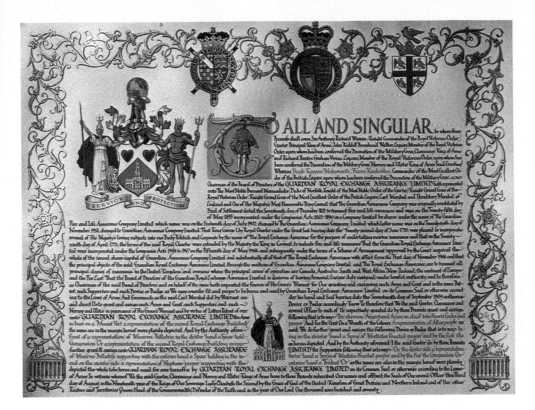

III   Grant of Arms, Crest, Supporters and Badge to The Guardian Royal Exchange Assurance Ltd, by Letters Patent dated August 3rd, 1970 of Garter, Clarenceux, and Norroy & Ulster Kings of Arms.

IV   Approval sketch for the armorial bearings of the Kingdom of Trinidad and Tobago, signed by Sir Learie Constantine, on behalf of his Government.

V   On the steps of St George's Chapel in Windsor Castle after the annual Service of the Order of the Garter in 1980, when H.M. Margrethe II, Queen of Denmark, was installed as a Lady of the Order.

VI   Lord Reilly (*centre right*) with his two Supporters and Richmond Herald, deputising for Garter King of Arms, shortly before his Introduction to the House of Lords in 1978.

England and not from Scotland.

A plaintiff in such a case would have to produce evidence that the arms in question were indeed his own. To do this he would have to produce the original Letters Patent granting the arms to himself or one of his forebears. In the latter event a direct male line descent would have to be proved. Failing that he would have to obtain the testimony of the English Kings of Arms certifying, from their official records, the arms and his descent from an armigerous ancestor. In view of the fact that the Commonwealth court would be administering law of English heraldic origin, it is possible that a certificate of Lord Lyon might be acceptable in so far as a right to arms was claimed in virtue of a Lyon grant to a person who was undoubtedly domiciled in Scotland at the time of the grant.

In the circumstances it will be seen that the English Kings of Arms are acting correctly in granting arms to persons or corporate bodies domiciled in Commonwealth countries or British colonies, but grants of arms by Lord Lyon to such persons, even of Scottish descent, might need to be covered by a confirmatory grant or certificate of the English Kings of Arms. There is another reason for this, and that is that the English Kings of Arms would have to be in a position to certify that the arms in question are unique within the Commonwealth to the plaintiff. Grants by Lord Lyon to persons domiciled outside his jurisdiction would, therefore, need to be checked through Garter's Ordinaries before being granted. At the same time a simultaneous English grant or confirmation would have to be made, so that the new arms were recorded in Garter's Ordinaries and thus made unique, and not granted to anyone else in future.

In the case of grants to persons in Commonwealth countries which have not inherited English heraldic law, and to Americans and others outside the Commonwealth, the protection of their arms would possibly be achieved by registration under appropriate copyright or trademark legislation, or the like, if the law of the country provided for this.

Armorial Bearings for Commonwealth countries go through a different process. The Prime Minister of the colony discusses direct with Garter King of Arms the design for the arms to be used by them on achieving independence. When agreement on the design has been reached, Garter submits a Royal Warrant to The Queen through the Secretary of State for Foreign and Commonwealth Affairs. If approved, The Queen signs it at the top and the Secretary of State at the foot, with a direction to the Earl Marshal to record it in the official registers of the College of Arms (Plate IV).

EIGHTEEN

ANCIENT ARMS AND GENEALOGICAL RESEARCH

ENEALOGISTS CAN CLAIM that theirs is the oldest profession in the world. When men first clung together in extended family groups and coherent speech was developed, bards and minstrels studied the genealogies of the chieftains in whose rudimentary and barbaric courts they lived, and sang of the deeds and lineage of their ancestors.

In western European countries one is entitled to arms by inheritance, if one can prove a direct male line descent from an ancestor who is on record as being entitled to a particular coat of arms. It is not, of course, hard to prove a descent from a grandfather, but it becomes increasingly difficult the further back one has to go, and it requires proportional skill and experience of a high order.

As a consequence of their duties as military staff-officers and at tournaments, the heralds came to be regarded as authorities on the more prominent local families, but this was a far cry from having an expertise in genealogy in the modern sense. Nevertheless, it would have been useful for them to be able to say that, as the grandfather and father of a particular knight had borne certain arms, it would be appropriate for him to use the same arms. I have recently made a preliminary study of medieval heraldic treatises, but in none of them is anything said about genealogy. The most one finds is that the devices depicted in a coat of arms should call to memory the deeds or fame of the first bearer of them. It was left to the lawyers to adduce the pedigrees of their clients in lawsuits over the descent and inheritance of manors or lands.

One of the duties of the Kings of Arms which they promised on creation to fulfil, was to have knowledge of all noblemen and gentlemen dwelling within their provinces, and to register their arms and descents. In consequence the heralds assumed a competence to examine and check the evidences submitted by the gentry in support of their claims to particular coats of arms by descent. Sir Anthony Wagner, in his classic book *Heralds and Heraldry in the Middle Ages*, dealt in considerable detail with the Visitation functions of the Kings of Arms, and has shown that Visitations were being undertaken by the Kings of Arms in the fifteenth century, as part of their official duties. Here again, the heralds were merely examining descents submitted to them, and accepting or rejecting these.

The Letters Patent dated April 19th, 1530, issued by Henry VIII to Thomas Benolt, Clarenceux King of Arms, required local authorities to assist him in the execution of his normal duty to visit the counties in his province in order to take note of the descents of the local gentry, with a view to recording their arms, or disown false pretentions to arms.

During the later seventeenth century the Kings of Arms, or their deputies, used printed forms, which were sent to the Bailiffs of the various Hundreds in the counties to be visited. The wording was the same in all cases. The circular sent out by Henry St George, Clarenceux, on July 5th, 1682, to the Bailiff of the Hundred of Gromboldash, in Gloucestershire (of which the original is in the College of Arms), is a good average example. It reads as follows:

These are to require you, and in His Majestys Name to charge and command you, that forthwith upon sight hereof you warn these Baronets, Knights, Esquires and Gentlemen, whose names are within written, personally to appear before us Thomas May Esq, Chester Herald, and Gregory King, Rougedragon, Officers of Arms, Deputies and Marshalls to Clarenceux King of Arms, for the County of Gloucester, at the Bell in Sodbury on Thursday the 3rd day of August next by nine of the Clock in the morning, where we intend to sit for Registering the Descents and Arms of all the Gentry within the said Hundred. And that they bring with them such Arms and Crests as they use and bear, with their Pedigrees and Descents, and such other Evidence or matter of Record and Credit as (if need require) may justifie the same: that we knowing how they use and challenge their Titles, and by what right and authority they bear, or pretend to bear, Arms, we may accordingly make entrance thereof, and Register the same in the College of Arms, or else to proceed as his Majesties Commission under the Great Seal of England Injoyneth in that behalf.

The list attached to this particular summons contained forty-six names, listed by parishes, and we find short comments entered against many of them. One 'lives beyond London', so could not appear; the next was 'lame and broke his legg', so evidently he did not turn up at the Bell Inn. Another was 'disowned but refuses to disclaim'. Several were persuaded to disclaim their right to arms. Two innkeepers were disclaimed; another was '3rd son of Samuell Stokes entered in the last Visitation', and so on. In all these cases it will be seen that the onus is on the person who claims a right to arms to adduce proof of descent from an armigerous ancestor. This was clearly the form in all earlier Visitations — the heralds were acting as examiners of evidence, and not as genealogists.

Nevertheless, the fact that the heralds were intimately concerned with handling pedigrees inclined several of them to become interested in genealogy, and it was not long before we find them acting as professional genealogists, and charging fees for their work. This development had begun in Tudor times, when the gentry developed an insatiable thirst for elaborate pedigree rolls, embellished with paintings of arms and often including fabulous ancestors.

Genealogical work comes to the Officers of Arms either directly because of their reputation or by recommendation, or through 'waiting'. The present system of waiting, first established in 1568, whereby each herald and pursuivant is on duty for a week at a time, means that a 'wait' comes round once in ten weeks. During that week all genealogical enquiries, whether by visitors, telephone or letter, which are not addressed to a particular officer by name, are handled by the Officer in Waiting.

Many visitors will confidently tell one that their ancestors came over with the Conqueror, a myth to which they cling with unshakable conviction. Although William the Conqueror's army numbered some 7,000 of all ranks, the names of only thirty-three are definitely known, and not all of them actually fought at the Battle of Hastings. While the Malets and Giffards could probably prove a male-line descent from one or other of these, even this has not yet been put on record in the College of Arms.

There is a slightly better chance of proving a descent from an ancestor whose name occurs in Domesday Book, but as it was compiled twenty years after the Conquest, it does not follow that someone then alive had fought at Hastings. All that can be said is that if he was aged over forty in 1086 he could have done, but that is not proof. In fact very many Normans were called over to England after the Conquest to help govern the country, and, at the same time, adventurers flocked to England on the chance of picking up a manor or a good job. In any case, it is very rare to be able to prove a male-line descent from a Domesday ancestor. The rate of extinction of families of the higher nobility in England throughout the Middle Ages has been remarked on by modern historians. Some have put it down to a genetic tendency to barrenness of heiresses, but the country gentry managed to marry heiresses almost as often, and their families did not die out so regularly.

It is, more often than not, impossible to trace with any certainty a pedigree to a period before the sixteenth century. Indeed, many cannot be traced as far back as the early eighteenth century. The social position of people of British origin does not usually give an indication of the origins of their family, for social mobility has been common in England, particularly since the Middle Ages. Many today who are well-to-do and regarded as pillars of the establishment have grandfathers of very humble origins; and the converse is also true.

The heralds are in a better position than professional genealogists outside the College of Arms to provide this service to the public, and there has developed in the College an expertise in the techniques of genealogical research. The heralds' other advantage is that they possess the only official genealogical and armorial registers in the country, as well as an unrivalled collection of manuscripts, some of which are of the utmost importance. Thus when any outside genealogist wishes to ascertain if a pedigree or arms are on official record, he or she must consult the College of Arms sooner or later, because although a pedigree produced outside might have been most carefully and accurately researched, it carries only the authentication of the person who researched it.

Pedigrees officially registered at the College of Arms are put through a strict process. Not until the Officer of Arms concerned with the research is satisfied that his proofs for each and every statement in the pedigree will stand up to criticism does he submit it for registration. Experience over many centuries has taught the heralds that genealogy is a science and not an art, and no evidences are accepted if not authenticated by some primary record. Having reached this stage the Officer concerned submits the pedigree to the Chapter of the College, which nominates two Examiners, normally a herald and a pursuivant who have had no part in the research. The documentary evidences are produced to the junior Examiner first, who studies them critically and accepts or rejects them. The same procedure is gone through separately with the senior Examiner. They ultimately report their findings to Chapter, which usually accepts their views and then orders the pedigree to be officially recorded.

There is also a Special Examiner of baronets' pedigrees. This is because, apart from a simple father to son succession, the Home Office will not recognise the title without a certificate of descent from Garter King of Arms. If the successor is descended from a cadet branch of the family, possibly linking up four or five generations ago, proof of descent can be a laborious job, because one has to prove not only that the claimant is lineally descended from his baronet ancestor, but also that none of the males ahead of him had any sons and male descendants. Proving a positive descent can be bad enough, but proving a series of negatives is much more difficult.

While in earlier times people came to the College of Arms to prove their descent from an armigerous ancestor and, indeed, still do, very many now come just to find out something about their forbears, what kind of people they were, what they did and where they lived. Nowadays, unlike formerly, we record a much greater volume of biographical detail in our recorded pedigrees, almost on the lines of *Who's Who*, so that they are becoming most useful sources for sociologists and demographers.

NINETEEN

OVERSEAS WORK OF THE HERALDS

URING the last ten years or so the English heralds have been called upon to undertake official duties in several Commonwealth countries and also in the United States of America, wearing their uniforms and often tabards as well. These ceremonies attract considerable attention in the countries concerned, receiving extensive press and television coverage, and are invariably favourably commented upon. In consequence they help, in particular, to keep in the public mind overseas the outward significance of the Crown and generally to keep alive ties with Britain.

Because the English Kings, Heralds and Pursuivants of Arms are members of the Royal Household, directly responsible to the Sovereign through the Earl Marshal, they can function in those Commonwealth countries, with the exception of Scotland, of which The Queen is Sovereign, or Head of the Commonwealth. Were we civil servants, subject to a U.K. Department of State and paid salaries from the Treasury, Commonwealth countries would probably feel that our visits had potential political undertones and be reluctant to invite us. The same considerations no doubt weigh with the U.S.A. authorities.

These visits are made only at the invitation of the appropriate authorities in the Commonwealth country concerned; we do not invite ourselves, although naturally some discussion takes place before an official invitation is made. The drill for these visits has been evolved over the last decade and is now pretty straightforward. Depending on the country, state, province, or Commonwealth territory concerned, the governor-general, governor, or lieutenant-governor, using the appropriate and customary channel of communication, writes to The Queen for permission for a named herald to carry out his duty in uniform and tabard. In the case of America, the governor of the state concerned takes up the matter with the British ambassador.

While the Earl Marshal can give authority for heralds to wear uniform on duty, together with their Collars of SS, tabards of the Royal Arms are now normally worn only when in attendance on The Sovereign. There is occasionally some misunderstanding about our tabards, which are embroidered with the Royal Arms as used in England. These are not the national arms of England. They are the Arms of The Sovereign alone and may not be used even by the loyallest of subjects. The reason the government departments in England use them is that ministers and their departments are servants of the Crown. The Royal Arms are not symbolic of England or the United Kingdom. Only The Queen may fly a flag of the Royal Arms, and her heralds wear tabards of the Royal Arms. Within Scotland the Arms of Sovereignty are used with the Scottish Royal Arms in the first and fourth quarters and England second. The flag of the English has, since the Middle Ages, been the red cross on white of St George, while that of Scotsmen has been the white saltire on blue of St Andrew, and that of Welshmen the red dragon on white and green. Those who wish to demonstrate their citizenship of the United Kingdom may fly the Union Flag, better known as the Union Jack.

When heraldic duties are being performed overseas, the governor or the British ambassador, or an appropriate representative, attends in uniform; this is because he is there as the personal representative of The Queen, and the herald is technically in attendance on him.

There is an increasing demand for the heralds to undertake these duties, for which the host country underwrites the cost. A glance at some recent years will give an idea of what is involved. In 1969 York Herald of Arms, in uniform and tabard, and in the presence of various dignitaries and citizenry of St George, attended upon the Governor of Bermuda when he presented to the Mayor and Council of the City of St George, the old capital, Letters Patent of the three English Kings of Arms, granting them armorial bearings, the terms of which York Herald proclaimed. A similar ceremony took place in Hamilton, the present capital, when a Patent of Arms was presented to the Bank of Bermuda. This was the first time that an English herald, wearing his tabard, had performed such a duty on the western side of the Atlantic. The procedures then worked out have proved of great value in subsequent ceremonials of this kind.

The State or Commonwealth of Virginia, the first permanent English settlement in America, had had a chequered early history, and its heraldry was equally muddled. It had evidently been intended by the then Clarenceux King of Arms to make a Grant of Arms to the Virginia Company of London, otherwise called the Virginia Merchants, and a docquet exists with a rough drawing of a proposed design for their arms. Unfortunately the Virginia Merchants went broke about 1619 and the grant was never issued. However, the design was clearly well-known in Virginia, and successive Governors of Virginia subsequently used it. The Commonwealth of Virginia decided that it would be appropriate, on the bicentenary of the Declaration of Independence, if their historic arms could be put on an official footing. In response to this request the English Kings of Arms, by Letters Patent dated June 3rd, 1976, devised for Virginia the arms which it had originally been intended to grant to the Company, and had been used since by the State.[1] The Queen, who had expressly authorised this grant, took part in the celebrations at Williamsburg, with Richmond Herald of Arms in attendance, in his tabard. Her Majesty presented the Letters Patent of Arms to the Governor. It was, for heralds, an historic occasion, because it was the first time that an Officer of Arms had worn his tabard on the mainland of America. At the same time a Devisal of Arms was made to the Senate of the Commonwealth of Virginia.[2]

The then Colony, now State of Queensland, in Australia had been assigned arms and crest by Royal Warrant in 1893, the first such colonial grant since that of Charles II in 1661 to Jamaica. The Arms of Queensland are, therefore, the oldest of their kind in Australasia and have the added distinction of being the earliest grant by the Crown anywhere south of the Equator. To celebrate The Queen's Silver Jubilee Year, the Government of Queensland petitioned for a Grant of Supporters to their arms and this was, of course, readily conceded. It was arranged that when The Queen visited Brisbane on March 9th, 1977, York Herald of Arms, wearing uniform and tabard, should be in attendance on Her Majesty. During a State Reception in the evening, The Queen signed the Royal Warrant, in her capacity as Queen of Australia, and York Herald proclaimed its terms. This was an occasion of constitutional interest, as Her Majesty was there as Queen of Australia, with one of her Heralds in attendance.

The Legislative Assembly of Queensland, established in 1860, had never had a mace, that traditional symbol of their power and authority derived from the Crown, and exercised by the elected representatives, a convention inherited from the Parliament at Westminster. In recent times, when a previous colonial territory has been granted independence, the British House of Commons has given the Parliament a mace, and a delegation of British Members of Parliament has taken it out and presented it. In the case of Queensland, independence had happened too long ago and, by some oversight, their Legislative Assembly had never been equipped with this essential symbol of sovereignty.

The Government of Queensland decided that this omission should be repaired, and directed their Agent-General in London to have one made. It so happened that for some years I had been occasionally advising the Agent-General's Office on certain matters, so I was asked to advise on the form of their new Mace and the armorial embellishments to be put upon it.

I consulted the Speaker of the House of Commons at Westminster, the Serjeant-at-Arms and other officers of the House, who were most helpful. A number of maces from elsewhere, which were considered relevant, were also examined. Indeed, it is surprising how many old maces still exist and how wide is the variety of their size and decoration. It was finally decided that the Queensland Mace should be based on that of the British House of Commons, being approximately the same size and shape. It was agreed that the new Mace should not be a slavish copy of the House of Commons' Mace, but that it and its heraldic embellishments should be good examples of the work of modern goldsmiths and silversmiths. The Birmingham firm commissioned to make the Queensland Mace fortunately have good craftsmen and an excellent artist, who was prepared to follow a Herald's guidance. (So many outside artists, alas, think they know better, seize the wrong end of the stick and scamper away before one can stop them.) In the event the Queensland Mace turned out to be a beautiful, dignified and interesting example of its kind.

The next problem was how best to inaugurate the Mace. It could hardly be presented as a gift from the British House of Commons, as they had not paid for it, and the ceremonial followed on such occasions did not really fit the special circumstances of Queensland. I finally suggested, and it was agreed, that the simplest procedure would be for the Governor, as The Queen's personal representative, to present the Mace to the Speaker of the Queensland Legislative Assembly, thus symbolising the fact that it represented the power and authority they had derived from the Crown. The attendance upon the Governor of Somerset Herald of Arms, in uniform and tabard, was requested and The Queen agreed.

It was then necessary to work out an appropriate ceremonial for the occasion, and this having been done, it was agreed by the Governor, Premier of Queensland, and Speaker. There came a last-minute telex request for a suggested speech for the Governor to make when handing over the Mace, which I prepared in consultation with the Serjeant-at-Arms at Westminster. This too was approved and, indeed, followed closely during the proceedings. The Agent-General's Office looked after me with efficiency and solicitude and flew me to Brisbane in the greatest comfort.

The Queensland Legislative Assembly met in the afternoon of November 29th, 1978 and, after the speaker had taken his seat, the

Serjeant-at-Arms informed him that the Governor, attended by Somerset Herald of Arms and members of His Excellency's staff, were present outside the Chamber. After the Speaker had ascertained that it was the wish of the House that they be admitted, the Serjeant-at-Arms went to the room where the Governor was waiting, picked up the Mace and, carrying it on his shoulder, led the procession into the Chamber, followed by Somerset Herald of Arms, the Governor and members of his staff. The Serjeant-at-Arms stopped at the Table, facing the Speaker, while the Governor and I took up our positions to the Speaker's right, and the A.D.C.s went to his left. The Governor addressed the House and declared the Mace to be inaugurated for the purpose of the Legislative Assembly. The Serjeant-at-Arms then placed the Mace upon the Table and went to his seat. The Premier expressed his thanks to the Governor and Somerset Herald, followed by the Leader of the Opposition, and the Speaker concluded the proceedings with a short speech. The procession departed in the same order, but without the Serjeant-at-Arms or Mace. Thereafter the Premier moved an Address of Loyalty to Her Majesty.

The Chamber of the Legislative Assembly is one of the most charming of any Commonwealth country, and provided a most suitable setting for the ceremony, which was followed by a reception in the quadrangle outside. However, herald's uniform, with the tabard, weighs over a stone and, as it was the beginning of the Australian summer, I was remarkably hot. The ceremony was extensively covered by television, which was seen in most parts of Australia, and also received favourable press notices.

Dr Conrad Swan, York Herald of Arms, is a Canadian by birth and has therefore maintained close links with that country. In September 1978 he was summoned to Toronto to attend in uniform upon the Lieutenant-Governor of Ontario (the first lady to hold such an appointment), when in her presence the Vice-Chancellor of the University of St Michael's College was formally installed. The ceremony took place in the historic St Basil's Church and, despite the sudden death earlier that day of Pope John Paul I, the ceremony caught the imagination of the Canadian media and was widely reported. In November 1979 the same Herald was requested to attend upon the Lieutenant-Governor of British Columbia, when Letters Patent of Arms were presented to the Mayor and Council of the town of Richmond, during the centenary celebrations of the municipality. As so often happens on these occasions, not only is the herald required to proclaim the terms of the Patent of Arms, but he is also asked to address the meeting on the significance and uses of armorial bearings. Both the present Norroy & Ulster King of Arms and York Herald have circumnavigated the world – the latter twice – to undertake heraldic duties and extensive lecture tours.

In November 1980 York Herald again visited Toronto to attend upon the Lieutenant-Governor of Ontario, when Letters Patent of Arms were presented to St Michael's College. Earlier that year Bluemantle Pursuivant of Arms had undertaken an exhausting twenty-one days lecture tour of nearly half the States of America, mainly in the east and mid-west, and including Texas. And in December that year Norroy & Ulster King of Arms, at the request of the Governor visited the State of South Carolina for the presentation of Letters Patent of Arms to Winthrop College.[3]

An important overseas activity of the heralds is lecturing, within the Commonwealth and America, and in many other countries too. The marked growth of interest in heraldry in Commonwealth countries can be largely attributed to these lecture tours, and they have led to the formation of many heraldic societies in the Commonwealth, helping to strengthen the invisible links between its member countries.

Further evidence of the part heraldry plays in this respect is the appointment in 1978, by Her Majesty as Queen of New Zealand, at the specific request and advice of the Government of New Zealand, of Mr Phillipe O'Shea as New Zealand Herald of Arms Extraordinary. Mr O'Shea is himself Advisory Officer (Honours) in the Prime Minister's Department in the Cabinet Office at Wellington, New Zealand. He is a well-known numismatist and has designed several New Zealand medals and the insignia of The Queen's Service Order of New Zealand.

Only by being attached to the College of Arms was New Zealand Herald able to attend the Service of the Order of the Garter at Windsor Castle in June 1980, when Sir Keith Holyoake, Governor-General of New Zealand, was installed as a Knight of the Garter.

In recent years the English and Scottish heralds have strengthened their links with the European mainland and several of us, of whom the present Garter is the most notable, have had the honour to be elected Members, and some Académiciens, of the Académie Internationale d'Héraldique, the most important and prestigious of the international heraldic societies. Its congresses, held in a different European city every two years, where papers on a wide variety of heraldic subjects are read, give many opportunities for discussions with our official colleagues from abroad and others active in the diverse world of heraldry, and much good results from these contacts.

TWENTY

THE HERALDS AND THE ORDERS OF CHIVALRY

RDERS OF CHIVALRY were the accidental by-product of the crusades. After the capture of Jerusalem in 1099 pilgrims from all over Europe came to make their devotions at the Church of the Holy Sepulchre and marvel at the sights of the city. Many fell sick because of the unhygienic conditions, or had been wounded by brigands on their way up from the coast, so a group of men, under a certain Gerard, banded together to found and run the Hospital of St John the Baptist in Jerusalem.

Their good work was widely talked about and soon contributions of money flowed into the coffers of the Hospitallers, as they were known. Before long, lands, houses, castles and privileges were given to them on a generous scale. The weight and importance which they thus acquired attracted royal patronage, backed by a charter of the Patriarch of Jerusalem in 1112. In 1113 a Papal Bull recognised their status and independence and took them under papal protection.

Continual warfare with the neighbouring Muslim states forced them to become a military order to protect their widely scattered possessions in the Latin Kingdom of Jerusalem and the crusader principalities in the Levant. Their numbers were augmented by knights dedicated to lifelong service to the Order by vows of the strictest obedience and chastity. Their military organisation reflected the tactics of feudal warfare, but their command structure was more efficient. These tough, skilled soldiers provided the backbone of the armies of the Latin Kingdom of Jerusalem. Numerous priories, with their subordinate commanderies, were established in every western European country, for the purpose of recruiting knights and men-at-arms to replenish casualties and to raise funds.

When the last crusader stronghold in the Holy Land was captured in 1291 the Knights of St John transferred their headquarters to the Kingdom of Cyprus, but this proved unsatisfactory and they looked elsewhere for a base which would be under their independent control. Luck favoured them and in 1308 they captured the castle and island of Rhodes, where they remained until it was taken by the Turks in 1523, after a remarkably gallant defence.

With great versatility the Knights of St John switched from the land to the sea and quickly became a maritime power of considerable consequence in the Mediterranean. Some eight years after the fall of Rhodes the Order settled in Malta. It was there that the Order reached the peak of its fame, during the Great Siege of Malta in 1565, when for some four months of a scorching hot summer, the Knights beat off the Turkish army many times the size of their garrison, under the command of their redoubtable Grand Master, Jean de la Valette. His successor in 1798 was incompetent and timid and Napoleon captured the island without much difficulty. The knights were again homeless, but just managed to keep the Order in being, and they finally found a home in Rome, where the headquarters of the Sovereign Military Order of St John of Jerusalem, of Rhodes and of Malta (to use its full name) remains to this day, directing and organising charitable works and several hospitals about the world.

The Order of Malta served as the model for the other crusading Orders which grew up during the early Middle Ages, and as the inspiration for the many orders of chivalry established by the sovereigns and princes of Europe since the fourteenth century, which were attached to the throne and under the direct control of the ruler. These were all secular orders and therefore linked in one way or another with the heralds who formed part of the household of the sovereign.

Other crusading orders were founded in the early Middle Ages, such as the Knights Templar and the Teutonic Knights, but their history does not concern us here.[1] What does concern us is that they, too, provided the inspiration for the foundation of the secular orders of chivalry, which, although in a less proselytising way, have some religious content; but it is not their primary purpose, as with the crusading orders, which followed a monastic regimen and regarded themselves as the sword of God. The secular orders were confraternities created by the greater and lesser rulers of western Europe, sometimes as knightly societies of brothers in arms, sometimes as a way of rewarding distinguished service to the crown, at little expense to the sovereigns for appointments were unremunerated, the honour and glory being its own reward.

The earliest and most illustrous of these secular orders is the Most Noble Order of the Garter, founded about the end of 1348 by Edward III. The founder knights, consisting of twenty-five Knights Companions, were all young, few being over the age of thirty, and most, if not all, had fought alongside the Black Prince at the Battle of Crécy. While there are today several very distinguished sailors, soldiers and airmen as Companions, the exclusively military character of the Order has been much diluted by distinguished civilians.

In 1415, just before sailing for France on the expedition which ended with the Battle of Agincourt, Henry V created the appointment of Garter King of Arms, the first time a King of Arms was appointed an officer for the special service of an order of chivalry. Since that time each Garter has been, *ex officio*, the senior officer of the Order and Principal King of Arms of England. The present Secretary of the Order is Sir Walter Verco, lately Norroy & Ulster King of Arms and now Surrey Herald Extraordinary. He has been responsible for the planning and organisation of the annual Service of the Order, for many years now held in mid-June, and also for the occasional investitures and installations of new Knights. The colourful Procession to St George's Chapel, Windsor, has frequently been filmed for television and photographed by the press, and is one of the most popular ceremonial occasions (Plate V).

In very early times, when the rude beginnings of knighthood and feudalism were emerging, knights were little more than free warriors. On coming of age a young man, born of free parents, was formally admitted to the military aristocracy of the tribe, and given the requisite arms and equipment. As feudalism and with it the institution of knighthood developed over the centuries, and warfare became more sophisticated, a knight exercised certain command responsibilities over units of mounted men-at-arms and infantry. As a consequence the ceremony of knighting became more elaborate and the Church began to participate in it, except when knights were dubbed just before or after a battle, when only the essential ceremony was used.

The religious element in the ceremony of knighthood led to the introduction of a ritual bath, to cleanse away the aspirant's sins, followed by a night-long vigil in the local church, royal chapel or cathedral. The next morning he would be dubbed knight, by the King for preference as that carried with it more prestige, or by his overlord. In the early Middle Ages any knight could dub another who qualified, but by Tudor times this had died out and dubbing thereafter was always by the Sovereign. From an early time knighthood was regarded as an 'order', not in the modern sense of the term, but rather as a confraternity of men dedicated to uphold certain virtues and ideals.[2] The ceremony of dubbing was obviously designed to impress the new knight with the importance of his responsibilities and, of course, to strengthen his allegiance to his king or overlord.

The great crusading orders, like that of St John of Jerusalem, were sovereign and self-governing. Their Grand Masters dubbed their Knights of Grace or of Justice and their governing councils promoted them as and when necessary. No outside rulers, not even the Pope, could interfere with their autonomy. The secular orders, of which the Garter is the earliest, are all strictly controlled by the kings and rulers and, of course, their successors, who brought them into being.

In the United Kingdom no one may be advanced to a knighthood in any of the Orders of Chivalry who is not already a Knight Bachelor. Sir Ivan de la Bere, for some fifteen years Secretary of the Central Chancery of the Orders of Knighthood and a great authority on the subject, stated that:

> every person who is appointed to be a Knight Companion of the Orders of the Garter or Thistle, or a Knight Grand Cross or Knight Commander of any of the other Orders of Chivalry, must be dubbed a Knight Bachelor before he is invested with the appropriate insignia of the Order to which he has been appointed.

In discussing certain expulsions from the Order of the Bath, he made the point that 'though Lord Cochrane and Sir Eyre Coote lost their appointments as Knights of the Bath, they were not deprived of the dignity of Knight Bachelor, and to this day there is no statute which would authorise such deprivation.'[3]

The bath of purification, although only one of several rituals observed during the knighting ceremony, caught the imagination of later generations, and by the end of the fourteenth century we find Knights Bachelor being referred to as knights of the bath, and this becomes increasingly common as time goes on, although there never was an actual order of knighthood of that name. With this precedent in mind John Anstis, Garter King of Arms, persuaded George I in 1725 to found the Most Honourable Order of the Bath. The idea was strongly supported by Sir Robert Walpole, the Prime Minister (as we would now describe him), who saw in it a convenient and economical way of rewarding his political supporters.[4]

The original Order of the Bath consisted of a First and Principal Companion, a Great Master, and thirty-six Knights. The statutes of the Order of the Garter clearly influenced the new Order, and George I intended it to have a military orientation, as the early statutes show. Fortunately succeeding prime ministers were not so cynical as Sir Robert Walpole, and it was not long before it became an important and much coveted way of rewarding distinguished service by senior naval and military officers.

VII Henry VIII opening Parliament on April 15th, 1523, the earliest known picture of Parliament. On his right sits the Bishop of London and beyond him, Cardinal Wolsey. In front are the lords spiritual (*left*) and earls and barons (*right*).

VIII   H.M. The Queen and H.R.H. The Prince Philip leaving the House of Lords after the State Opening of Parliament in 1977. On Her Majesty's right stands the Earl Marshal.

The Napoleonic wars produced a large number of successful naval and army commanders whose service and merits had to be rewarded. Sir George Nayler, then York Herald, able, ambitious and not too scrupulous, had taken an active part since 1793 in the affairs of the Order of the Bath, as Genealogist. In 1803 he directed the production for George III of a sumptuous book entitled *History of the Sovereigns of the Most Honourable Military Order of the Bath*, commonly called 'The Bath Book'. It cost Nayler £2,000 (a vast amount of money in those days) and George III refused to pay, so Nayler kept it and, after his death, it eventually came to the College of Arms, where it is regarded as one of the College's finest treasures. Nayler took an active part in the expansion and reorganisation of the Order in 1815, when his appointment as Genealogist was confirmed.

He was involved in a running battle with his brother heralds over the next thirty years, because he claimed the exclusive right to record the pedigrees and arms of the Knights and Esquires. His activities produced a series of forty-seven beautifully bound Bath registers of the pedigrees and arms of almost all the great naval and military figures of the period, including the pedigree and arms of Admiral Nelson, signed by him shortly after recovering from the loss of his right arm, possibly the earliest example of his signature with his left hand. Nayler also asked all those admitted to the Order to furnish him with their *curriculum vitae*. These have been bound into some fifty volumes and provide much valuable autobiographical material on all the leading naval and military figures of this most important period.

At present the Order of the Bath, after several reorganisations, consists of two divisions, a Military and a Civilian, and three ranks, Knights Grand Cross (G.C.B.), Knights Commanders (K.C.B.), and Companions (C.B.). After the Garter and the Thistle it is the most illustrious and highly regarded of the British Orders of Chivalry. Until comparatively recent times the King of Arms of the Order was usually Garter King of Arms, but now a distinguished sailor, soldier or airman, being already a Knight of the Order, is appointed. While it is understandable that there should be a wish to honour a member of the Order in this way, it does not follow that the King of Arms of the Order is very conversant with heraldry and the ways in which it can be harnessed to the service of the Order. Fortunately the Genealogist of the Order of the Bath is always a herald, at present Dr Conrad Swan, York Herald of Arms. The Chapel of the Order is the Henry VII Chapel in Westminster Abbey.

As the Order of the Bath during the Napoleonic wars was essentially a military order, it became necessary to create an order of chivalry which could be given to civilians who had rendered outstanding service, particularly British officials serving in the Mediterranean and including natives of Malta and the Ionian Islands. Accordingly the most Distinguished Order of St Michael and St George was formed in 1818. It was modelled more or less on the Order of the Bath, and has been remodelled several times since its foundation, but remains a civilian Order. It consists of three grades, Knights Grand Cross, Knights Commanders and Companions. The majority of awards in this Order are made to officers of the Foreign and Commonwealth Office, but other civilians who have rendered important services at home or in connection with Commonwealth countries are also eligible. The King of Arms of the Order is usually, as at present, a distinguished diplomat or senior member of the Foreign and Commonwealth Office. It is surprising that this important Order has no official genealogist. The Chapel of the Order is in St Paul's Cathedral.

Patronage helps to oil the wheels of the machinery of government, and by the late nineteenth century a long series of ambitious prime minsters had gradually gained control over the award of honours, tending to make them into rewards for political service rather than marks of distinction for service to the Crown. Accordingly Queen Victoria proposed to Lord Salisbury, then Prime Minister, that a new order be instituted, which would be entirely in the personal gift of The Sovereign. Lord Salisbury agreed on condition that the Government was not asked to foot the cost.[5] In consequence the Royal Victorian Order was founded on April 21st, 1896. The Garter and the Thistle have also now been brought within the personal gift of The Sovereign, as has the Order of Merit. The Royal Victorian Order consists of Knights or Dames Grand Cross, Knights or Dames Commander, Commanders, and Members of the Fourth and Fifth Classes; and there is also a Royal Victorian Medal, in silver, silver-gilt and bronze. There is no King of Arms of the Order, but the Genealogist is normally one of the English Officers of Arms, at present Sir Walter Verco, K.C.V.O., Surrey Herald. The Chapel of the Order is The Queen's Chapel of the Savoy.

The First World War created the immense problem of how to reward the services of innumerable people, not only at the Front, but also on headquarters and lines of communication duties, as well as numerous civilians, of both sexes, doing essential war work. The possibility of expanding the Order of the Bath and the Order of St Michael and St George was considered, but abandoned as likely to detract from the standing of those Orders by over-dilution. Accordingly in 1917 the Most Excellent Order of the British Empire was established, consisting of a Military and a Civil Division, and five ranks: Knights and Dames Grand Cross; Knights and Dames Commanders; Commanders; Officers; and Members. The King of Arms is normally a distinguished and senior sailor, soldier or airman; while the Genealogist of the Order is at present Sir Walter Verco, K.C.V.O., Surrey Herald. The Chapel of the Order is in the crypt of St Paul's Cathedral.

So long as Garter King of Arms had to deal only with the Order of the Garter and the Order of the Bath before its enlargement, the many administrative problems involved could be handled by him and his staff. With the growth in the number of Orders of Chivalry and the great inflation of their membership, this became more of a problem. Sir Albert Woods, Garter King of Arms, died in 1904 at a very advanced age, leaving his work on the Orders of Chivalry in a state of some confusion. In mitigation, it should be said that Garters then, as now, have been required to undertake this work on an honorary basis; it is therefore difficult for them (unless they happen to be very wealthy men) to maintain a staff sufficient to cope with the work. In consequence it was finally decided, after much discussion at the very highest levels, that a Central Chancery of the Orders of Knighthood should be established, to deal with the day-to-day administrative work involved with the Orders.

Knights of the Garter and of the Thistle, and Knights and Dames Grand Cross of the other Orders of Chivalry are entitled to supporters to their arms. In many cases they already have personal family arms of their own, which are on record in the official registers of the College of Arms as being indeed theirs. In that case they need only petition the Earl Marshal for a Grant of Supporters, which are granted by Garter King of Arms alone. In other cases it may be that there are arms on record for their ancestors, so it is only necessary to place on record a continuation pedigree proving their right to arms by descent, and then they are in a position to petition for supporters. It may be, however, that a search of the official registers of the College shows that they are not entitled to arms; indeed, it sometimes turns out that arms which their families have been using for the last two or three generations are, in fact, the arms of some totally different and unconnected family. In that case it would be necessary to petition the Earl Marshal for a Grant of Arms and Supporters.

After that the stall-plates, where appropriate, of the Knights of the Garter and Knights Grand Cross have to be designed by a Herald Painter of the College of Arms and engraved on brass and enamelled, or sometimes painted, by an outside craftsman. These have to be checked for accuracy and subsequently affixed to the back of the stall in the chapel of the Order. Banners of the Knights' arms also need to be made. Those for Knights of the Garter are five feet square and those for G.C.B.s six feet square. At the same time a 'life-size' carving in wood of the Knight's crest has to be made and coloured. All these have to be made and put in place before the new Knight is installed. When the Knight dies, his banner and crest are taken down, in order to make room for his successor, but the stall-plate remains as a permanent memorial.

Knights Bachelor have continued to be created from the earliest times until today, but it was not an Order of Chivalry, as the term was

177

understood after the end of the Middle Ages. Before then, all Knights regarded themselves as brothers in arms, but not as members of a closely-knit confraternity. King James I instituted a Register of Knights Bachelor, but it lapsed. The creation of new Orders of Chivalry and their great expansion led a number of Knights Bachelor to form a 'Society of Knights' in 1908, but this was only a voluntary association. It received royal interest and patronage and, by royal command, it was put on a more formal basis and the name changed to The Imperial Society of Knights Bachelor, which is very much alive. The chief officer is the Knight Principal, who has normally been Garter King of Arms, but as, at the time of writing, the present Garter has not yet been dubbed, Sir Anthony Wagner, the previous Garter, is continuing the appointment.

The English priory and commanderies of the Order of Malta were suppressed by Henry VIII at the time of the dissolution of the monasteries. There followed a period of eclipse, but in the early nineteenth century certain people became interested, no doubt as a result of the romantic revival of that period, in reconstituting an English 'langue' of the Order of Malta. It was at first no more than a voluntary society with an Anglican flavour, and was quite separate from the Sovereign Order of Malta, which adheres to the Church of Rome, and the religious animosities of the time precluded any liaison. However, the English association grew in size and importance over the next fifty years and in 1888 Queen Victoria gave them a charter formally incorporating and founding the Venerable Order of the Hospital of St John of Jerusalem. The Queen is Sovereign of the Order, and admissions to it and promotions within it require her approval. As the Knights of the Order are, however, not dubbed before investiture they cannot use the style 'sir', although the star and badge of the Order may be worn on official occasions after all other U.K. orders. The Genealogist of the Venerable Order is always an Officer of Arms, the present one being Dr Conrad Swan, York Herald, who is responsible for certifying the armorial suitability of candidates. The Venerable Order does much charitable work, founding and running an ophthalmic hospital in Jerusalem, and it is also responsible for the St John Ambulance Brigade. Indeed, it is in the great tradition of the ancient crusading orders, and now maintains amicable relations with the Sovereign Order.[6]

TWENTY-ONE

Parliamentary Duties of the Heralds

S SENIOR household officers of The Sovereign, the heralds have been associated with Parliament from its earliest days, but the public records are unhelpful about their activities, as the duties of royal officials would not normally merit special mention, being taken for granted. Nowadays our duties in this respect are:

settling the style and title of new peers;
settling the armorial bearings of new peers;
introduction of new peers into the House of Lords;
the State Opening of Parliament.

SETTLING THE STYLE AND TITLES OF NEW PEERS

Simultaneously with the gazetting of the creation of a new peer, normally in the New Year Honours or Birthday Honours Lists, the Prime Minister's Office informs Garter King of Arms of the names of those ladies or gentlemen on whom a life barony is to be conferred. Each then calls on Garter at the earliest opportunity to discuss what his title shall be. Obviously, it cannot be so close to an existing or even extinct peerage title as to be mistaken for it, so Garter and his assistant in these matters — for many years now Sir Walter Verco, Surrey Herald — have to check the records of the College of Arms. If the proposed title passes this scrutiny and conforms to the practice in these matters and to the regulations which apply, which were drawn up between the Prime Minister and The Queen in 1966, and is otherwise suitable, Garter informs the Prime Minister's Office of the title recommended. Garter simultaneously informs the Crown Office in the House of Lords where the Peer's Letters Patent of Creation are prepared, and the Privy Council Office prepares the Writ of Summons to Parliament. When completed this is sent to the new Peer and notice of the creation is published in the *London Gazette*.

The wording of the Writ of Summons follows ancient form and recalls the High Middle Ages, when kings were kings and expected instant obedience. The delightfully feudal wording of the Writ, which has been in use since the fourteenth century, runs thus:

> Elizabeth the Second, by the Grace of God of the United Kingdom of Great Britain and Northern Ireland and of Our other Realms and Territories Queen, Head of the Commonwealth, Defender of the Faith, to Our right trusty and well-beloved [full name and place of residence of the new Peer], Chevalier, Greeting. Whereas Our Parliament for arduous and urgent affairs concerning Us, the State and defence of Our United Kingdom and the Church, is now met at Our City of Westminster. We strictly enjoining command you upon the faith and allegiance by which you are bound to Us, that considering the difficulty of the said affairs and dangers impending (waiving all excuses) you be personally present at Our aforesaid Parliament with Us and with the Prelates, Nobles and Peers of Our said Kingdom to treat and give your counsel upon the affairs aforesaid. And this as you regard Us and Our honour and the safety and defence of the said Kingdom and Church and despatch of the said affairs in nowise do you omit.

SETTLING THE ARMORIAL BEARINGS OF NEW PEERS

Unlike the practice in the mainland European countries, the Letters Patent under the Great Seal creating a new peer do not include a grant or confirmation of armorial bearings, so a non-armigerous gentleman so created must petition the Earl Marshal for a grant of arms, crest and supporters (the last being a privilege of peers). The procedure for granting armorial bearings to peers is similar to that for gentlemen (described in Chapter 18) and, while it is not obligatory for a peer to establish arms for himself, most newly created peers do so. A peer without armorial bearings looks remarkably naked.

INTRODUCTION OF NEW PEERS INTO THE HOUSE OF LORDS

Sir Antony Wagner and Mr J. C. Sainty, in a paper read to the Society of Antiquaries in 1966, discussed the origin in the Middle Ages of the ceremony of investing new peers, and traced its subsequent history. They also discussed the separate ceremony of placing peers, new or succeeding, into their places in the House of Lords. They then related the factors which led to the abandonment of these two ceremonies, and their supercession in 1621 by the ceremony of the introduction of new peers into the House of Lords, which has been followed to this day. Their paper has been published,[1] so there is no need to traverse this ground again.

What does emerge, as one would expect, is that the heralds were closely associated with these aspects of Parliament from an early time. In the Middle Ages officials seldom enjoyed salaries or retainers sufficient for them to live on, and were dependent on occasional fees and 'droits' for certain services, as well as on casual largesse. Their parliamentary duties produced these. For instance, a scale of fees was due to the Officers of Arms when the King, the Prince of Wales, a duke, marquess, earl, baron or banneret first displayed his banner,[2] that is to say on succession or creation. Fees were also claimable when peerage dignities were created. This also applied to bannerets and knights. After the creation of the office of Garter King of Arms in 1415, Garter received as perquisite the gowns and garments these people were wearing at the time of their investiture. These were splendid and costly garments, made of the rarest and most expensive materials and sewn with pearls and precious stones. There is a record that in 1514 Garter claimed from Charles Brandon, on his creation as Duke of Suffolk, a gown worth £200, an enormous sum. The Duke redeemed it the next day for a substantial sum of money and an annuity of £4 for life.[3] These fees and perquisites on Introductions were only abolished in comparatively recent times. No longer do peers parade like peacocks, and a modern Garter would be at a loss as to what to do with a rather shiny morning dress coat and trousers baggy at the knees, plus a pair of well-worn, down-at-heel Lobb shoes.

The ceremony of the Introduction of New Peers into the House of Lords is simple, dignified and colourful. The usual form today is that the new Peer gives a luncheon party in the Lords' dining-room for his family and friends, to which he invites Garter and Black Rod and his Supporting Peers. Apart from courtesy, the reason for this is that Garter can ensure that the new Peer and his Supporters (two Peers of like degree) leave the table in good time to have a rehearsal before the House sits. The Moses Room (one of the Lords' committee rooms next to the entrance to the Lords' Chamber) is used for the putting on of their scarlet and furred

181

parliamentary robes and Garter's tabard, collar of silver-gilt SS, and his silver-gilt and enamel badge of office. It is here too that Garter picks up the new Peer's Letters Patent of Creation. The Peer brings his Writ of Summons with him (Plate VI).

It is worth describing this ceremony in some detail, as it has never been photographed or recorded on television. The House of Lords usually sits at 2.30 p.m., so shortly before that Garter forms up the procession, led by himself carrying a scroll with the Great Seal pendant, representing the Peer's Letters Patent in his left hand and wand of office in his right, followed by the junior Supporter, the new Peer carrying his Writ in his right hand, and then the senior Supporter. The three Peers carry their cocked hats in their left hands. On occasion the Earl Marshal and the Lord Great Chamberlain also take part in the proceedings. They then wait in the Moses Room until prayers in the Lords are over, when Black Rod comes out to summon them, leading the procession into the Lords' Chamber. The full procession looks like this (although the third and fourth are usually absent):

> Gentleman Usher of the Black Rod
> Garter Principal King of Arms, carrying the Patent
> The Earl Marshal, with his Baton
> The Lord Great Chamberlain, with his White Staff
> The Junior Supporter
> The New Peer, bearing his Writ of Summons
> The Senior Supporter

At the Bar each member of the procession gives a head bow in turn to the Cloth of Estate, which is in fact the Throne, and the custom goes back to the days when the King attended in person. They then proceed up the Temporal (or Opposition) side, and go towards the Woolsack, bowing in turn for the second time as each reaches the Table, and for the third time as each reaches the Judges' Woolsack. On reaching the Lord Chancellor, Black Rod passes round the back of the Woolsack and stands to the right of the Lord Chancellor. At the Woolsack, Garter stops by the Lord Chancellor's left hand and turns to face the new Peer approaching the Lord Chancellor. The Junior Supporter, as he arrives, makes way for the Reading Clerk to move forward from a position that he has been occupying by the rails of the Throne. On reaching the Woolsack the new Peer stops and, kneeling on his right knee, presents his Writ, while Garter simultaneously presents the Patent to the Lord Chancellor, who hands both to the Reading Clerk. The Peer then rises and turns towards the Table. At the same time the Senior Supporter, who has been following the Peer up to the Woolsack, turns about and leads the new Peer, the Reading Clerk and the

Junior Supporter — in that order — back to the Table.

As these four move to the Table, Black Rod and Garter move at the same time down the Spiritual (or Government) side of the House — so called because the Bishops sit on that side — and stand behind the seats of the Clerks at the Table. When the Reading Clerk has reached the Despatch Box, the procession on the Temporal side halts and turns inwards, the new Peer placing his hat on the Table beyond the Despatch Box. Peeresses wear their hats throughout the ceremony.

The Reading Clerk reads the Patent and the Writ, both crucial documents in the making of a peer, and administers the Oath of Allegiance (or the solemn Affirmation) to the Peer, who then signs the Roll upon the Table. The Peer takes up his hat from the Table and moves with his Supporters across the Chamber, each turning and bowing in turn to the Cloth of Estate as they cross the House.

The procession then re-forms, with Black Rod leading, followed by Garter and the Peer with his Senior Supporter in front and his Junior behind; and moves down the Spiritual side of the House towards the Bar, where the procession crosses the House again between the cross benches and the Bar, each member in succession turning as he reaches the centre of the Chamber and bowing to the Cloth of Estate. Black Rod halts, facing the lower end of the Earls' Bench, that is, what is normally the front Opposition Bench. The Peer and his two Supporters are now conducted by Garter to the bench appropriate to his degree in the peerage of the United Kingdom, normally the top or Barons' Bench on the Opposition side, where Garter ensures that by bows and doffing their hats they acknowledge the Lord Chancellor.

Finally, the procession re-forms and moves down the temporal side of the House, each member bowing in turn to the Cloth of Estate on reaching, successively, the Table and the Woolsack. The Peer pauses, bows and shakes hands with the Lord Chancellor. The procession then passes into the Prince's Chamber through the door on the Temporal side of the House. The whole ceremony takes about fifteen minutes, and is very dignified and impressive. Having disrobed after his introduction, identification and acceptance by the House, the new Peer returns and takes his seat for a short time.

The Peers take it amiss if Garter does not conduct Introductions personally, but on occasion, when there is good reason why he cannot do so, one or other of the senior Heralds deputises for him. I have done so several times, and the first was rather alarming, as the House was pretty full, and completely quiet. Having conducted the new Peer and his Supporters to the Barons' Bench, the Herald stands in the row below and tells them to put on their hats and be seated, to rise, take off their hats and bow to the Lord Chancellor. This is done three times. One has to speak in a firm but not over-loud voice. The first time I did it I was naturally rather nervous and, after I had got the Peers lined up in front of me on the Barons' Bench, told them somewhat peremptorily to 'sit', after which the rising and bowing took place. Afterwards Black Rod came up to me and said, 'That went very well, but', with a grin, 'I think you had better say "Be seated" in future. It sounded exactly as if you were speaking to your retriever.'

THE STATE OPENING OF PARLIAMENT

The annual State Opening of Parliament, usually about the first week of November, is one of the most splendid, colourful and dramatic of all state occasions, and marks the beginning of the ensuing parliamentary session, when The Sovereign, crowned and enthroned, reads The Queen's Speech, outlining the Government's political and executive programme for the coming year. It is probably well known to many people, as it is regularly televised (Plate VII is the earliest picture of the occasion.)

As it is one of the Great Ceremonies of State the Earl Marshal is responsible for its planning and organisation, with Garter King of Arms as his chief-of-staff. In recent times Garters, because they are very busy people, have enlisted the aid of one of the senior Heralds to deal with the day-to-day planning, because considerable work is entailed, lasting over many weeks, and many different royal, parliamentary, service and governmental departments have to be consulted and co-ordinated, and a wide variety of people briefed and brought together in the right sequence at the right time. While the ceremony follows the same pattern each year, planning is not just a matter of taking the previous year's Ceremonial (as the printed programme is called) out of the files, dusting it down and using it again. Each time there is some small (and sometimes not so small) amendment which has to be accommodated and which may have a domino effect on the whole procession. The ceremony must be perfect in every detail so that it looks effortless. For many years Sir Walter Verco, Surrey Herald, has been assisting Garter King of Arms in its detailed planning.

The heralds always enjoy the State Opening of Parliament because we all know the others taking part, so that there is a kind of family feeling about the occasion, although it is so grand and formal, and glittering with pomp. Because the heralds always parade as a group, we are used to acting together, and can thus be a steadying influence on any procession. The junior Pursuivants always lead the procession and set the pace, and this needs exact timing because the Earl Marshal and the Lord Great Chamberlain have to walk backwards. If the pace is too quick the procession tends to pull out, leaving untidy gaps; if too slow it bunches up, thus making The Queen slow down to accommodate it, which would draw a rebuke afterwards. All royal processions are conducted at a slow walking pace, mainly because it gives greater dignity to the occasion and allows the onlookers to see more of the procession and its composition. An incidental advantage is that if someone new to it makes an accidental deviation he can recover his position unobtrusively, provided he rectifies his mistake at the same unhurried pace.

The heralds arrive at the House of Lords about an hour before the ceremony begins and, having checked that our tabards, collars of SS and wands are in the committee room allotted to us, we spend much of the rest of the time, in our scarlet uniforms embroidered with gold oak-leaves, conversing with the peers and peeresses we know, or with our wives and friends taking their places in the Royal Gallery. On these occasions it is a very colourful sight, with the women in their gay hats, standing against the painted and gilded walls, and everyone looking happy. About half an hour before the start, the heralds go to their room and put on their tabards, thereafter going in procession to the Princes' Chamber, where the Honourable Corps of Gentlemen at Arms are on duty. All retired senior army officers, they are an impressive sight in their scarlet uniforms and white plumed hats. We pause there for a while before proceeding through the Royal Gallery to the stairs leading to the Norman Porch.

The walls and ceiling of the stairway are covered with brightly painted shields of the arms of the royal dynasties of Britain. The stairs are lined with a dismounted party of the Household Cavalry; Life Guards in scarlet tunics, the Blues and Royals in blue tunics, both with steel helmets, from the top of which hang horsehair plumes, white and red respectively, and all wearing their steel cuirasses, polished like looking-glasses. The heralds line the stairs in front of them, our tabards adding a further splash of colour. There we wait while the Earl Marshal, wearing his Duke's Parliament Robe, and the Lord High Chancellor billow down the stairs, with the Lord Great Chamberlain and others. Then, with a clatter of horses' hooves, Members of the Royal Family arrive in their carriages and, with a flashing of swords in a Royal Salute, they come up the stairs, tiaras and orders a-glitter.

While the military bands outside play the National Anthem, there is a terrific clatter of hooves and rumble of carriage wheels as The Queen drives into the Norman Porch. About a minute later the Earl Marshal and Lord Great Chamberlain emerge into sight, walking backwards, the former raising his baton as a signal for the heralds to turn and lead the procession up the stairs and into the Royal Gallery. The front part stops about half-way along the Gallery, while The Queen's part peels off and goes to the Robing Room.

There we wait for about twelve minutes, although it seems longer, standing between the lines of The Queen's Bodyguard of the Yeomen of the Guard. Founded by Henry VII in 1485, they are the oldest military corps in England, with an unbroken history, and about half a century older than the Honourable Corps of Gentlemen at Arms. Their red tunics, with purple facings and stripes and much gold lace, with white ruffs, have hardly changed since Tudor times.

The doors of the Robing Room slowly open and, to a fanfare by trumpeters of the Household Cavalry, The Queen enters the Royal Gallery wearing the Imperial State Crown, the diamonds flashing in the lights, on which is set the Black Prince's ruby. She is preceded by two peers carrying the Cap of Maintenance and the Sword of State and is usually accompanied by the Duke of Edinburgh and the Prince of Wales. We all turn about and lead the Procession through the Princes' Chamber into the Lords' Chamber, the heralds and front half of the Procession grouped to the left of the Throne; the Kings of Arms and rear half to the right.

Although I have taken part in some twenty Openings of Parliament, I am just as enchanted now by the sight as the first time I saw it. Before the arrival of the procession the lights in the Lords' Chamber are lowered, and as the heralds enter through the door the lights are turned up gradually, so that they are at full strength as The Queen enters. The judges sit on the Woolsack in their scarlet or black robes, with full-bottomed wigs; the massed ranks of peers on the benches, in their scarlet Parliament Robes with rows of white ermine round the right shoulder: two for a baron, two and a half for a viscount, three for an earl, three and a half for a marquess, and four for a duke. On the Temporal benches sit the peeresses, in long dresses of every colour, their tiaras flashing back the lights from the ceiling, while opposite, on the Spiritual side, sit the Bishops, with a couple of rows of foreign Ambassadors behind them, glinting with orders and decorations.

When The Queen is seated she nods to the Lord Great Chamberlain, who turns to the Bar of the House, where Black Rod is waiting, and raises his long, thin white wand to signal to the latter that he must go to the House of Commons to summon the Speaker and Members of Parliament to the Bar of the House of Lords. There is then a pause, which seems to last for ages, with The Queen and the Duke of Edinburgh sitting completely motionless on their thrones awaiting the Commons. At last there is a distant sound of conversation as the Speaker, with the Prime Minister and Leader of the Opposition come to the Bar of the Lords, where they stand, with the Commons grouped behind them.

As soon as all are silent the Lord Chancellor walks forward and goes down on one knee before The Queen. He takes The Queen's Speech from his large, square purse, embroidered with the Royal Arms, and hands it to her. He then has to return to his place, moving backwards; a difficult thing to do as there are three steps to negotiate, and Lord Chancellors are often elderly and sometimes unsteady. The Queen then reads the Speech, after which, the Lord Chancellor collects it from her; but the heralds do not see this part, as we have to hurry out discreetly and form up in the Royal Gallery, where The Queen and her part of the procession soon join us. We proceed to the top of the stairway to the Norman Porch, while The Queen's part of the procession goes to the Robing Room.

We line the stairs and wait for The Queen to depart. By this time the rest of the procession has dispersed and the heralds alone, followed by the Earl Marshal and the Lord Great Chamberlain, no longer having to walk backwards, lead The Queen out into the Norman Porch, where we line the outside steps while The Queen, the Duke of Edinburgh and the Prince of Wales get into their State Carriage. The carriage steps are folded up, the door shut and the footmen clamber briskly on to the back of the carriage, and they are off to clattering of hooves and martial music, with the Imperial Crown in a following carriage (Plate VIII).

One is reminded strongly of the continuity of English history and institutions, and it is always agreeable on these occasions to reflect that the heralds have been organising and taking a prominent part in this unique ceremony from time out of mind. The printed Ceremonial which follows gives a better idea of its complexity and the detailed timing of all its component parts.

THE CEREMONIAL
TO BE OBSERVED AT THE

OPENING
OF PARLIAMENT

BY

Her Majesty
The Queen

ON THURSDAY THE TWENTIETH DAY
OF NOVEMBER 1980

PROCEEDING TO PARLIAMENT

HER MAJESTY THE QUEEN, accompanied by His Royal Highness The Prince Philip, Duke of Edinburgh, and His Royal Highness The Prince of Wales, having proceeded from Buckingham Palace, will arrive at 11.15 o'clock at the Royal Entrance to The Palace of Westminster, where Her Majesty will be received by the Great Officers of State and others there assembled and conducted to the Robing Room.

Her Majesty, having put on the Royal Robes and wearing the Imperial Crown, will join the procession awaiting her in the Royal Gallery at 11.27 o'clock and will proceed in State into the Chamber of the House of Lords, the procession moving in the order following:

Rouge Dragon
Pursuivant
P. L. DICKINSON, ESQ.

Bluemantle Pursuivant
P. L. GWYNN-JONES, ESQ.

Rouge Croix
Pursuivant
T. WOODCOCK, ESQ.

Surrey Herald Extraordinary
W. J. VERCO, ESQ.

Wales Herald Extraordinary
F. JONES, ESQ.

Norfolk Herald Extraordinary
G. D. SQUIBB, ESQ.

Richmond Herald
M. MACLAGAN, ESQ.

Windsor Herald
T. D. MATHEW, ESQ.

Chester Herald
D. H. B. CHESSHYRE, ESQ.

Lancaster Herald
F. S. ANDRUS, ESQ.

York Herald
C. M. J. F. SWAN, ESQ.

Somerset Herald
R. O. DENNYS, ESQ.

Gentleman Usher to
Her Majesty
COLONEL GERARD LEIGH

Gentleman Usher to
Her Majesty
CAPTAIN MICHAEL TUFNELL, R.N.

The Private Secretary to
H.R.H. The Prince of Wales
HON. EDWARD ADEANE

The Private Secretary to
H.R.H. The Duke of Edinburgh
LORD RUPERT NEVILL

Serjeant at Arms
EDMUND GROVE, ESQ.

Serjeant at Arms
PETER WRIGHT, ESQ.

Equerry in Waiting
to Her Majesty
CAPTAIN CHARLES MACFARLANE

The Crown Equerry
LIEUTENANT-COLONEL
SIR JOHN MILLER

Equerry in Waiting
to Her Majesty
LIEUTENANT-COLONEL
BLAIR STEWART-WILSON

The Comptroller of
Her Majesty's Household
SPENCER LE MARCHANT, ESQ.

The Treasurer of
Her Majesty's Household
JOHN STRADLING THOMAS, ESQ.

The Keeper of
Her Majesty's Privy Purse
MAJOR SIR RENNIE MAUDSLAY

The Private Secretary
to Her Majesty
THE RIGHT HON. SIR PHILIP MOORE

Norroy and Ulster King of Arms
J. P. B. BROOKE-LITTLE, ESQ.

The Lord Privy Seal
THE RIGHT HON.
SIR IAN GILMOUR, BT.

The Lord High Chancellor
THE LORD HAILSHAM OF
SAINT MARYLEBONE

The Gentleman Usher of
The Black Rod
LIEUTENANT-GENERAL
SIR DAVID HOUSE

Garter King of Arms
LIEUTENANT-COLONEL
COLIN COLE

The Earl Marshal
THE DUKE OF NORFOLK

The Lord Great Chamberlain
THE MARQUESS OF CHOLMONDELEY

THE SWORD OF STATE
FIELD MARSHAL
THE LORD CARVER

THE CAP OF MAINTENANCE
THE LORD SOAMES

THE QUEEN'S MOST EXCELLENT MAJESTY

accompanied by

HIS ROYAL HIGHNESS THE PRINCE PHILIP, DUKE OF EDINBURGH

Pages of Honour

RICHARD LYTTON-COBBOLD, ESQ.
VISCOUNT CARLOW

JAMES MAUDSLAY, ESQ.
HON. THOMAS COKE

HIS ROYAL HIGHNESS THE PRINCE OF WALES

Woman of the
Bedchamber
HON. MARY MORRISON

The Mistress of the Robes
THE DUCHESS OF GRAFTON

Lady of the
Bedchamber
THE COUNTESS OF AIRLIE

Gold Stick in Waiting
MAJOR-GENERAL
LORD MICHAEL
FITZALAN HOWARD

The Lord Steward
THE DUKE OF
NORTHUMBERLAND

The Master of the Horse
THE EARL OF WESTMORLAND

Lord in Waiting to
Her Majesty
THE LORD HAMILTON OF DALZELL

The Rear-Admiral of the
United Kingdom
ADMIRAL SIR WILLIAM O'BRIEN

The Captain of the Yeomen
of the Guard
THE LORD SANDYS

The Captain of the Honourable
Corps of Gentlemen at Arms
THE LORD DENHAM

Air Aide-de-Camp
to Her Majesty
AIR CHIEF MARSHAL
SIR MICHAEL BEETHAM

Flag Aide-de-Camp
to Her Majesty
ADMIRAL SIR
RICHARD CLAYTON

Aide-de-Camp General
to Her Majesty
GENERAL
SIR JACK HARMAN

The Comptroller
Lord Chamberlain's Office
LIEUTENANT-COLONEL
SIR ERIC PENN

The Gentleman Usher to the
Sword of State
AIR CHIEF MARSHAL
SIR JOHN BARRACLOUGH

Field Officer in Brigade
Waiting
COLONEL RICHARD HUME

Silver Stick in Waiting
COLONEL SIMON COOPER

The Lieutenant of the Yeomen
of the Guard
COLONEL HUGH BRASSEY

The Lieutenant of the Honourable
Corps of Gentlemen at Arms
COLONEL HENRY CLOWES

The Queen being seated on the Throne, the Peer bearing the Cap of Maintenance will stand on the right and the Peer bearing the Sword of State on the left of Her Majesty, on the steps of the Throne.

The Lord High Chancellor, the Lord Privy Seal and the Earl Marshal will stand on the right of Her Majesty; the Lord Great Chamberlain will stand on the steps of the Throne, on the left of Her Majesty, to receive the Royal Commands. The Officers of Her Majesty's Household will arrange themselves on each side of the steps of the Throne in the rear of the Great Officers of State.

At Her Majesty's Command the Gentleman Usher of the Black Rod will proceed to summon the Speaker and Members of the House of Commons to the Bar of the House of Lords.

DEPARTURE

When Her Majesty retires, the Procession will return in the same order as before to the Robing Room, where Her Majesty will unrobe and be conducted thence to the State Carriage by the Lord Great Chamberlain and the Earl Marshal, preceded by the Officers of Arms.

As soon as Her Majesty has departed, the Crown, the Sword of State, and the Cap of Maintenance will proceed under escort to the Regalia Room.

Her Majesty's Judges will proceed through the Royal Gallery to the Royal Entrance.

The Gentlemen at Arms, having handed in their Axes, will proceed to the Norman Porch, followed by the Yeomen of the Guard.

DRESS (A Collar Day)

Peers: Robes over Full Ceremonial Day Dress, Full Dress Uniform or Morning Dress. The Master of the Horse, the Captain of the Honourable Corps of Gentlemen at Arms and the Captain of the Yeomen of the Guard: Full Dress Uniform without Robes.

Gold Stick in Waiting, the Gentleman Usher of the Black Rod, the Comptroller Lord Chamberlain's Office, Silver Stick in Waiting, Field Officer in Brigade Waiting, Officers of Arms, Gentlemen at Arms and Yeomen of the Guard: Full Dress Uniform.

Others: Full Ceremonial Day Dress or Morning Dress with which Stars of Orders limited to two in number, a neck Badge, Decorations and Medals may be worn. Knights of the several Orders will wear their respective Collars if in Robes or in Uniform but not if wearing Morning Dress.

NORFOLK, *Earl Marshal*

10.30 The Honourable Corps of Gentlemen at Arms and The Queen's Bodyguard of the Yeomen of the Guard assemble at the top of the stairs leading from the Norman Porch.

10.45 Doors closed to the public.

10.45 A dismounted party of the Household Cavalry arrive at the Norman Porch and proceed to line the staircase.

10.47 The Queen's Bodyguard of the Yeomen of the Guard enter the Royal Gallery.

10.52 The Honourable Corps of Gentlemen at Arms proceed to the Princes Chamber.

10.52 The Crown, the Sword of State, and the Cap of Maintenance arrive at the Royal Entrance and proceed to the Regalia Room.

10.55 The Crown, the Sword of State and the Cap of Maintenance arrive under escort in the Royal Gallery.

10.57 The Officers of Arms leave the Princes Chamber and proceed to the stairs leading from the Norman Porch.

11.02 The Members of the Royal Family not in the Procession arrive at the Norman Porch and proceed to the Robing Room.

11.05 The Crown is borne by the Lord Great Chamberlain into the Robing Room.

11.07 The Lord High Chancellor proceeds from the Princes Chamber to the foot of the stairs leading from the Norman Porch.

11.09 The Members of the Royal Family not in the Procession leave the Robing Room and proceed to the Chamber of the House of Lords.

11.15 Her Majesty The Queen arrives at the Royal Entrance and proceeds to the Robing Room.

11.20 The Peers carrying the Sword of State and the Cap of Maintenance join the Procession in the Royal Gallery awaiting Her Majesty The Queen.

11.27 Her Majesty enters the Royal Gallery and the Procession advances into the Chamber of the House of Lords.

TWENTY-TWO

THE CEREMONIAL DUTIES OF THE HERALDS

ROM BEING military staff-officers it was a short step for the heralds to become closely involved in the organisation of tournaments, those schools of war. As tournaments turned into social occasions, the expertise and experience of the heralds was employed in organising a variety of other ceremonial occasions. Robert Little (Parvus), King of Heralds, who officiated at the Feast of the Swans in 1306 is mentioned as having been responsible on several occasions during his career for arranging Court festivities.[1] In the Middle Ages offices were not defined in such a tidy way as they are today, and one man could play many parts.

So many and so varied were the ceremonial duties of heralds that one would need more than a volume to describe them fully. The Ceremonies of State in which The Sovereign is most importantly concerned have been discussed pretty fully by John Brooke-Little, in *Royal Ceremonies of State* (Country Life Books, 1980), so that what follows complements what he has written, and is therefore selective.

Ceremonial duties of the heralds in recent times have included:

> The Proclamation of the Accession of the new Sovereign
> The State Funeral of the late Sovereign
> The Coronation of the new Sovereign

The Investiture of the Prince of Wales
State Funeral of Sir Winston Churchill.

The Earl Marshal is the Great Officer of State who is directly responsible to The Sovereign for the planning, organising and marshalling of the Great Ceremonies of State. As the officer responsible for the heralds, he naturally oversees their other ceremonial duties too. It is on these occasions that the heralds appear wearing their uniforms and colourful tabards of the Royal Arms, and are seen, through television and the newspapers, by a world-wide public. Indeed, I have found that the heralds' ceremonial work is a most popular subject for lectures.

Until the eighteenth century the Earl Marshal was also responsible for a wider range of public ceremonies, such as Royal Marriages. Towards the end of the seventeenth century, the Lord Chamberlains (not to be confused with the Lord Great Chamberlain) began to encroach upon these other responsibilities. In 1702 when Queen Anne, according to custom, went to St Paul's Cathedral to give thanks on her accession, the then Lord Chamberlain persuaded the Privy Council to declare St Paul's to be a Chapel Royal for that one day, thus making it a private royal ceremony and transferring responsibility from the Earl Marshal to the Lord Chamberlain, which the heralds of that day regarded as an unsporting trick.

This situation was subsequently rectified and the heralds were required by later sovereigns to be on duty at various royal ceremonies and occasions. For instance, in 1851 when Queen Victoria opened the Great Exhibition in Hyde Park, nine Officers of Arms were in attendance. In 1935, at the Jubilee Service of King George V, five heralds were on duty; in 1948, for the Twenty-Fifth Anniversary Service of the marriage of King George VI and Queen Elizabeth, four were on duty. At The Queen's Silver Jubilee Thanksgiving Service in St Paul's Cathedral in 1977, all the Officers of Arms were in attendance. There is a policy memorandum, dated February 11th, 1948, resulting from a conference between the Earl Marshal (Bernard, Duke of Norfolk), the Lord Chamberlain (the Earl of Clarendon) and Garter (Sir Algar Howard), in which it was agreed 'that on particular occasions such as Thanksgiving Services, Weddings of The Sovereign's children, and such like ceremonies, it should be recommended to The King that some of the Heralds should be summoned, the number to depend on the nature of the ceremony and other factors.' Indeed, this agreement covered a pretty wide spectrum of duties, for in 1965 Portcullis, Bluemantle, Rouge Dragon and Rouge Croix Pursuivants of Arms attended on The Queen, in their tabards, at the Service in St Paul's Cathedral to celebrate the 750th anniversary of the sealing of Magna Carta. We had also been involved in the planning of the ceremonial.

The planning of a Great Ceremony of State is a highly complicated matter. Broadly speaking, the principal authorities directly concerned are the Earl Marshal, who has overall responsibility and command; the Lord Great Chamberlain, who is concerned with Ceremonies of State in the Palace of Westminster; the Lord Chamberlain's Office, which has responsibility for The Sovereign and other Members of the Royal Family; and the Prime Minister's Office, which is responsible for initiating Government action, activating the Cabinet Office and arranging through the Whips' Office the conduct of the necessary Parliamentary action. The Cabinet Office is responsible for activating Government and Service Departments and other authorities, such as the police, and the Ministry of Defence for the Commands within which the Ceremony of State will take place. Needless to say the Earl Marshal's Office is in constant and direct liaison with all these authorities, including television, radio and press, not only as soon as they come under 'starter's orders', but also in the run-up planning period, which may be anything from a week to a year or more.

When a Great Ceremony of State is to be performed The Sovereign consults the Prime Minister and parliamentary approval is sought. At the same time The Sovereign commands the Earl Marshal to organise the ceremony, and the Cabinet Office activates all the governmental machinery involved in the support of the Earl Marshal.

Garter King of Arms is, to use a military analogy, the Earl Marshal's Chief-of-Staff, and the Earl Marshal's Office is run with only a handful of officers and secretaries mostly drawn from the College of Arms, with some additional support from H.Q. London District (who command all the troops in the London area) and the Civil Service. The Office is normally formed into four divisions: (i) Ceremonial, (ii) Invitations and Seating, (iii) Administration and (iv) Public Relations. The Ceremonial division is assisted on the actual day and during the rehearsals by ushers specially recruited to conduct the minor processions and those invited. They are called Gold Staff Officers for a Coronation, Green Staff Officers for a Prince of Wales's Investiture, and Purple Staff Officers for a State Funeral, from the colour of the batons which they carry. The Earl Marshal sees to it that contingency plans for those Ceremonies of State which might have to be organised at very short notice are made well in advance, and reviewed from time to time.

PROCLAMATION OF THE ACCESSION OF THE SOVEREIGN

Possibly one of the most important of the duties undertaken by the heralds is the proclamation of the Accession of The Sovereign, and its significance is often overlooked. It is part of the constitution which probably has its roots in the earliest years of the Dark Ages, the period of the Germanic migrations, when the political features of modern England were being formed.

Recent research has thrown much light on to this period of the Dark Ages. In general the qualifications for kingship appear to have rested on an acknowledged or claimed descent from a ruling dynasty sprung from a tribal god, election and, later, consecration, and this applied to those Germanic tribes, the Angles, Saxons and Jutes, who settled England from the sixth century onwards.

> The early medieval King did not come to the throne through a simple personal right of inheritance. He did, it is true, as a rule possess a certain hereditary reversionary right, or at least a 'throne-worthiness' in virtue of his royal descent. But it was the people who summoned him to the throne with the full force of law, inasmuch as they chose from among the members of the ruling dynasty either the next in title or the fittest. The part played by the people or their representatives in the election of the monarch fluctuated between genuine election and mere recognition (or acceptance) of a king already designated. But at least the community gave legal assent to the prince's accession to the throne and solemnly installed the new king in power.[2]

Although there were a few possible exceptions, king-worthiness included all those members of a royal family, like the Kings of Wessex in England, claiming (with hindsight) descent from a common ancestor, such as the Germanic god Woden. With the variations brought about by time and differing circumstances, this was the general pattern followed by the Germanic peoples. We find it with the West Germans, who included the Franks, Angles, Saxons and Jutes, as well as other tribal groups, and with the east Germans, who included among others the Ostrogoths and Visigoths, Burgundians and Lombards. By the third quarter of the fourth century the Germanic peoples, fleeing from the onslaughts of the Huns, had begun their migrations, and carried with them their customs.

Thus we find in Anglo-Saxon England the same general pattern regarding the accession of their kings.

> The descent of a great executive office such as the kingship could not be settled by the rules which would govern the devolution of a private estate, and in the past it had often been hard to determine which member of the royal house should succeed to the crown on a vacancy ... Under such conditions it was the obvious duty of the late King's Council to take the initiative in the choice of his successor, and this, combined with traditions of the time when it had been for a dead lord's followers to proclaim and protect his heir, brought a strong elective element into English Kingship.[3]

The ceremonial concerned with the accession and proclamation of an English sovereign is evidence of the continuity of our history, where customs and traditions survive with remarkable tenacity while being adapted to contemporary circumstances.

Immediately after the death of The Sovereign is certified by the doctors in attendance, The King's Private Secretary informs the Prime Minister, the Earl Marshal and Garter King of Arms, as well as the Clerk of the Privy Council. The Prime Minister's Office forthwith informs the Cabinet Office which activates the government departments concerned, while the Privy Council summons the Accession Council, the shadowy modern descendant of the Anglo-Saxon *witenagemot*, the great council of the realm, a fluctuating body with, apparently, no set rules or procedures. It consists of all available Privy Councillors, who include the Prime Minister and Cabinet Ministers, and also the Lord Mayor and Aldermen of the City of London together with other magnates and important men of the realm.

The last occasion it met was in 1952. An announcement dated February 6th, 1952 and published in the *London Gazette* the following day[4] stated that:

> Upon the intimation that our late Most Gracious Sovereign King George the Sixth had died in his sleep at Sandringham in the early hours of this morning, the Lords of the Privy Council assembled this day at St. James's Palace and gave orders for Proclaiming Her present Majesty ... We, therefore, the Lords Spiritual and Temporal of this Realm, being here assisted with these of His late Majesty's Privy Council, with representatives of other members of the Commonwealth, with other Principal Gentlemen of Quality, with the Lord Mayor, Aldermen and Citizens of London, do now hereby with one voice and Consent of Tongue and Heart publish and proclaim that the High and Mighty Princess Elizabeth Alexandra Mary is now, by the Death of our late Sovereign of Happy Memory, become Queen Elizabeth the Second, by the Grace of God Queen of this Realm and of all Her Realms and Territories, Head of the Commonwealth, Defender of the Faith, to whom Her lieges do acknowledge all Faith and constant Obedience, with hearty and humble affection ...

There assembled at St James's Palace 191 people. The Accession Council was presided over by the Lord President of the Council. They appear to have signed in any order, as peers and commoners are all mixed up; the Lord Chancellor signed first, Winston Churchill second, the Earl Marshal − although the premier Duke − thirteenth, and Garter King of Arms seventieth. The City was well represented. The names of Clement Attlee, then Prime Minister, Herbert Morrison, Lord Home, Harold Wilson, 'Rab'

Butler and Aneurin Bevan catch the eye, as does also that of V. K. Krishna Menon, Indian High Commissioner in London.

Two days later, on February 8th, in pursuance of the Orders in Council (the Accession Council) of February 6th, the Officers of Arms 'made Proclamation declaring the Accession of Her Majesty Queen Elizabeth II'. The Earl Marshal and the heralds assembled at St James's Palace and, attended by the Serjeants-at-Arms carrying the Maces, preceded by State Trumpeters, the Proclamation of the new Sovereign's accession was read from the balcony in Friary Court of St James's Palace by Garter Principal King of Arms, the Hon. Sir George Bellew. The Earl Marshal and Garter remained at St James's Palace, and the rest proceeded in state carriages, flanked by an escort of Life Guards, to Trafalgar Square, where the Proclamation was read a second time by Lancaster Herald. Thence they proceeded to the boundary of the City of London at Temple Bar, where a temporary barrier had been set up. The City is very jealous of its ancient privileges. At this point Portcullis Pursuivant (the most junior herald there) advanced between two State Trumpeters who were preceded by two of the Life Guards, and demanded admission to the City. He was conducted by the City Marshal to the Lord Mayor, who was waiting in state, attended by the Aldermen, Sheriffs and other senior officers of the City. After the Order in Council had been read, the Lord Mayor directed the temporary barrier to be removed, and the procession continued to the corner of Chancery Lane, where the Proclamation was read a third time by Norroy & Ulster King of Arms. The Lord Mayor and his entourage joined the procession and went to the Royal Exchange, where the Proclamation was read a fourth time by Clarenceux King of Arms.[5] The Officers of Arms were then entertained by the Lord Mayor at the Mansion House before their return.

THE STATE FUNERAL OF THE LATE SOVEREIGN

The death of a ruling Sovereign in recent times entails the following public action: (i) the declaration by the Earl Marshal of national mourning; (ii) the Lying in State in Westminster Hall; (iii) the Procession thence to Paddington Station and the railway journey to Windsor; (iv) the Great Procession from Windsor Station to St George's Chapel, Windsor Castle; (v) the Funeral Service and the Interment.

The basic ceremonial does not change very much from one reign to another, so that there are plenty of precedents to aid the planning of it. Even Sovereigns are human and sooner or later they must die, and in the modern world one can never rule out the possibility that an assassin may hasten their end. Naturally, therefore, every Earl Marshal must make contingency plans, because adequate and seemly arrangements could scarcely be made if left to the last minute, and the ceremony would have an appearance of hastily thrown together amateurishness about it, and would lack dignity. It is here that the centuries-old experience and expertise of the heralds can be so valuable.

A glance at the State Funeral of King George VI will show the procedure followed and the kind of action which is taken on these occasions. The King's health had been giving much concern for some time, so that when his last illness occurred, plans had been more or less finalised for his State Funeral, but naturally there is much which cannot be put into action until after the death and the formal activation of the arrangements. The King died in the early hours of February 6th, 1952.

The Prime Minister's Office immediately informed the Earl Marshal and instructed the Cabinet Office to arrange for the Privy Council to summon the Accession Council forthwith, and this met the same day. Simultaneously the Prime Minister's Office put the Whips Office into motion, and alerted the Lord Great Chamberlain and the Minister of Public Building and Works, who had to make arrangements for the Lying in State. The Lord Chamberlain's Office, as permanent Court officials, would know about the death in any case, and immediately begin taking action to convey the body from Sandringham to Westminster Hall for the Lying in State. The Cabinet Office also instructed the Home Office to alert the police and railways and the Postmaster General to make the necessary arrangements for communications. Apart from alerting the Service Departments to implement their plans, the Cabinet Office also requested the Foreign Office to arrange for the invitation of Foreign Heads of State, and the Commonwealth Office and Colonial Office to take similar action.

The newly acclaimed Queen Elizabeth II sent a Gracious Message to both Houses of Parliament directing that there be a State Funeral for the late King. They passed Humble Addresses concurring with it, and the House of Commons underwrote the expense. The stage was set for a dramatic and solemn occasion, and on February 12th the Earl Marshal issued an 'Order for General Mourning for His late Most Gracious Majesty King George VI', in which it was expected that all persons 'do put themselves into mourning until after His late Majesty's Funeral'.[6]

The Lord Chamberlain's Office arranged for the conveyance of the Royal Coffin from Sandringham to the Palace of Westminster. Thence it was taken in Procession by the Lord Great Chamberlain, and the Minister of Public Building and Works, preceded by the Kings, Heralds and Pursuivants of Arms to Westminster Hall, where the new Queen and the Earl Marshal awaited its arrival, and they all proceeded to the catafalque on which the Royal Coffin was placed. The Peers and the Commons, with their two Speakers, occupied both sides of the Hall, and the Archbishop of

Canterbury conducted a short religious service. There the Coffin remained until the day of the Funeral, so that his loyal subjects could pay their respects to The King.

At the end of the Lying in State, the Bearer Party of the King's Company, Grenadier Guards, took the Coffin from the catafalque and placed it on the gun-carriage, draped with the Royal Standard, upon which were the Imperial State Crown, Orb and Sceptre, and the solemn procession moved from Westminster Hall to Paddington Station. The heralds went direct to Windsor, there to await the arrival of the Coffin and conduct it in a procession replete with kings, princes and heads of state, many of which no longer exist. The obsequies in St George's Chapel, Windsor captured the imagination of the public, for there can have been few State Funerals of a Sovereign who was more universally respected and loved. Here again the heralds took their place in the procession which they, under the direction of the Earl Marshal, had organised, and Garter King of Arms proclaimed the styles and titles of King George VI, and his Coffin was lowered into the crypt of St George's Chapel.

THE CORONATION OF THE SOVEREIGN

By Order in Council on June 6th, 1952, The Queen decreed that Her Coronation should take place on June 2nd, 1953, and accordingly on the following day the Earl Marshal and the Officers of Arms made 'Proclamation declaring Her Majesty's Pleasure touching Her Royal Coronation and the solemnity thereof'. The procedure was the same as for other royal proclamations. The Earl Marshal and the Officers of Arms, attended by two Serjeants-at-Arms carrying their Maces, and preceded by State Trumpeters, proceeded to the balcony in Friary Court of St James's Palace where, after the trumpets had sounded thrice, the Proclamation was read by Garter King of Arms. This was followed by a further fanfare and the playing of the National Anthem. The Earl Marshal and Garter remained behind, while the Officers of Arms and the Serjeants-at-Arms, with the Deputy High Steward of Westminster (the Mayor of Westminster) formed a procession, and the Proclamation was read at Charing Cross by Lancaster Herald. They then proceeded to Temple Bar, where the same formalities as for the Proclamation of Accession were followed, except that this time it was Rouge Dragon Pursuivant who demanded entry to the City. The Proclamation was then read at the usual places in the City of London.

Also on June 6th, The Queen in Council set up the Committee of Claims, known more generally as the Court of Claims, to investigate and adjudicate on claims made by a number of eminent, and not so eminent, people to perform certain hereditary serjeanty services at the time of the

Coronation. One of the most colourful is that of the Dymoke family, heirs in the female line of the ancient family of Marmion, who held the manor of Scrivelsby in Lincolnshire by the grand serjeanty of King's Champion at the Coronation of each Sovereign of England. In the days when the Coronation was followed by a banquet in Westminster Hall, the Champion rode into the Hall supported on either side by the Lord High Constable and the Earl Marshal, and a Herald read out his Challenge which included the words 'any person, of what degree soever, high or low, [who] shall deny or gainsay our Sovereign Lord ... to be the right heir to the Imperial Crown of this realm of Great Britain and Ireland ... is a false traitor', and challenged him to fight. The Coronation Banquet was discontinued after 1821, and the King's Champion now has the duty of bearing the Banner of England at the Coronation.

A coronation is so much easier to plan than, for example, a state funeral, because there is no need for confidentiality. The fact that it will take place, and its date, are announced about a year in advance, and all the machinery of government is overtly at the disposal of the Earl Marshal. This means that discussions with the various ministries and authorities concerned can be conducted quite openly. The work is, nevertheless, every bit as exacting, because a coronation is the biggest of the Great Ceremonies.

So, planning for the Coronation of Queen Elizabeth II could proceed apace. It is a very complicated service which has been made even more complicated over the centuries by alterations introduced by various Archbishops of Canterbury. Some amendments were sensible, but some, dare one say it, seem to have been rather capricious. It was Charlemagne who sold the pass when he accepted the Imperial Crown from Pope Leo III on Christmas Day 800. Originally the sovereign was acclaimed by the magnates and more important lieges, but the early Church, with the encouragement of several tough Popes, introduced the notion that a king who had been anointed by the Church had the edge over other kings. From this it has grown up, over the centuries, that a western European sovereign has not established a claim to divine right unless anointed by the Church. In fact, as we have seen, not so many years ago, the title to the throne of King Edward VIII was completely valid, although he was never crowned, for the Accession Council had proclaimed him King and this was his title to the throne.

The Coronation has been written about very fully at the time and since, so there is little that can usefully be added here. It is of interest that the service begins with the Recognition, when the Archbishop of Canterbury presents the new Sovereign to all those assembled in Westminster Abbey; on the last occasion with the words, 'Sirs, I here present unto you Queen Elizabeth, your undoubted Queen: Wherefore all you who are come this day to do your homage and service, Are you willing to do the same?' They all then said, in a loud voice, 'God Save Queen Elizabeth'. This is the other side of the penny to the Proclamation of Accession.

THE INVESTITURE OF THE PRINCE OF WALES

Edward of Caernarvon — known thus to his contemporaries, because he was born there — was created Prince of Wales by his father, Edward I, on February 7th, 1301 and was invested the same day, probably at Lincoln where Parliament was meeting. Nowadays the heir to the Throne is automatically from birth Duke of Cornwall, and also Duke of Rothesay, Earl of Carrick and Baron of Renfrew, Lord of the Isles and Great Steward of Scotland, but the creation of Princes of Wales is by Letters Patent under the Great Seal of the Realm; and their investiture with the Principality and with the Earldom of Chester may take place on the same day or years later. In the case of Prince Charles he was created Prince of Wales and Earl of Chester in 1958, but not invested until July 1st, 1969. The records are not complete, but it would appear that the first to be invested at Caernarvon Castle was Prince Edward (later King Edward VIII) on July 13th, 1911, his predecessors having been invested in Westminster, York, and elsewhere outside Wales.

It was David Lloyd George, then Chancellor of the Exchequer, who suggested that the Investiture be in Caernarvon Castle (of which he was Constable), no doubt because he was Member of Parliament for that constituency and the event would bolster his standing there. Nevertheless, whatever his motives, it was an inspired choice, because Caernarvon is in the heart of the ancient Welsh Kingdom of Gwynedd, and this ceremony emphasised the descent of the English royal line from Cunedda, King of Gwynedd about the year 400, just before the last of the Roman legions was withdrawn from Britain.

Like a coronation, an investiture of a Prince of Wales is publicised well in advance, so that the planning of it can be undertaken with full and open collaboration with all government and service department concerned. On the last occasion the Earl Marshal's Office was set up in a building in Northumberland Avenue, London, and it followed the administrative organisation which had been found successful for the Churchill Funeral (see pp. 205–33). I again had the honour of serving as senior ceremonial staff officer on the Earl Marshal's staff.

We were fortunate in discovering the existence of a film of the 1911 Investiture, so we arranged for this to be shown to most of those concerned with the planning, and it was extremely helpful because it brought the old papers to life. One of our problems was working out the timings for the many complicated movements of all those involved in the ceremonial and, at first, this entailed frequent visits to Caernarvon. By one of those happy chances it occurred to me that it might save all of us a deal of trouble if the Ministry of Works (as it then was) could lay out with white tapes on one of the lawns of Buckingham Palace a full-scale plan of those parts of Caernarvon Castle where the ceremony would take place. I put this to the Earl Marshal, who liked the idea, and instructed the Ministry of Works to arrange it. This proved a great help to the members of the royal family and government ministers.

At one of the press conferences a journalist asked Duke Bernard what would happen if it rained on the day, and he replied, 'They will get wet'. Duke Bernard was a pleasure to work with, because he always gave a decision promptly and stuck to it, and one soon learnt to condense one's thoughts and put up proposals to him on not more than one side of one sheet of paper.

A Great Ceremony of State should go smoothly and with effortless dignity, giving the impression of immemorial tradition. In point of fact, with the exception of the State Opening of Parliament and the Garter Service at Windsor Castle, only the central act, the focus of the Ceremony, such as the actual Investiture of the Prince of Wales with mantle, coronet and sword, remains unchanged. Movements leading up to it and going away from it are adapted to meet the requirements of different times and conditions. It is the responsibility of the Earl Marshal to sense the trends of public opinion and to decide what innovations can be introduced to meet these in a seemly way.

Thus, for the Churchill Funeral and the Investiture of the Prince of Wales, the worldwide public interest they aroused meant that much closer liaison with the press, radio and television was needed than hitherto. Very many more people, in particular local authorities, wished to take part in the Investiture proceedings, which entailed several different and separate processions, and each had to be shepherded by a herald or a Green Staff Officer. I therefore arranged with the Minstry of Works to put large clocks in every place in the Castle where we might need to check the timing of the various movements.

In the event, the timings of the Royal Procession and of the subsidiary processions and other movements went according to plan, and The Queen arrived at the Watergate Tower precisely on time for the flypast of the Royal Airforce, which marked the end of the ceremony. We had arranged for wireless communication between the Castle and the R.A.F. base, so that the aircraft would arrive above the Watergate about one second after The Queen reached the top of the steps, but that this was achieved reflects great credit on the efficiency of the R.A.F.

THE STATE FUNERAL OF SIR WINSTON CHURCHILL

It seems pretty clear that even in prehistoric times it was not only the kings who were given a ceremonial burial, but also tribal heroes, and it has been customary ever since to honour in this way those who have given outstanding service to their country, whether as warriors or as statesmen. Since 1773 State Funerals, organised and marshalled by the heralds, have been at the public expense, and there have only been seven of them: those of the Rt Hon. William (Pitt), 1st Earl of Chatham, Prime Minister, died 1778; Admiral The Viscount Nelson, died 1805; the Rt Hon. William Pitt the Younger, Prime Minister, died 1806; Field-Marshal The Duke of Wellington, K.G., and Prime Minister, died 1852; the Rt Hon. W. E. Gladstone, Prime Minister, died 1898; Field-Marshal The Earl Roberts, K.G., V.C., died 1914; and the Rt Hon. Sir Winston Spencer-Churchill, K.G., O.M., Prime Minister, died 1965. The papers on all these State Funerals are preserved in the College of Arms.

A State Funeral is one which is conducted at the direction of The Sovereign, with the concurrence of Parliament, the House of Commons passing a resolution that it shall be at the public expense. In consequence, State Funerals for national heroes are bound to be of rare occurrence. The very eminent are frequently Knights of the Garter, Knights of the Thistle, or Knights Grand Cross of the Order of the Bath, or of the other Orders of Chivalry, so that on their deaths they are given a Memorial Service with appropriate ceremonial in the chapels of the Orders of which they were members. For example, the funeral of Admiral of the Fleet The Earl Mountbatten of Burma, the last Viceroy of India, so tragically murdered in 1979, although held with considerable ceremony in Westminster Abbey, was in fact a private royal funeral, because Parliament had not decreed it a State Funeral.

The State Funeral of Sir Winston Churchill was undoubtedly one of the most magnificent that has ever been staged, and the first time that a conscious effort was made to give it a world-wide audience by bringing in television and radio as well as the press at an early point in the planning. It may therefore be of interest to describe it in some detail as few people are aware of the very complicated organisation and co-ordination which it involved.

In the autumn of 1953 the state of Sir Winston Churchill's health gave some cause for anxiety, and the Earl Marshal, Bernard, 16th Duke of Norfolk, suggested to Sir Alan Lascelles, The Queen's Private Secretary, that it might be advisable to ascertain Her Majesty's wishes should Sir Winston die. On November 5th, 1953 the Secretary of the Cabinet, Sir Norman Brook, received a letter from Sir Alan indicating that should Sir Winston Churchill die while The Queen was abroad that winter, she wished him to be given a public funeral, under the general direction of the Earl Marshal, on a scale befitting his position in history. Happily this contingency never arose, and the matter was shelved until early 1957.

By that time Sir Winston's health again caused some anxiety, and towards the end of February the Lord Great Chamberlain, then the 5th Marquess of Cholmondeley, informed the Earl Marshal that as a result of 'a few discreet enquiries at No. 10', he had been told that there would be a Lying in State in Westminster Hall and that the Earl Marshal would make the arrangements. In fact, no decision had yet been taken as to whether there should be a Lying in State, let alone where.

In May 1957, following an approach from the Dean of St Paul's Cathedral suggesting that Sir Winston ought to be buried in St Paul's following the precedent of Nelson and Wellington, Mr Harold Macmillan, the then Prime Minister, wished to know if those responsible for the planning and organising of a State Funeral for Sir Winston Churchill were in a position to move promptly should the need arise. This led to a flurry of activity.

As Sir Winston was known to be reluctant at that time to consider the question of his obsequies, he could not be consulted as to the place of his interment, so it was decided to ascertain the wishes of his family. At an informal meeting between representatives of the Prime Minister's Office, the Cabinet Office, and Sir Winston's Private Secretary, Mr Anthony Montague Browne, it was learnt that Sir Winston had at one time expressed a wish to be buried 'on the front lawn at Chartwell'. Further discreet consultations followed.

In November the Earl Marshal and Sir Norman Brook discussed the matter, and the former suggested that there should be a Lying in State in Westminster Hall, followed by a procession through London with a funeral service at St Paul's or Westminster Abbey. It was agreed that Garter King of Arms, then the Hon. Sir George Bellew, should examine the arrangements made for the State Funerals of Nelson and Wellington, the bound papers relating to these being in the library of the College of Arms. He was also to consider the merits of St Paul's and the Abbey, and to see if there were any precedents for a Lying in State in Westminster Hall other than for royalty.

Garter King of Arms had completed a comprehensive study of the precedents by December 6th, when the Earl Marshal and Sir Norman Brook met again to discuss further action. The funeral of Gladstone provided a precedent for the Lying in State in Westminster Hall of a former Prime Minister, so it was agreed that this should be accorded to Sir Winston Churchill. This was to be followed by a Procession to St Paul's Cathedral, as being a more appropriate place for the Funeral Service, in view of the precedents, and because the layout of St Paul's was much more

IX The personal
banner of Sir Winston
Spencer-Churchill, K.G.
(Churchill quartering
Spencer).

X The banner of the
Cinque Ports, of which
Sir Winston Spencer-
Churchill was Lord
Warden. Both banners
were borne in the
Procession at his State
Funeral, January 30th,
1965.

XI The Coffin being borne away from St Paul's Cathedral after the State Funeral of Sir Winston Spencer-Churchill.

convenient than that of Westminster Abbey for a ceremony of this size and kind. Thereafter, interment would probably be at Chartwell. Because of the state of Sir Winston's health it was not possible to consult him, but through Mr Montague Browne it was possible to keep in touch with the family's wishes. Indeed, Sir Winston's health had reached a stage which made it inadvisable to discuss with him the plans which were now being made, and I am told on the best authority that while he expected to be given a funeral out of the ordinary, he never knew that he was going to be given such a grand State Funeral, in the planning of which he would have shown in earlier days the closest interest.

A further recurrence of Sir Winston's illness caused some concern, and a meeting was called by Sir Norman Brook in the Cabinet Office on February 27th, 1958, attended by representatives of the Prime Minister's Office, the Whips' Office and the Home Office, and agreement was reached on the general procedure, both parliamentary and otherwise, to be followed in the event of Sir Winston's death. This also covered the extent to which broadcasting and the press were to be involved, and a public relations officer, Mr R. G. S. Hoare, Chief Information Officer at the Ministry of Transport, was designated for the Earl Marshal's Office a fortnight later. This conference also considered what arrangements should be made in the event of Sir Winston's death abroad.

By early March the Earl Marshal and Sir Norman Brook had agreed to put the Lord Chamberlain in the picture, as it was his responsibility to look after The Queen and Members of the Royal Family, and to arrange for the body to be conveyed to Westminster Hall. The Lord Great Chamberlain would also be consulted, as he was then responsible for the Palace of Westminster and thus, together with the Minister of Works, for the Lying in State in Westminster Hall. In fact, as we have seen, the Lord Great Chamberlain had been given a pretty good idea of the proposals about a year earlier. At the same time the Foreign Office and the Commonwealth Relations Office were asked to consider arrangements for representation of foreign and Commonwealth countries at the funeral.

By March 19th it was becoming clear that the news media already had an inkling that a State Funeral would be accorded to Sir Winston, and on March 21st Sir Norman Brook discussed it with Sir Ian Jacob, Director-General of the B.B.C., and assured him that the B.B.C. would be brought into consulation when plans were more advanced.

The Cabinet Office, after further correspondence and discussion with the Earl Marshal, then produced on May 9th, 1958, a comprehensive paper on *Procedure on the Death of Sir Winston Churchill*. This was revised and updated at least eight times before the final version appeared on November 2nd, 1964, which was the master plan for all action to be taken by the many different government departments and authorities concerned, in support of the Earl Marshal, on the day when Sir Winston Churchill died.

In June 1958 the Earl Marshal instructed Garter King of Arms to begin earmarking suitable heralds and pursuivants to form the nucleus of the Earl Marshal's Office when the time came to set it up, and meanwhile to assist with contingency planning.

By now so many people were getting to know what was afoot that the Earl Marshal felt it would be more convenient, as well as more secure, if the operation were given a code name. At a meeting at the College of Arms about this time, the Earl Marshal, Garter and Rouge Croix Pursuivant (then Mr W. J. G. Verco, now Sir Walter Verco, K.C.V.O.) discussed the question, and it seems that it was the fertile mind of Sir George Bellew, Garter King of Arms, which produced the code name 'Operation Hope Not'.

The last few months of 1958 were slightly bedevilled by a rather protracted but courteous wrangle about seating arrangements. This was finally resolved to the Earl Marshal's satisfaction by February of the next year. This enabled Lancaster Herald (Lieutenant-Colonel J. R. B. Walker) to complete the seating plans for the funeral service, and the agreement of the Dean and Chapter of St Paul's was obtained by the end of March.

Throughout the first half of 1959 planning proceeded apace, and the Permanent Under-Secretaries of State and their staffs in all the departments and ministries concerned proved most helpful and co-operative. The most important ingredient in the cake was, of course, the Armed Services, and H.Q. London District was a tower of strength. Discussions with the Controller of the Stationery Office, then Sir John Simpson, enabled much useful preliminary work to be put in hand forthwith, with the printing of both the Ceremonial and the tickets, omitting Sir Winston's name. The operational address of the Earl Marshal's Office had not been decided, so the writing-paper could not yet be printed. The very many pages of manuscript notes in his handwriting show that the detailed planning of the Ceremonial was being done by Mr Walter Verco, who had painstakingly to fit the many different and sometimes conflicting pieces of the jigsaw puzzle into their correct places. Fortunately he has a remarkable flair for ceremonial.

From the beginning of 'Hope Not', the Earl Marshal had insisted on being given eight clear days from the time of the death to the day of the State Funeral but by now the planning of both the Ceremonial and seating, and the Lying in State and the street Processions had advanced to such a degree that the Earl Marshal was in a position to assure Sir Norman Brook that not only could he guarantee this timing, but he might be prepared to accept seven days.

Lancaster Herald was responsible for the seating arrangements, and the papers throughout 1958 and 1959 show the many problems involved. The

Royal Family, as always, were most understanding and co-operative, and government departments and the armed services gave every help. The Dean and Chapter of St Paul's appear, from the papers, to have taken a little longer to realise that this was to be a Great Ceremony of State, when those invited are technically the guests of The Sovereign but common sense and some discussion ironed out most of the wrinkles which arose, and thereafter liaison was close and cordial. Naturally, the efficient ushering of the great and the not so great on grand ceremonial occasions is essential to the success of the operation, and towards the end of 1958 the Earl Marshal had appointed Major-General Sir Randle Feilden to take charge of this aspect of it, and he worked in close collaboration with Lancaster Herald. Eventually it was decided to employ one usher for every hundred seats, and this ensured the smooth running of the arrangements. They were known as Purple Staff Officers and mostly recruited from those who had some experience of handling people, for firmness is often needed.

The planning of the Ceremonial, from the foot of the west steps of St Paul's, into the Cathedral, the Funeral Service and the Withdrawal afterwards to the foot of the steps, had been pretty well worked out by the middle of 1959, and the Earl Marshal felt that the file could be put away for the time being. While H.Q. London District had completed much of the planning of the street or Grand Procession, it was not until the end of 1959 that general agreement was reached on the seating arrangements. The most important development, however, was that it was learnt in December 1959 that Sir Winston Churchill had expressed a wish to be buried in the churchyard at Bladon, near Woodstock in Oxfordshire, beside his parents. This entailed considerable rearrangement of the plans for the later part of the proceedings. The procession from St Paul's to Tower Wharf was retained, and it was decided that the coffin should be transported by river to the Festival Hall Pier and thence by hearse to Waterloo Station, whence it could be taken by special train to the railway station nearest Bladon.

It is essential that there should be only one man in full command of a state occasion, for otherwise there would be chaos, and it is fortunate that the Earl Marshal is hereditarily the Duke of Norfolk, who is not only the premier English Duke but usually a man of consequence in his own right, with ready access at the topmost levels. There had evidently been some query, towards the end of 1959, as to chains of command. On January 4th, 1960 the Prime Minister informed the Earl Marshal of a conversation he had had with The Queen that day, when he had explained the kind of problems involved. He added that: 'She understood this and wished me to let you know that not only will She, of course, immediately when the sad event takes place, issue Her Royal Command for a State Funeral, but She feels it is quite right that you should do as much of the detailed planning as is possible beforehand'. In a postscript to a letter to Garter dated January 8th, 1960, the Earl Marshal mentioned that he had: 'received a letter from the Prime Minister informing me that The Queen fully understands that I am making such arrangements as are possible: I discussed this matter with him, and feel the situation is now much clearer.'

Sir George Bellew retired in July 1961 and was succeeded as Garter King of Arms by Sir Anthony Wagner, but much of the credit for the successful outcome of 'Hope Not' some three and a half years later must go to George Bellew. He had a highly developed sense of 'theatre', in the placing and movement of people both in the mass and individually, which, combined with an unerring sense of colour, made him just the right man for planning 'Hope Not'. Highly intelligent and sophisticated, with a sardonic sense of humour, he is himself an artist of merit as well as being a discriminating collector and, from his few literary excursions, it is evident he could have been a notable author: indeed a Renaissance character. George Bellew and Duke Bernard made a remarkably good team, because each had qualities and experience which complemented the other's.

Duke Bernard had been Earl Marshal since 1917, when at nineteen he succeeded his father, and had since then directed the Great Ceremonies of State which followed, which include the annual State Opening of Parliament. His knowledge and experience of state ceremonial was thus unrivalled and made him the ideal man for the job. One of the last of the grandees, he knew what he wanted and expected to get his own way and did, and by the time I got to know him he had become a national institution. He had a great sense of occasion, but was equally interested in the smallest details involved in a ceremony and expected to be kept fully informed, often making helpful suggestions on some quite minor point of organisation or procedure. At the same time he had a splendid sense of the ridiculous and an endearing and kindly sense of humour, but his heralds found him rather unapproachable and stood in considerable awe of him. When he got cross — thankfully never with me — he was a formidable sight, and I have seen ministers tremble under his quiet fury. A simple, straightforward country gentleman, he was a great man.

Lieutenant-Colonel John Walker, Lancaster Herald of Arms (in 1968 promoted Clarenceux King of Arms), continued until the end to deal with the invitations and seating arrangements. The general principle was that he dealt personally, in collaboration with the Lord Chamberlain's Office, with the seating of the Royal Family and other distinguished persons, the Churchill family and personal friends, while the remaining seats were allocated in blocks to the Cabinet Office, the Houses of Parliament, and the different government departments and authorities concerned. The election of the Labour Government in November 1964 brought with it considerable rearrangement of the seating to accommodate the increased number of former Ministers, Permanent Secretaries and Privy Councillors who had served under Sir Winston Churchill and who, because they were now out of office, were not otherwise provided for.

In July 1960 Mr Walter Verco had been promoted to Chester Herald of Arms (being promoted to Norroy & Ulster King of Arms in 1971), and I was appointed Rouge Croix Pursuivant of Arms in August 1961. Much of our liaison with H.Q. London District had been with Lieutenant-Colonel Eric Penn and, on his retirement in 1960, he was appointed Assistant Comptroller in the Lord Chamberlain's Office. We had found him extremely efficient and invariably helpful, so this was a most welcome move. He was promoted Comptroller in 1964 and was thus himself virtually running that office during the last crucial few months of 'Hope Not'. I look back with gratitude on our collaboration. Eric Penn has recently retired from that arduous appointment, with a well-earned G.C.V.O.

In view of the changes in the College of Arms and changes among the personnel of London District and other authorities and departments concerned with the planning of 'Hope Not', the Earl Marshal called a meeting on November 15th, 1961 at H.Q. London District. This was attended by Garter, Lancaster, York, Chester, Rouge Croix and Mr Hoare, the Lord Great Chamberlain, Lieutenant-Colonel Penn for the Lord Chamberlain, Sir Norman Brook and his Private Secretary, Mr (later Sir) John Hewitt of the Prime Minister's Office, Sir Randle Feilden, representatives of the Metropolitan, City of London and Oxfordshire Police, and the officers concerned in H.Q. London District, the Admiralty, War Office, Air Ministry, and Ministry of Works. It was one of the most important conferences to be held and every aspect of 'Hope Not' was examined, decisions taken and action decided. The Earl Marshal reiterated his view that he would need eight clear days from the time of Sir Winston's death (D + 8), irrespective of the day of the week, and this would have been necessary had not Sir Winston's terminal illness given us sufficient warning for most of the arrangements to be completed in advance.

Because I was at that time working in Garter's Office as his assistant, he found it convenient for me to deal with the staff work on the ceremonial planning and organisational problems of 'Hope Not'; Walter Verco, promoted Chester Herald, had by then moved into his own chambers in the College. He continued to be of the greatest help, and all the careful and painstaking work which he had put into the planning of the ceremonial side of 'Hope Not' enabled us to build on the firmest of foundations. Much of the credit for its success is his.

In spite of all the work which had been done on 'Hope Not', very much still remained to be done. Among other things, it was agreed in principle that two banners should be carried in the Procession and into the

211

Cathedral, Sir Winston Churchill's personal banner, and the banner of the Cinque Ports of which he was Lord Warden. Garter banners are five feet square and thus too large for the normal Army colour-pike, while the Cinque Ports banner which had been used by Sir Winston was a curious Victorian concoction, a kind of do-it-yourself heraldry, which bore no relation to the correct arms of the Cinque Ports. After considerable discussion and searches in the records of the College of Arms, Treasury authority was obtained for the production of two banners, that of Sir Winston Churchill being Spencer-Churchill differenced by a small crescent in the centre (his father having been the second son of the 7th Duke of Marlborough), while that for the Cinque Ports was their correct ancient banner, both to be made three feet square. Both are now in the Heralds' Museum in the Tower of London (Plates IX and X).

It was then noticed that the timing and movements of The Queen and members of the Royal Family, foreign heads of state and royal representatives, and of the Lord Mayor, into and out of St Paul's were not quite synchronised with the timings and movements envisaged by the Dean and Chapter. A meeting was called by Garter on February 20th, 1962, attended by those of us working on 'Hope Not' in the College, the Comptroller, Lord Chamberlain's Office, and the Dean and the Canon dealing with the matter. In the course of a long discussion the Dean agreed to the timings and movements proposed by ourselves and the Lord Chamberlain's Office, and a few days later the Comptroller, Sir Norman Gwatkin, was able to let Garter have a complete timetable together with the order of The Queen's Procession. This enabled us to amend the Ceremonial and bring it up to date.

The question of command and authority for 'Hope Not' evidently again aroused some concern and Duke Bernard sought further clarification, which was forthcoming in a letter dated April 6th, 1962 from Sir Norman Brook. 'The Queen made it known as long ago as 1953 that she wished Sir Winston Churchill to be given a public funeral on a scale befitting his position in history. She said that She hoped the Earl Marshal would be entrusted with the arrangements, following the precedent set by the funeral of the Duke of Wellington in 1852. Thus it is with The Queen's authority that you have taken charge of the planning.'

A further small amendment to the street Procession became necessary in April, when Lord Mountbatten of Burma asked the Earl Marshal to include the Chiefs of Staff in the Procession and, after consultation with H.Q. London District, he agreed that they should march at the rear of their troops and in front of the Earl Marshal. It was decided that on arrival at the Cathedral, Lord Mountbatten, who would walk alone, would join the rest of the Pall Bearers at the foot of the steps, while the Chiefs of Staff were conducted to their seats. This relatively small point occupied the time of several authorities and a surprising amount of correspondence. The principal and slightly ridiculous snag was that the three Chiefs of Staff wanted to walk in the order of seniority of their services, telling off from the right, and it took them weeks to hoist in the fact that this would make the Navy junior to the Army, because the senior place in state processions is in the middle, followed by the right and then the left.

By July 10th, 1962, the Lord Great Chamberlain had completed his plans for the Lying in State in Westminster Hall and the movements into and out of it. Arrangements with the Ministry of Works, police, press and broadcasting were also finalised. By July 16th, all aspects of planning had advanced to such a stage that I was able to draw up the first draft of a detailed timetable, or operational order, running to some seven foolscap pages, of the minute-by-minute movements of the heralds and the Earl Marshal's Procession (as that part of the street or Great Procession which entered St Paul's was called). At this time it was envisaged that some of the heralds would march in the Earl Marshal's Procession from Westminster Hall, but the Earl Marshal subsequently ruled that all the Officers of Arms should go direct to St Paul's.

The question of what should be carried in the Earl Marshal's Procession in the way of 'achievements' then arose, and the Nelson and Wellington precedents were examined. The Earl Marshal ruled that only Sir Winston's Spurs, Sword, Crest and Shield (or Targe) should be borne by four of the Heralds. The two banners were to be borne by officers of The Queen's Royal Irish Hussars, while four more were to carry his orders and decorations on four cushions. He had three British orders and seventeen British medals, and five foreign orders and ten foreign medals.

By August, the problem of the time allowed from the day of death to the Funeral Service was again raised in an acute form. H.Q. London District said they could not possibly do it under eight days, the B.B.C. said they needed at least eight days to lay their cables, and the Stationery Office thought it would be impossible to complete the printing in less than eight days, while the family naturally wanted it over in the shortest possible time. The police said there would be chaos if it fell on a weekday unless it were declared a day of public mourning, but the Cabinet said they could not possibly agree to declaring a weekday a day of public mourning, as that would put it on the same footing as a Royal Funeral. The Earl Marshal, in a letter to Garter who had become concerned at the thought of the decision he might have to take should Sir Winston's death occur while the Earl Marshal was in Australia, told him not to worry and added that he was 'pretty sure the decision for the date would be taken by the Cabinet anyhow'. In the event it was, and the Cabinet decreed, when Sir Winston died, that the funeral should take place on $D + 6$, the following Saturday, which meant in effect that printing had to be completed by $D + 4$ and all loose ends had to be tidied up and rehearsals completed by D + 5. Very exhausting.

The correspondence shows that throughout 1962 and 1963 many points arose which required decisions, and in October 1963 the Earl Marshal held a conference at H.Q. London District which was attended by representatives of all those authorities concerned, and the new matters which had arisen since the last conference were dealt with. The Earl Marshal also ruled that the Lying in State should be for four days. Meanwhile the Lord Great Chamberlain's Office had drawn up detailed instructions for the police, and for the Members and officers of both Houses of Parliament, regarding the organisation of the Lying in State and the handling of the crowds of people expected to file past the coffin, as well as the ceremonies on the day of the funeral.

By February 1964 it had been agreed that the Earl Marshal's Office would be established on the ground floor of the Ministry of Defence in Horse Guards Avenue, London, and the Ministry of Public Building and works began to make the necessary plans for it, including painting the name-boards for fixing to doors and so on. We were also now in a position to give the Stationery Office the address of the Earl Marshal's Office, so that they could begin printing our black-edged writing-paper. By December we were in a position to finalise the Ceremonial and the Order of Service, and the Stationery Office produced proofs before Christmas.

On November 2nd, 1964 the Cabinet Office, after consultation with the Earl Marshal, issued a revised instruction on the procedure to be followed on the death of Sir Winston Churchill, detailing the action to be taken by all government authorities and departments of state in support of the Earl Marshal, immediately on notification of Sir Winston's death.

Duke Bernard appointed Brigadier H. L. Green, lately Chief of Staff at H.Q. London District, as his personal staff-officer, mainly in order to ensure the closest liaison with London District. We also took the precaution of putting ourselves in a state of readiness, and I prepared a draft order for Garter to issue when the time came, detailing the action to be taken to set up the Earl Marshal's Office. We were now 'under starter's orders' and there was not much more to be done until the starting-gate went up.

On January 12th, 1965, H.Q. London District issued their revised 'Hope Not Orders', combining in one fat folder an inch and a half thick all previous orders, consisting of fourteen parts, the last containing fifteen maps. Reading it through made one realise what a remarkably complicated and all-embracing operation 'Hope Not' had become.

It was just as well that we had completed all the Ceremonials, with their split-second timings, that the Cabinet Office had issued their instructions to all the authorities concerned, and that London District had just issued their detailed orders, for we were informed on January 15th that Sir Winston was dangerously ill and that his doctor expected him to die at any time.

Garter immediately issued a circular to all Officers of Arms giving them guidance on how to handle press enquiries, and simultaneously issued another instruction to all Officers of Arms detailing the action which was to be taken to set up the Earl Marshal's Office, directly the death was announced, and what action was to be taken by the different officers. I made my bed in the College.

Both the Foreign Office and the Commonwealth Relations Office had underestimated the number of heads of state and Commonwealth representatives who now announced their intention to attend. This produced some tricky problems of seating and timing, which had to be fitted in.

On January 17th the Lord Chamberlain's Office produced a bulky memorandum detailing the movements and timings worked out, in consultation with us, for The Queen, the Duke of Edinburgh, Queen Elizabeth the Queen Mother and members of the Royal Family. The Lord Chamberlain's Office also took care of Commonwealth and foreign heads of state. Members of the Royal Family are always looked after by the Gentlemen Ushers to The Queen and not by Purple (or other) Staff Officers. It was a relief to find that all our timings synchronised exactly.

As it was clear that 'Hope Not' was imminent, the Earl Marshal convened a meeting of all those concerned in the Conference Room at H.Q. London District on January 18th, to ensure that each authority was completely co-ordinated with every other authority, that no loose ends remained untied, and to make final decisions. It was attended by some thirty people, each of whom had an important part to play in the organisation of the State Funeral.

For the last five years the B.B.C. had been in close touch with us, and Richard Dimbleby had paid several visits to the College of Arms, to keep abreast of developments. We, in our turn, were delighted to be of help, not only because he was a particularly agreeable and intelligent man, but because we were as anxious as the B.B.C. to ensure that their coverage of the Funeral would be as accurate as possible. It frequently happens during state occasions that there is a pause in the proceedings, or patches during a procession when the principal figures have not yet appeared. For instance, in Royal Processions the senior places are those nearest The Sovereign, with the more junior people in the lead. The television commentator is thus left with several minutes at a time which have to be filled up smoothly and interestingly. We were able to provide Richard Dimbleby with suitable background information on the lesser people taking part in the Procession, why they were there and why certain things were done in certain ways. He impressed us considerably by the remarkable care with which he did his homework on 'Hope Not'. He thoroughly deserved the acclaim he received for his commentary on the Churchill State Funeral. The press were dealt with almost entirely by the Earl Marshal's Press Officer with whom, of course, we were in the closest touch.

On January 21st, John Hewitt of the Prime Minister's Office telephoned me to say that the Prime Minister, Mr (later Sir) Harold Wilson, was concerned about what action should be taken if Sir Winston died on the morrow, Friday, or during the weekend, as it would not be possible to recall the Houses of Parliament before Monday. The problem was that, on Sir Winston's death, the Prime Minister would issue a statement (which was ready prepared) to the effect that it was understood that The Queen would be sending a Gracious Message to both Houses conveying her wish that a State Funeral be held, on a day to be appointed. The Houses would then receive the Message and pass Humble Addresses concurring with her wishes, and the Commons then vote the funds for it. Until that had been done the Funeral could not, theoretically, take place. The question was what form of words should be used by the Prime Minister and the Earl Marshal to indicate what was being planned without appearing to anticipate the action which the two Houses of Parliament would be taking. John Hewitt and I discussed the various implications and the form of words which we submitted for consideration was, in fact, approved by the Earl Marshal and the Prime Minister.

Throughout these days we were kept constantly informed by Anthony Montague-Browne of the progress of Sir Winston's illness, and it became clear that the end was only a matter of hours away. I had taken the precaution soon after the onset of Sir Winston's last illness to ensure that the Ministry of Public Building and Works completed their work on the rooms in the Ministry of Defence building which were to be occupied by the Earl Marshal's Office. The G.P.O. had made special arrangements for handling the post and for franking letters and telegrams, and they also installed a special telephone exchange. H.Q. London District had direct telephone lines from the Earl Marshal's room to the G.O.C. London District and his Chief-of-Staff, with another direct line for the rest of us to the Assistant Adjutant-General. They also placed Army despatch riders at our disposal, and military policemen to man the entrance to the Earl Marshal's Office, as well as Army orderlies. The Treasury, Admiralty, War Office and Air Ministry put ten clerical officers and typists at our disposal. Entry passes to the Ministry of Defence building had to be arranged. The Stationery Office provided sufficient (more than sufficient as it turned out) stocks of black-edged writing-paper and the Ministry of Works supplied a number of official motor cars and drivers, as well as a van for moving our files from the College of Arms. I was able to report on Saturday January 23rd that all arrangements had been completed.

In the early morning of Sunday January 24th, Anthony Montague-Brown telephoned me to say that Sir Winston Churchill had just died. I immediately informed Garter and the Earl Marshal and we were able to mobilise the Earl Marshal's Office and move into our operational headquarters during the course of that morning. We were in business.

The Cabinet Office advised that the State Funeral should take place on the following Saturday, January 30th, 1965 (D + 6), but we were able to accept this with equanimity because all plans and preparations had been completed.

Our Press Office issued a press release, which unfortunately was not cleared with Garter or me beforehand. They not only managed to get the sequence of events in a muddle, but stated in their opening paragraph that: the following arrangements have been made by London District Headquarters for the State Funeral of Sir Winston Churchill at St Paul's Cathedral. Not only was there no mention of the work on 'Hope Not' put in by the Earl Marshal and two Garter Kings of Arms and several heralds over some eight years, but the only mention of us was that 'the' Garter King of Arms and Heralds would be walking in the street Procession from Westminster Hall to St Paul's, which was not in any of the ceremonials we had given them. Such sloppiness made us wonder what further curious information would be fed to the press. The Earl Marshal called a press conference for the following Monday afternoon. We learnt our lesson during 'Hope Not', and during the Investiture of The Prince of Wales a few years later the Ceremonial Division of the Earl Marshal's Office kept a tight hand on all press releases.

Although all plans had been completed, there was still a remarkable amount of work to do, because on an occasion of this kind the plans cannot be put into operation, with some discreet exceptions, until after the death. It was a very hectic five days with precious little sleep. For instance, one cannot print the final editions of the Ceremonial and of the Order of Service until after the death, but preliminary printing had been put in hand when Sir Winston's terminal illness began, so immediately the death was announced, the Stationery Office sent me the page proofs and I was able to telephone them, as soon as these had been checked, to go ahead with printing the final editions. They made a remarkably good job of it, working round the clock, so we had Ceremonial and Order of Service completed in good time. We were lucky in having ten days' warning before Sir Winston's death, so that much could be put in train in advance, a necessary step, for although newspapers are geared to printing their editions within a few hours, the Stationery Office is not, and while one is prepared to accept spelling mistakes in a newspaper, or the transposition of several lines, it would be quite unacceptable in the ceremonial of a state occasion, when even a misplaced comma would be regarded as extreme carelessness. The reason why it is not possible to print until almost the last minute is that unexpected alterations sometimes need to be made and this may throw out of place several people in a procession. A printed ceremonial issued by the Officers of Arms must be immaculate.

The Coffin was brought to Westminster Hall and placed upon the catafalque on the Tuesday night, where the Royal Family visited it to pay their respects and, for the next three days and nights, immense crowds of people filed silently past it — a very moving sight. On the Friday night, watched by the Earl Marshal, the Lord Great Chamberlain and the Major-General Commanding London District, and other dignitaries, there was a very private rehearsal of the Bearer Party, to run through the drill for lifting the Coffin off the catafalque and carrying it to the gun-carriage at the door of Westminster Hall. The Coffin had been brought to the Hall by the undertakers, so the Bearer Party of six soldiers from the Brigade of Guards, who had had no previous experience of handling it, had to be rehearsed. The Coffin was made of solid oak and the body inside it was encased in thick lead, and they weighed altogether over five hundred-weight, so that each soldier would be carrying nearly one hundredweight. Any of us who have tried to lift a hundredweight sack of corn or cement will know how very heavy it is. At the word of command the Bearer Party stepped smartly forward — and were unable to lift the unwieldy coffin. A stunned and scandalised silence followed; then the Earl Marshal got very cross indeed that this problem had not been sorted out sooner. The undertakers were summoned from their beds and rushed to Westminster Hall. Fortunately it turned out that there is a knack about these things which they were able to demonstrate to the soldiers, who were finally able laboriously to lift the Coffin and march with it to the door, carrying it, three a-side, on their shoulders, with a sergeant marching behind, so that he could grasp a short rope which hung from the end to steady it from time to time. The Bearer Party deserves the highest credit for what must have been a most tiring and exceedingly uncomfortable task. The next day, after the Funeral Service in St Paul's was over and the heralds had led the way out of the Great West Door to line each side of the steps, the Bearer Party had the hazardous task of carrying the Coffin on their shoulders down the long flight of steps. I was standing near the bottom of the steps and as the Bearer Party, with the sweat pouring down their white faces, came abreast of me they faltered and swayed. I watched with horrified alarm expecting catastrophe, but fortunately the sergeant saved the day by grabbing the rope and steadying them. It was a great relief to think that I had not been responsible for the planning of the coffin part of 'Hope Not'. Steps have since been taken to ensure that this sort of thing does not happen again.

The Earl Marshal's Office had completed their work and all loose ends were neatly tied up by Thursday, so Friday could be devoted to rehearsing the various elements taking part in 'Hope Not'. These went as smoothly as rehearsals usually do. At the time they look a pretty good shambles and one wonders if it will ever go right on the day. Fortunately the heralds always provide a steadying influence on any procession, because we are so used to it and, being a closely knit body, can act in concert and set the pace for the rest.

On the Friday afternoon the Israeli Embassy telephoned me, in some agitation, to say that they had just realised that as Dr Weitzmann, the President of Israel, was a very strict Orthodox Jew, he could not possibly travel to St Paul's in a wheeled vehicle the next day, as it was the Sabbath. It was essential that he should reach St Paul's at the precise minute laid down, so I sent an officer with a stop-watch to walk from the Savoy Hotel at the pace which he thought a very elderly gentleman might take, so that I could tell the Israeli Embassy when to launch the President on his way. He did, in fact, arrive on the dot.

Saturday January 30th, 1965 was a comparatively fine but bitterly cold day. All the Officers of Arms breakfasted at the College of Arms, where we put on our scarlet uniforms, with black knee-breeches and silk stockings, and then went to St Paul's Cathedral at eight o'clock. There we went to the North Crypt, where the College tailors dressed us in our tabards of the Royal Arms, with black crepe mourning sashes worn diagonally across them.

After that we waited in the All Souls' or Kitchener Chapel, from which we could watch others carrying out the work we had planned for them, for there was nothing more for us to do until we formed up into procession at 10.10 a.m., with the four senior heralds carrying the Sword, Targe, Crest and Spurs. These have always been carried in State Funerals of persons other than sovereigns, and in former times were also carried at the funerals of the nobility and greater gentry. The Sword was Sir Winston's Army sword and so were his Spurs; the Crest was that from above his garter-stall in St George's Chapel, Windsor. The Targe or Shield had to be specially made and, of course, bore his own Arms. The last two are now on view at the Heralds' Museum at the Tower of London.

We went out through the Great West Door of the Cathedral and lined the steps, fanning out in front of the dismounted party of the Household Cavalry. There we stood for three-quarters of an hour, shivering so much with cold that it was difficult to hold our wands steady or keep our teeth from chattering. As each of the great arrived at the foot of the steps I began to fear they were running late, but dared not to look at my watch, as an enormous television camera was quite close and pointing in my direction.

As it turned out, after the end of the Service the Great Procession was only two minutes behind in leaving the Cathedral.

The printed Ceremonial of this State Funeral gives a comprehensive picture of a great occasion, which may perhaps be the last of its kind, so it is worth printing in full:

CEREMONIAL TO BE OBSERVED
AT THE FUNERAL OF

The Right Honourable
Sir Winston Leonard
Spencer-Churchill

K.G., O.M., C.H.

30th January 1965

ORDER OF THE CEREMONIAL

GUARDS OF HONOUR will be mounted by the Brigade of Guards at New Palace Yard, the Royal Air Force in the Forecourt of the Cathedral Church of St. Paul, the Royal Marines at Tower Hill, and the Royal Navy on Tower Wharf.

At 9.35 o'clock in the morning THE COFFIN will be removed from Westminster Hall by a Bearer Party of the Brigade of Guards and placed upon a Gun Carriage drawn by a Royal Naval gun crew and escorted by a detachment of the Royal Air Force.

THE COFFIN will be covered by the Union Flag and laid thereon will be the Insignia of the Most Noble Order of the Garter.

At 9.45 o'clock precisely the Procession, having been formed, will move, proceeding by way of New Palace Yard, Parliament Square, Parliament Street, Whitehall, Trafalgar Square (South-East corner), the Strand, Fleet Street, and Ludgate Hill to the Cathedral Church of St. Paul.

The Clock in the North Tower of the Palace of Westminster will strike 9.45 o'clock and will thereafter remain silent for the remainder of the day.

The Procession to St. Paul's Cathedral will move in the Order following:

Two Bands of: The Royal Air Force

Detachments of: Battle of Britain Aircrews
The Royal Air Force
The 4th/5th (Cinque Ports) Battalion The Royal Sussex Regiment (T.A.)
The 4th Battalion The Essex Regiment (T.A.)
The 299th Field Regiment Royal Artillery (T.A.)
(Royal Buckinghamshire Yeomanry, Queen's Own Oxfordshire Hussars and Berkshire)

The Honourable Artillery Company (T.A.)

The Royal Military Academy, Sandhurst

Two Bands of: Her Majesty's Foot Guards

Detachments of: The Welsh Guards

The Irish Guards

The Scots Guards

The Coldstream Guards

The Grenadier Guards

Two Bands of: The Royal Marines

Detachments of: The Royal Marine Forces
Volunteer Reserve

The Royal Marines

The Royal Naval Reserve

The Royal Navy

A Drum Horse and State Trumpeters of the Household Cavalry

First Detachment of the Household Cavalry

Two Bands of: Her Majesty's Foot Guards

Air Chief Marshal	Admiral of the Fleet	General
Sir Charles Elworthy,	Sir David Luce,	Sir Richard Hull,
G.C.B., C.B.E., D.S.O.,	G.C.B., D.S.O., O.B.E.,	G.C.B., D.S.O.,
M.V.O., D.F.C., A.F.C.,	Chief of Naval Staff	Chief of the
Chief of the Air Staff	and First Sea Lord	General Staff

Admiral of the Fleet
The Earl Mountbatten of Burma, K.G.,
Chief of The Defence Staff

Orders and Decorations of the Deceased borne by
Officers of The Queen's Royal Irish Hussars

Major	Major	Major	Major
D. A. R.	J. J. Graham	C. D. B.	R. O. G. Wood
Murray-Brown		Troughton, M.C.	

The Banner of the Cinque Ports	*The Banner of Spencer-Churchill*
borne alternately by Officers of	*borne alternately by Officers of*
The Queen's Royal Irish Hussars	*The Queen's Royal Irish Hussars*
Major G. K. Bidie	Lt.-Col. J. M. Strawson, O.B.E.
Major J. L. Sutro, M.C.	Major T. W. Tilbrook

A.D.C. to the General Officer	Brigade Major of the
Commanding London District	Household Brigade
Captain J. F. C. Festing	Major P. J. N. Ward
(Grenadier Guards)	(Welsh Guards)

The Chief of Staff London District
Brigadier J. W. Berridge, M.B.E.

The General Officer Commanding London District and
Major-General Commanding the Household Brigade
Major-General E. J. B. Nelson, C.B., D.S.O., M.V.O., O.B.E., M.C.
(Commanding Troops on Parade)

The Earl Marshal
The Duke of Norfolk, K.G.

Bearer Party of Her Majesty's Brigade of Guards	Royal Naval Gun Crew (Forward Detachment)	Bearer Party of Her Majesty's Brigade of Guards

Escort of the Royal Air Force   **THE GUN CARRIAGE**   Escort of the Royal Air Force

Royal Naval Gun Crew
(Rear Detachment)

The Family
and Other Principal Mourners

Second Detachment of the Household Cavalry

Band of the Royal Artillery

Band of the Metropolitan Police

Contingents of: The Police

The Fire Services

The Civil Defence Corps

ON ARRIVAL at St. Paul's Cathedral the head of the Great Procession proceeds by way of the south side of the Churchyard into Cannon Street and halts there.

The Earl Marshal's Procession halts at the south side of the Forecourt, and the Chiefs of Staff, and the G.O.C. London District, accompanied by his Chief of Staff, Brigade Major, and A.D.C., enter the Cathedral.

The Officers bearing the Orders and Decorations, and the Banners, go to their places on the Steps among the Officers of Arms stationed there.

The Family and Other Principal Mourners go to the north side of the Forecourt, where those in carriages alight.

The Earl Marshal goes to the foot of the Steps.

The Bearer Party then takes THE COFFIN from the Gun Carriage and goes to the south side of the Forecourt, where the Pall Bearers, having awaited it, turn about and precede it to the foot of the Steps.

The Earl Marshal's Procession, led by the Officers of Arms, proceeds up the Steps, and the Family and Other Principal Mourners follow it.

The Royal Naval Gun Crew, the Escort of the Royal Air Force, and those in the rear of the Procession wait in their appointed places.

The Earl Marshal's Procession then moves into the Cathedral by the
Great West Door and advances into the body of the Church in the
Order following:

A Virger

The Sacrist

The Canon in Residence

Rouge Dragon Pursuivant C. M. J. F. Swan, Esq.	Fitzalan Pursuivant Extraordinary C. W. Scott-Giles, Esq., O.B.E.	Rouge Croix Pursuivant R. O. Dennys, Esq., O.B.E.

Portcullis Pursuivant A. C. Cole, Esq.	Bluemantle Pursuivant J. P. B. Brooke-Little, Esq.

Orders and Decorations of the Deceased borne by
Officers of The Queen's Royal Irish Hussars

Major D. A. R. Murray-Brown Major J. J. Graham	Major R. O. G. Wood Major C. D. B. Troughton, M.C.

The Banner of the Cinque Ports *borne by an Officer of* *The Queen's Royal Irish Hussars* Major G. K. Bidie	*The Banner of Spencer-Churchill* *borne by an Officer of* *The Queen's Royal Irish Hussars* Lt.-Col. J. M. Strawson, O.B.E.

Wales Herald Extraordinary Francis Jones, Esq.	Arundel Herald Extraordinary Dermot Morrah, Esq.	Norfolk Herald Extraordinary G. D. Squibb, Esq.

Richmond Herald R. de la Lanne-Mirrlees, Esq.	Chester Herald W. J. G. Verco, Esq., M.V.O.

York Herald The Lord Sinclair, M.V.O. Bearing the Spurs	Lancaster Herald J. R. B. Walker, Esq., M.V.O., M.C. Bearing the Crest

Somerset Herald
M. R. Trappes-Lomax, Esq.
Bearing the Targe

Windsor Herald
R. P. Graham-Vivian, Esq.,
M.V.O., M.C.
Bearing the Sword

Norroy and Ulster
King of Arms
A. J. Toppin, Esq.,
C.V.O.

Clarenceux King of Arms
Sir John
Heaton-Armstrong,
M.V.O.

Garter Principal King of Arms
Sir Anthony Wagner, K.C.V.O.

The Earl Marshal
The Duke of Norfolk, K.G.

The Pall Bearers

The Rt. Hon.
Harold Macmillan

The Rt. Hon.
Sir Robert Menzies, K.T.

Field Marshal
Sir Gerald Templer, K.G.

The Lord Normanbrook,
G.C.B.

The Lord Bridges,
G.C.B., G.C.V.O., M.C.

The Lord Ismay, K.G.

Field Marshal
The Viscount Slim, K.G.

Marshal of the R.A.F.
The Viscount Portal
of Hungerford, K.G.

The Earl of Avon, K.G.

The Earl Attlee, K.G.

Field Marshal
The Earl Alexander
of Tunis, K.G.

Admiral of the Fleet
The Earl Mountbatten
of Burma, K.G.

THE COFFIN
borne by the Bearer Party of
Her Majesty's Brigade of Guards

The Family and Other Principal Mourners

On arrival at the Crossing all those in the Procession go to their appointed places, being conducted there by Purple Staff Officers, and THE COFFIN is placed upon the Bier.

The Bearer Party then withdraws and the Funeral Service begins.

THE SERVICE BEING ENDED THE COFFIN is removed by the Bearer Party and the Procession, with the Officers of Arms leading and in the same order as it entered, is conducted by the Canon in Residence to the Great West Door.

The Officers of Arms and the Bearers of the Orders, Banners, and Achievements take up their stations upon the Steps, while the remainder of the Earl Marshal's Procession and the Pall Bearers proceed to the bottom of the Steps where they go to their appointed places.

The Bearer Party, on arrival at the foot of the Steps, proceed to the Gun Carriage when THE COFFIN is placed upon it, and those going before and after it take their places in the Procession.

At the signal given by the Earl Marshal the Procession advances, by way of Cannon Street, Eastcheap and Great Tower Street, to Tower Hill where it halts at the appointed place and those in carriages alight.

THE COFFIN is removed from the Gun Carriage and, preceded only by the Earl Marshal, and followed by the Family and the Principal Mourners, is borne aboard the Port of London Authority launch *Havengore* and there placed on a Bier.

The Launch bearing THE COFFIN of the Deceased casts off and, escorted by launches of the Port of London Authority, Trinity House, and others, proceeds upstream to the Festival Hall Pier where THE COFFIN is taken ashore and conveyed by motor hearse to Waterloo Station and thence by train to Long Handborough Station, near Blenheim Palace.

The interment will be in Bladon Churchyard and the ceremonies there will be private.

During the Procession in London Minute Guns will be fired from St. James's Park and from the Tower of London. During the River Procession there will be a Fly Past by the Royal Air Force.

DRESS

OFFICERS OF THE SERVICES: *Ceremonial day dress with greatcoats and black armbands.*

CIVILIANS: *Morning dress or lounge suits. Those not wearing overcoats may wear Stars of Orders, Decorations and Medals.*

LADIES: *Day dress.*

NORFOLK
Earl Marshal

TIME TABLE

8.45 The doors of St. Paul's Cathedral open for the public.

9.40 The Representatives of France, The United States of America, and Union of Soviet Socialist Republics arrive at St. Paul's.

9.45 THE COFFIN Procession leaves Westminster Hall.

9.50 The Aldermen and High Officers arrive at St. Paul's.

9.55 The Members of The Royal Family, not being Royal Highnesses, will have arrived at St. Paul's.

10.00 The doors of St. Paul's are closed to the public.

10.04 The Speaker arrives at St. Paul's.

10.05 The Lord Chancellor arrives at St. Paul's.

10.15 The Heads of State and Royal Representatives of Foreign Heads of State arrive at St. Paul's.

10.23 Queen Elizabeth The Queen Mother and the Members of the Royal Family arrive at St. Paul's.

10.25 The Lord Mayor of London arrives at St. Paul's.

10.30 The head of THE COFFIN Procession reaches St. Paul's.

10.35 The Queen and The Duke of Edinburgh, accompanied by The Prince of Wales, arrive at St. Paul's.

10.45 THE COFFIN arrives at St. Paul's.

10.49 The Earl Marshal's Procession enters St. Paul's and THE COFFIN is borne up the Nave.

11.00 The Service begins.

11.30 The Service ends.

11.50 THE COFFIN leaves St. Paul's.   [Plate XI]

12.25 THE COFFIN arrives at Tower Hill.

12.50 Launch leaves Tower Pier for Festival Pier.

12.52 Royal Air Force Fly Past.

The Service was remarkably impressive and moving and, for such a sombre occasion, very colourful too. The sonorous words of the Authorised Version of the Prayer Book, now becoming a fading memory to so many, are so appropriate for an occasion such as this. The hymns included John Bunyan's 'Who Would True Valour See', and 'The Battle Hymn of the Republic', which I always find very stirring. The Service ended by a trumpeter in the gallery above the Great West Door of the Cathedral sounding the Last Post, which was followed after a brief silence by Réveillé. There were few there who were not affected by emotion. The trumpeter was a brilliant touch and I cannot, after all these years, remember who first thought of it. It probably came up in the course of one of our many discussion, the sort of discussion when all those who were there are convinced that it was their idea.

On returning to Buckingham Palace after the Funeral, Sir Michael Adeane, The Queen's Private Secretary, wrote to Duke Bernard to say that:

The Queen and The Duke of Edinburgh were enormously impressed by the dignity and perfection of today's ceremonies, especially the Funeral Service in St. Paul's Cathedral. I am to convey Her Majesty's sincere thanks to you for the manner in which you implemented her instructions after the death of Sir Winston Churchill. The Queen knows how hard you and your staff have been working and she hopes that you will pass on to them and to those who helped them her thanks and her very warm appreciation of all they did to make this occasion worthy of the great man whose death we are all mourning and a true expression of the world wide respect for his memory.

This very kindly message was a great encouragement to us all.

Lady Churchill was understandably exhausted by this ordeal and went abroad for a holiday to recuperate. On her return, she most generously gave those of us in the College of Arms who had worked in the Earl Marshal's Office — Garter King of Arms, Lancaster, York and Chester Heralds, and Bluemantle, Portcullis and Rouge Croix Pursuivants, four of the Officers' secretaries and two members of the College staff — copies of Sir Winston Churchill's books, which we were allowed to select; I chose *Frontiers and Wars* and *A History of the English-Speaking Peoples*. This was a most thoughtful gift, accompanied by a warm letter of thanks to each of us, which will always remain a treasured possession.

Another letter, which will be carefully preserved, was from Richard Dimbleby, whose B.B.C. commentary of the occasion was widely acclaimed. He died soon afterwards. Although his letter was addressed to me, his remarks applied to all of us: 'I must say that your careful preparations resulted in one of the most magnificent and moving pieces of ceremonial that this country has ever seen.' We all of us received letters of congratulation from most of those with whom we had collaborated and who therefore knew what was involved, but one of the most gratifying was from the Earl Marshal, a few days after the Funeral: 'Thank you so much for all the work you put into our last effort and all the help you were to me. We seem to [have] pleased a lot of people and I am so grateful to you.'

Until recently the Officers of Arms working on Ceremonies of State did not receive any fees for the time spent on them, and they had accepted this as a public duty which they were happy to undertake at their own expense. In those days most heralds had adequate private means, so that the loss of time which would otherwise have been devoted to their private practices could be borne, but by the 1960s, not only did far fewer heralds have sufficient private means, but their office overheads and staff costs were very much higher than formerly, and the shoe was beginning to pinch. Sir Anthony Wagner, on succeeding as Garter King of Arms, took the matter up with Sir Robert Knox, Permanent Secretary of the Treasury, in 1961. After some correspondence it was finally agreed that the Treasury would pay Garter £3.10.0 an hour, Chester Herald £1.10.0 an hour, and all other Officers of Arms £1.0.0 an hour for work on 'Hope Not', while Officers' secretaries engaged on 'Hope Not' would be remunerated at their normal rates of pay, calculated on an hourly basis. These fees were to be claimed when 'Hope Not' was over, and detailed time-sheets were to be submitted to the Treasury. When one is working flat out it is very difficult to remember precisely how many hours one did actually spend. Even in those days this was felt to be taking a pretty dim view of the heralds' abilities. However, it was better than nothing, and anyway we regarded it as an honour to be asked to work on 'Operation Hope Not'.

The Civil Estimates for 1964–5, presented to the House of Commons on March 4th, included a Supplementary Estimate for 'Hope Not' which shows that its cost to public funds was only £48,000. Without appearing smug, I think one can say that the country got its money's worth:

(10A)

FUNERAL OF THE
LATE RT. HON. SIR WINSTON CHURCHILL, K.G.

I. ESTIMATE of the amount required in the year ending 31 March 1965 to defray the expenses of the funeral of the late Rt. Hon. Sir Winston Churchill, K.G.

Forty-eight thousand pounds
(£48,000)

II. Head under which this Vote will be accounted for by the Treasury, and additional detail.

EXPENSES OF THE FUNERAL OF THE LATE RT. HON. SIR WINSTON CHURCHILL, K.G.	£	£ 48,000
(1) Earl Marshal's Office: Expenses connected with the funeral arrangements, including the service at St. Paul's Cathedral .	15,000	
(2) Ministry of Defence: Travelling, &c., expenses of Naval, Military and Royal Air Force personnel	19,000	
(3) Travelling, &c., expenses of representatives of the Fire, Police and Civil Defence Services	2,000	
(4) Ministry of Public Building and Works: Expenses in connection with the Lying-in-State at Westminster Hall, works services along the route of the funeral procession, &c.	7,000	
(5) H.M. Stationery Office: Printing, &c.	3,000	
(6) Expense of Departments of H.M. Household	1,000	
(7) Other expenses	1,000	

NOTE

As regards expenses of Departments of H.M. Household, the accounts will be submitted to the Auditor of the Civil List. The remaining accounts will be audited by the Comptroller and Auditor General.

NATIONAL ACCOUNTS CLASSIFICATION

The whole of this Estimate is classified as current expenditure on goods and services.

Postscript

HEN I began this book I was conscious, as we all are in the College of Arms, that we really are uncommonly busy. Now that I have finished I am surprised by the wide range and variety of the activities we undertake. Our friends wonder why such an elegant and restful job requires us to commute daily to the College of Arms, and our families wonder what on earth can keep us so late from returning.

There is nothing here about the work of the heralds in connection with Regimental Colours, R.A.F. Badges, and Royal Naval Badges. The chapter on this had to be omitted owing to the demands of space. It is in fact a very important part of the work of the Officers of Arms, with an interesting history, reflecting the development of the British and Commonwealth armed services. In 1806 (Sir) George Nayler was appointed Inspector of Regimental Colours and every Garter King of Arms since has held this appointment, often enlisting one of his colleagues as Deputy Inspector. In 1936 one of the Officers of Arms was appointed Inspector of Royal Air Force Badges. Later he was appointed by the Australian government Inspector of Royal Australian Air Force Badges. Another Officer was appointed in 1954 Adviser to the Admiralty on Royal Naval heraldry.

Neither have I discussed the many contributions of the heralds to

234

scholarship, which consist not only of books or monographs, but also of articles in learned journals and in the popular press. Lectures and talks on all aspects of heraldry are given frequently by most of the heralds, while some of us give talks and interviews on radio and television. For many years exhibitions of heraldic art have been organised in London and various provincial cities, under the guidance of the heralds.

By a happy chance the heralds were able to realise in 1980 a long held ambition to have a museum of heraldry. Through the kindness of the Governor and the Master of the Armouries of H.M. Tower of London, and the Department of the Environment, we were allotted a gallery in one of the buildings of the Tower. The credit for achieving this must go to Sir Anthony Wagner, now Clarenceux King of Arms, who is Director of the Heralds' Museum; I am Deputy Director. The Department of Education and Science has recently become interested in heraldry as a subject for school projects, and we are actively discussing with them and with the Education Department at the Tower ways in which we can be of assistance. I feel that this is where we might be able to make a useful contribution.

The modern craze for souvenirs of every conceivable sort and size, in gold, silver, base metals, or materials, has led to an extensive use of armorial emblems, often without the owners' permission. The use of the Royal Arms and Badges is strictly controlled and permission to use them for souvenir purposes is normally confined to coronations, investitures of Princes of Wales, royal weddings, and anniversaries such as The Queen's Silver Jubilee. By direction of the Lord Chamberlain manufacturers have to apply to the College of Arms for approved line drawings or coloured paintings. But in other cases responsibility for protection rests with the owners of the arms, which is unsatisfactory because the damage has often been done before the owner learns about it. Apart from that, the general standard of such armorial art has been at best dull and often deplorable. In consequence the more important of the firms producing heraldic souvenirs have lately been turning to the heralds for advice and guidance, and asking us to obtain the agreement of the owners of the arms. Several of our herald painters are excellent designers and their products more imaginative than and much superior to outside work. Norroy & Ulster and I have been engaged in these activities to a greater extent than our colleagues. We will consider collaboration only with a firm of the highest repute, and only if some academic body or charitable organisation benefits by way of royalties. Over the last five years we have raised close on £100,000 for such charities.

The activities of a modern herald are remarkably varied and never dull. We work in a historic house with a very friendly atmosphere. One's colleagues are intelligent and congenial, with a breadth of vision cultivated by a wide range of outside interests. We have an Earl Marshal whose distinguished career in the Army and subsequent career as a merchant banker made him very much a product of the modern world. What more can one want? At the same time we cost the country nothing.

1981   R.D.

GLOSSARY OF SOME COMMON HERALDIC TERMS

Although it was originally published in 1894, James Parker, *A Glossary of Terms Used In Heraldry* (Newton Abbot: David & Charles, 1970), is still the essential reference book for anyone seriously interested in the subject and, fortunately, it is again obtainable. *Boutell's Heraldry*, edited by J. P. Brooke-Little (Frederick Warne, revised edition 1978), has an excellent glossary and it, too, is readily obtainable. Indeed, most good books on heraldry have a glossary, but they tend not to be as comprehensive as these two, and are usually intended only as a help to readers of the particular book, as is the case with this glossary. An indispensable reference book which all armorists should have on their shelves is Baron Stalins et al., *Vocabulaire-Atlas Héraldique en Six Langues* (Société du Grand Armorial de France, 1952), published under the auspices of the Académie Internationale d'Héraldique, to which I am greatly indebted. No heraldic library is complete without Professor Gerard J. Brault, *Early Blazon* (Oxford University Press, 1972), which is a most comprehensive study of the heraldic terminology in the twelfth and thirteenth centuries.

ACHIEVEMENT
The complete display of all the armorial bearings to which an armiger is entitled, which in the case of gentlemen, knights and baronets includes the shield, with the crest standing upon the helm within its wreath or coronet, with the mantling hanging from behind it; and in the case of Peers, Knights of the Garter and Thistle, and Knights Grand Cross of the Orders of Chivalry, supporters.

237

ADDORSED Fr. *Adossés*; Ge. *Abgewendet*
Charges in the shield which are placed back to back; and also in the case of winged creatures, where the wings are drawn extended and elevated above the back so that they are themselves, as it were, back to back.

AFFRONTÉ
Used to describe a creature in a shield or crest which is shown as looking directly at the observer and showing its full front view. But see also Caboshed.

AMBULANT
Walking. The term more frequently used is 'passant'.

ANNULET Fr. *Cyclamor*; Ge. *Grosser Reif*
A plain ring. Also in English heraldry the cadency mark of a fifth son.

ARGENT Ge. *Silbern*
Silver, one of the two metals of armory, usually white in heraldic art. The abbreviation in an armorial trick is usually 'a' or 'arg'. Sometimes in English heraldry blazoned as 'silver'. In the Middle Ages held to symbolise purity and justice, and the age of childhood and hope. Silver paint is never satisfactory, while modern silver-type paints act like a looking-glass, reflecting other colours in a most confusing way. It is best to use Chinese white, or just to leave the white paper to show through.

ARMED Fr. *Armé*; Ge. *Bewehrt*
When the teeth, tusks, horns or claws of a beast, whether real or fabulous, are of a different colour from its body, it is blazoned as 'armed' of a particular metal or colour, but the hooves of beasts of the chase and other ungulates are blazoned as 'unguled'. Birds of the chase or falconry are also said to be 'armed', but other birds are blazoned as 'beaked and membered' of a particular colour. When used in connection with human bodies or limbs it means 'armoured'. In the case of eagles, the French equivalent is *aigle onglé*, and in German *mit Krallen*.

ARMIGER
Technically one who is entitled to legitimate heraldic arms, and in earlier times synonymous with Esquire. Now an armigerous gentleman.

ARMORY
Specifically the art or science concerning the devices borne on the shield and its accompaniments.

ARMS
Specifically the devices and emblems painted on the shield, pennoncel, gonfanon, banner, surcoat or jupon, and also on the horse-trappers. It is now used more loosely to include all the elements in an achievement.

ATTIRES
A stag's antlers; blazoned as 'attired' of such-and-such a colour.

AUGMENTATION
An honourable addition to arms, granted for special services.

AZURE Fr. *Azur*; Ge. *Blau*
The colour blue, from the Old French *azur*, resulting from the crusader contacts with the Arabs and Persians in Outremer. It is derived from a corruption of the Persian word for lapis-lazuli. Described by an early writer as the heavenly colour, and by another as being like the sky on a clear sun-shining day. Ultramarine and cobalt are good colours, and both can be lightened with a little white if required.

BADGE
A device which was quite distinct from the shield, and which became popular with the magnates of England during the fifteenth century, when private armies and contingents needed emblems to demonstrate their allegiance. These in the following century often became transmuted into supporters or crests.

BANNER Fr. *Bannière*; Ge. *Fahne*
A flag borne on a lance or staff, rectangular in shape. Originally of greater height than width, it became square in the fifteenth century and has so remained. In the Middle Ages it was the distinctive flag of a knight banneret, but today in England it can be used by any armiger.

BAR Fr. *Divisé*; Ge. *Querfaden*
A diminutive of the fess. Theoretically there can be any number, but more than four would be inconvenient and messy, and it would be better to make the shield Barry.

BARRY Fr. *Fassé de* ... (so many) *pièces*; Ge. ... (so many) *Geteilt*
When the field is divided into an equal number of bars of alternating tinctures. The earlier term Barrulé or Burulé is equally correct.

BARS GEMELLES
When bars are placed in pairs, close together, they become bars gemelles, or twin bars. It is almost unknown to have more than two pairs.

BARWISE
Charges placed on a shield in a horizontal line, like a bar.

BASE Fr. *Pointe*; Ge. *Schildfuss*
The lower part of the shield and a charge placed there is blazoned as 'in base'.

239

BELLED
Eagles, falcons and hawks used in falconry have a bell and jess (or thong) tied to one leg, and are blazoned as 'belled and jessed' proper, or of a particular metal or colour.

BEND Fr. *Bande*; Ge. *Schrägbalken*
One of the major ordinaries, being a diagonal band from the dexter chief to the sinister base of the shield. The opposite diagonal is the bend sinister, which in French armory is the *barre*, no doubt the origin of many a novelist's 'bar sinister', a term unknown to English heraldry. In the fourteenth century, bastards placed the arms of their father on a bend, e.g., Clarendon (Figure 15) and Beaufort (Figure 16).

BENDLET Fr. *Cotice*; Ge. *Schrägleiste*
The diminutive of the bend and usually more than one, but however many the field of the shield must show above the top one and below the bottom one, otherwise the field is blazoned as bendy of so many pieces. Both the bend sinister and the bendlet sinister have been used as marks of bastardy.

BENDWISE
When charges in a shield are placed in a diagonal line like a bend.

BENDY Fr. *Bande de* … (so many) *pièces*; Ge. *Schräggeteilt* … (so many times)
When the field is divided into an equal number of bendlets of alternating tinctures.

BEZANT Fr. *Besant*; Ge. *Münze*
A gold roundel, so named from the gold coin of Byzantium. It is flat and should never be shaded because it is not a ball.

BILLET Fr. *Billette*; Ge. *Schindeln*
A rectangular charge of any tincture.

BILLETY Fr. *Billetté*; Ge. *Mit Schindeln besät*
When the shield is powdered with billets. In the early Middle Ages a cross billeté was what is now blazoned as a cross potent.

BLACK: see Sable

BLAZON
The technical description in words of heraldic devices and insignia. If, say, in a patent of arms the painting of the armorial bearings differs in any way from the blazon, it is the latter which is regarded as correct.

BLUE: See Azure

BORDURE Fr. *Bordure*; Ge. *Schildrand*
One of the ordinaries, being a narrow border around the edge of the shield
or banner. It may be plain, or its inner edge may be engrailed, indented
and so on. It may be of any tincture or combination thereof. The bordure is
the normal form of differencing the arms of cadet branches of a family in
Scotland. In England the bordure wavy is the modern form of differencing
the arms of bastards.

BRIZURE
A mark of cadency.

BURULÉ: see Barry

CABOSHED, *or* **CABOSSED**
The head of an animal depicted affronté, or full-faced, without any of the
neck being visible.

CADENCY
The position of younger members or cadet branches of a family in relation
to the head of the family, and hence the system of differencing their arms
to indicate this. In England the cadency marks are as follows: the eldest son
a label during his father's lifetime; second son a crescent; third a molet;
fourth a martlet; fifth an annulet; sixth a fleur de lys; seventh a rose; eighth
a cross moline; ninth a double-quatrefoil. All cadency marks are small and
placed not too obtrusively at some convenient point at the top or middle of
the shield.

CANTING ARMS
Arms which contain a charge or charges which allude to, or are a pun on,
the bearer's name.

CANTON Fr. *Canton*; Ge. *Obereck*
A square ordinary smaller than the quarter, and always placed in the dexter
chief of the shield on top of any charges which may already be there. It is
almost always charged, and is often used for containing an honourable
augmentation.

CAP OF ESTATE *or* **CAP OF MAINTENANCE**
An early symbol of high rank, originally borne by princes or peers of the
realm. Subsequently more widely used, but still uncommon, and in
England now reserved for life peers.

CARBUNCLE *or* **CARBOCLE**: see Escarbuncle

CHARGE
Anything, whether living or inanimate, placed or charged upon the field of
the shield. Charges can themselves be charged with another object, but this

is discouraged as it tends to produce a messy design.

CHECKY *or* CHEQUY Fr. *Échiqueté*; Ge. *Geschacht*
The field, or an ordinary, or a charge, coloured in small squares of alternate metal and colour, like a chessboard.

CHEVRON Fr. *Chevron*; Ge. *Sparren*
One of the major ordinaries, like an inverted letter V. A chevron reversed is like a V.

CHEVRONEL Fr. *Etai*; Ge. *Sparrenleiste*
The diminutive of the chevron, usually used when there are more than three. As with the other diminutives of ordinaries, they can be of any reasonable number, but the field must appear above the top one and below the bottom one.

CHEVRONNY Fr. *Écu Chevronné*; Ge. *Gesparrt*
When the field itself is divided evenly, chevronwise, in alternating colours.

CHIEF Fr. *Chef*; Ge. *Schildhaupt*
Regarded as one of the major ordinaries, it can also be used as one of the divisions of the shield and thus sometimes escapes the rule against putting metal on metal, or colour on colour. It lies horizontally across the top part of a shield and its depth can be varied a little, deeper if it carries a charge or charges, narrower if not. Like all heraldic art this is a matter of common sense. Charges placed at the top of a shield are said to be 'in chief', or 'in dexter chief' and so on, as the case may be.

CINQUEFOIL Fr. *Quintefeuille*; Ge. *Fünfblatt*
A conventionalised flower of five equal petals, probably in the early days of heraldry based on the wild rose.

CLOSE
When the wings of a bird are depicted as folded shut against the body; also applied to a helm with the visor closed.

COGNIZANCE
In the very early days of heraldry, when arms were borne mainly as lance-flags or pennoncels rather than being painted on shields, the Norman-French word *conoisances* was used in the sense of 'arms', literally ensigns by which a man could be known. It may still be used today, although a little affected.

COMBATANT Fr. *Affrontés*; Ge. *Zugewendet*
When two ferocious beasts, such as lions, are depicted facing each other and rampant, as if fighting. The more pacific creatures and birds are termed 'respectant'.

COMPARTMENT
The base, often depicted as a grassy mound, on which the supporters stand to hold up the shield.

COMPONY Fr. *Componné*; Ge. *Gestückt*
A single row of chequers, of alternate metal and colour, by which a bordure or one of the minor ordinaries is coloured. Its alternative form is gobony.

CONJOINED Fr. *Aboutés*; Ge. *Mit den spitzen aneinanderstossend*
Joined together.

CONTOURNÉ Fr. *Contourné*; Ge. *Abnehmend*
Used of a creature depicted with its body facing to the sinister. Not to be confused with 'reguardant'.

CONTRE-HERMINES: see Ermines

COTISE (earlier sometimes Cost)
The smallest diminutive of the fess, bend and chevron, always depicted lying close alongside them on both sides, when it is blazoned as 'a fess cotised' and so on. In the case of the pale the same thing is usually blazoned as 'a pale endorsed'. But beware: in French armory *coticé* means bendy of many pieces.

COUCHANT
Term used for blazoning an animal lying down with its head held up, but a stag or hart thus is blazoned as 'lodged'. When the beast's head is down on its paws or the ground it is 'dormant'.

COUNTERCHANGED Fr. *De l'un á l'autre*; Ge. *In verwechselten Farben*
When a field is party of two different tinctures and a charge over the whole field has these colours reversed.

COUNTER-COMPONY
A double row of chequers, usually used for colouring one of the major ordinaries.

COUNTER-PASSANT
Passant in opposite directions; but counter-rampant or counter-salient when one is behind the other doing this.

COUPED Fr. *Alésé*; Ge. *Schwebend*
Term used to describe the head or limb of a person or creature which is cut off cleanly at the neck or elsewhere.

CRESCENT Fr. *Croissant*; Ge. *Liegender Halbmond*
This is self-evident, but in armory it is always drawn with the horns

pointing upwards. If the horns of a crescent or moon point to the sinister it becomes 'desrescent', and if to the dexter 'increscent'.

CREST Fr. *Cimier*; Ge. *Helmzier*

The device which was and is set upon the helm. Sometimes within at its base a crest-coronet, but normally a crest-wreath, more usually just wreath.

CROSS Fr. *Croix*; Ge. *Kreuz*

In the thirteenth century the heralds recognised twelve different crosses: cross passant (passing across the shield from side to side); cross engrailed; cross piercée (voided); cross recerclée (like a cross moline, but with the ends more curled); cross fourmée (formy); cross à les degrees (the Calvary cross, set on three steps); cross crosslet; cross potent; cross pomelée (pommé); cross floretty; cross patée; and 'un Croice entier saunz nulle diversitee', which St George bears (a plain cross, but it is difficult to see how it differs from the first cross). The saltire was also in use then, but evidently not regarded as a cross. By the fifteenth century some twenty-eight different kinds of cross were recognised. Today the ingenuity of many generations of heralds has produced nearly 400 different varieties of cross; the majority have only been used to meet a particular case and then abandoned, and some are pretty ugly and best forgotten. Those who are interested in pursuing this recondite backwater of armory should consult the standard text-books on heraldry.

CRUSILLY

When the field of a shield is powdered with little crosses.

DANCE Fr. *Vivré*, Ge. *Zickzack*

Sometimes spelt Daunce. A kind of fess depicted in a bold zigzag way, the indentations much larger than when an ordinary is 'indented'. Party lines or the edge of an ordinary, such as a chief, can be depicted as 'dancetty'.

DEBRUISED

Used when a charge is overlaid by an ordinary.

DECRESCENT

A moon or crescent with the horns to the sinister.

DEMI

Usually the upper half of any creature, from the waist upwards, but it can be used for inanimate objects.

DEXTER Fr. *Dextre*; Ge. *Rechts*

The right side. When applied to an armorial shield it refers to the part which would be towards the right side of the man holding it, thus the part to the viewer's left.

DIFFERENCE

Different marks or charges on the basic family arms to distinguish one cadet branch from another. See also Cadency.

DIMIDIATED

The earliest method of impaling two different shields of arms, whereby each was cut in half down the middle and the dexter half of one joined to the sinister half of the other. It was fairly soon abandoned in favour of impalement.

DISPLAYED

When an eagle or other bird is depicted with its belly to the viewer and wings spread open on either side.

DOUBLE-EAGLE Fr. *Aigle bicéphale*; Ge. *Doppleadler*

An eagle with two heads, like the Imperial eagle. It may also be blazoned a double-headed eagle or an imperial eagle. The anonymous author of *De Heraudie* (*c.* 1300) stated that the Emperor bore an 'eagle de sable ove double bek' because of his 'graunt seignourie'. It would, I feel, be prostituting this noble bird to grant him to commoners.

DOUBLE-QUEUED

Having two tails, or a forked tail; usually blazoned as queue-fourché.

DRAGON: see Wyvern

ÉCARTELÉ

French for quarterly.

ELEVATED

When the wings of birds and other flying creatures are raised.

EMBATTLED Fr. *Crénelé*; Ge. *Zinnenförmig*

When a particular line or the edge of an ordinary is shown like the battlements or crenellations of a castle.

EMBOWED Fr. *Ployé*; Ge. *Eingebogen*

Bent, as of an arm.

ENFILED

When a charge, say, a sword, is encircled by another, e.g., a coronet. From the Fr. *enfiler*, to thread.

ENGRAILED Fr. *Engrêlé*; Ge. *Dornen*

A particular line or the edge of an ordinary shown with semi-circular indentations, the points outwards.

ENHANCED Fr. *Haussée*; Ge. *Erhöht*
When a charge is depicted above the normal position.

ERADICATED Fr. *Arraché*; Ge. *Bewurzelt*
Of a tree, with the roots showing, as if pulled out.

ERASED Fr. *Arraché*; Ge. *Abgerissen*
Used to describe the head or limb of a creature which has a ragged base, as if torn off.

ERECT Fr. *Ravissant*; Ge. *Aufrecht*
Upright.

ERMINE Fr. *Hermine*; Ge. *Hermelin*
This is the principal fur of heraldry, and was made of the white winter coats of stoats, with the black tips of their tails, or 'spots', sewn on in a regular pattern. Stoats only change their coats in countries with very cold winters, with permanent snow, so the fur had to be imported from eastern Europe, mainly by western merchants trading to the Crimea, and it was therefore expensive. It became a status symbol of rulers and nobles. It is still used on the coronation robes of English peers. It is depicted in heraldry in various conventional ways.

ERMINES Fr. *Contre-hermine*; Ge. *Gegenhermelin*
The ermine colours reversed: white tails on black.

ERMINOIS
Similar to ermine, but with black tails on gold.

ESCUTCHEON OF PRETENCE
A small shield of the wife's arms placed in the middle of the husband's shield, to indicate that she is an heraldic heiress.

FESS O.Fr. *Fesse*; Fr. *Fasce*; Ge. *Balken*
One of the ordinaries, being a broad horizontal band across the middle of the shield.

FESS-POINT Fr. *Abime*; Ge. *Herzstelle*
The middle point of the shield.

FESSWISE
A charge of charges depicted in a horizontal position.

FIELD
The surface of the shield or flag on which the charges are placed.

FIMBRIATED Fr. *Bordé*; Ge. *Gerändert*
Edged with a narrow border of a different tincture from the ordinary.

FITCHY Fr. *Croix au pied fiche*; Ge. *Fuss spitzkreuz*
With the lower arm of a cross pointed.

FLEUR DE LYS
Originally the white lily, emblematic of the Virgin Mary, as opposed to the fleur de gley, the yellow wild iris; but by the fourteenth century the term was applied to both.

FLORY Fr. *Croix florencée*; Ge. *Glerenkreuz*
Embellished with fleurs de lys, especially the ends of the arms of a cross.

FORMY Fr. *Pattée*; Ge. *Tatzenkreuz*
Of a cross, with the ends of the arms considerably wider than their bases. Nowadays more usually blazoned as 'patty'.

FRET Fr. *Frette*; Ge. *Mit einer fensterraute verschränkter leistenschragen*
A saltire interlaced with a mascle. When the field or a charge is covered with narrow interlacing diagonal bands it is termed 'fretty'.

FUSIL
A lozenge elongated vertically. Hence 'fusilly' when there are several.

GOBONY
A synonym for compony.

GOLD Fr. *Or*; Ge. *Golden*
The terms 'gold' and 'or' are equally valid in English blazoning. See under Or, below.

GONFALON, later **GONFANON** Fr. *Gonfanon*; Ge. *Kirchenfahne*
A type of flag, usually placed at the end of a lance, more or less square or rectangular in shape, usually with three tails or streamers at the fly. It was sometimes suspended from a cross-bar.

GORGED Fr. *Gorgé*; Ge. *Kehlig*
When a beast, bird or reptile has a collar or coronet around the neck. If the latter, the German term is *Halsgekrönt*. Creatures may be gorged with any suitable object, which should always be blazoned.

GREEN: see Vert

GUARDANT
When a beast is passant or rampant, etc., but looking at the observer; e.g., a lion passant guardant.

GUIDON Fr. *Guidon*; Ge. *Lanzenwimpel*
A flag or pennon, forked at the fly. Now borne by English dragoon regiments.

GULES Fr. *Gueules*; Ge. *Rot*
The colour red, which can be of any tint or shade so long as it is recognisably red. In early armory no distinction was made between red and purple. In the Middle Ages considered symbolic of boldness. Vermilion or scarlet are the best paints.

GUTTÉ, GUTTY, *or* GOUTTE Fr. *Goutté*; Ge. *Mit Froppen besät*
When the field or a charge is depicted as powdered with little droplets. When white they are blazoned as *gutté d'eau* (i.e., water); when red as *gutté de sang* (i.e., blood); when blue as *gutté de larmes* (i.e., tears); when green as *gutté d'huile*(i.e., oil).

GYRONNY Fr. *Gironné* ... (of so many) *piéces*; Ge. ... (so many times) *Geständert*
When the field is parted per cross and per saltire, thus forming eight wedge-shaped divisions of alternate colours. In English armory eight is the normal number.

HABITED
When a person or limb is clothed.

HAUBERK Fr. *Haubergeon*; Ge. *Brünne*
The shirt of mail armour worn by knights and men-at-arms. Land held by knight-service was known as a *fief de hauberk*.

HELM Fr. *Heaume* or *Casque*; Ge. *Helme*.
In English armory a gold helm with bars affronté is reserved to The Sovereign and members of the Royal Family; a steel helm with bars and depicted sideways is reserved for peers, although there are three or four exceptions. A steel helm with visor open and affronté is reserved for baronets and knights, and a steel helm with visor closed and depicted sideways is the mark of esquires and gentlemen, and also corporate bodies. In English armory it is permissible to adjust the position so as to bring the axes of helm and crest into line with one another.

HONOUR POINT Fr. *Point d'Honneur*: Ge. *Ehrenstelle*
The middle point in the chief or topmost part of a shield.

HURT
A blue roundel.

INDENTED Fr. *Émanché*; Ge. *Mit spitzen geplanten*
When a party line or the edge of an ordinary is of small zig-zag indentations. Not to be confused with dancetty.

INESCUTCHEON
A small shield placed usually at the centre point of another shield. See also Escutcheon of pretence.

INVECTED Fr. *Cannelé*; Ge. *Lappen*
The converse of engrailed.

ISSUANT Fr. *Issant*; Ge. *Wachsender*
Used of a creature which is issuing out of, e.g., a crest-wreath, and usually only the upper half of it is shown.

JESSANT DE LYS
When a fleur de lys is depicted as issuing out of the mouth of a creature, such as a leopard's head jessant de lys.

JESSED Fr. *Longé*; Ge. *Gefesselt*
Eagles, falcons and hawks used for falconry have a small bell tied to one leg; to each leg are also tied leather thongs for attaching the bird to its perch when at rest. This is blazoned as 'belled and jessed', either proper or of a particular colour.

JUPON
A sleeveless surcoat worn outside the body armour.

LABEL Fr. *Lambels*; Ge. *Turnierkragen*
A narrow band from which three or five tags depend, fixed across the top of a shield. Used as a mark of cadency for the eldest son during his father's lifetime, and then removed when the heir succeeds. In the Middle Ages it was probably loose and not painted on the shield.

LANGUED Fr. *Lampassé*; Ge. *Gezungt*
When the tongue of a creature is of a different tincture from its body, it is blazoned as 'langued' of a particular colour. The gold Leopards of England on their red field are always langued azure.

LODGED
Term used for a beast of the chase when depicted lying down with its head raised. See also Couchant.

LOZENGE Fr. *Losange*; Ge. *Raute*
One of the sub-ordinaries, being a diamond-shaped figure. When the field or a charge is completely covered with lozenges of alternating tinctures it is 'lozengy'.

MANTLING Fr. *Lambrequin*; Ge. *Helmdecken*
A piece of cloth hanging down the back of the helm, from below the crest-wreath or coronet, which has been depicted in various fanciful ways and is usually shown arranged on both sides of the shield.

MARSHALLING OF ARMS
The grouping in a single shield of two or more distinct arms, by means of dimidiation, impalement, quartering, or by means of an escutcheon of pretence or augmentation.

MARTLET O.Fr. *Merlete, Merlot*; Fr. *Merlette*; Ge. *Gestümmelte Amsel*
In the thirteenth century and earlier this bird was often called a 'merle', and later sometimes a 'merlion'. It is depicted without proper legs and with the wings close, and is an amalgam of the swift, swallow and house martin.

MASCLE Fr. *Macle*; Ge. *Fensterraute*
A voided lozenge.

MAUNCH Fr. *Manche mal taillée*; Ge. *Altertümlich geschmitten*
A medieval lady's sleeve, usually drawn in a very conventionalised way.

MEMBERED Fr. *Membrée*; Ge. *Mit beiren*
If the legs and beak of a bird are of a different colour from its body, it is blazoned as 'membered' of a particular colour.

MOLET Fr. *Étoile*; Ge. *Stern*
In the early Middle Ages, a five-pointed gold star represented a spur-rowel; when of gules it was called a 'molet', and when of silver a 'star', but for some centuries molets have been of all colours and still termed molets, while stars or estoiles are now drawn with wavy points. In England a molet is also the cadency mark of a third son.

MOLINE (CROSS) Fr. *Croix ancrée*; Ge. *Aukerkreuz*
A cross with the ends of the arms slightly divided and curling a little outwards. From Fr. *fer de moline*, a mill-iron or mill-rind.

MULLET: See Molet

NAIANT Fr. *Naissant*
Swimming.

NEBULY Fr. *Nebulé or Enté*; Ge. *Gewelkt*
When a party line or the outline of an ordinary is more exaggerated than when wavy, to an extent that it resembles conventionalised clouds.

NOMBRIL POINT Fr. *Nombril*; Ge. *Nabelstelle*
Literally the navel point in the shield, halfway between the fess point and

the bottom of the shield.

NOWED: See Nowy

NOWY Fr. *Noué*; Ge. *Pfropfbalken*
When a line is interrupted in the middle to form a small arch. Not to be confused with 'nowed', which is used of a snake or a creature's tail and means 'knotted'.

OGRESS
A black roundel, originally representing a cannon ball. Also called a pellet, and when the field is strewn with them it is 'pellety'.

OR Fr. *Or*; Ge. *Golden*
In English blazon both 'or' and 'gold' are equally correct. In the Middle Ages regarded as the noblest colour, fit only for princes, but in fact widely used. If you are feeling rich and know how to put it on, use gold leaf or powdered gold; otherwise chrome yellow is most suitable.

ORDINARY
The basic geometrical charges used in armory, usually divided into the (honourable) ordinaries and the sub-ordinaries. An ordinary of arms is an index of arms arranged according to the charges thereon; e.g., all the different lions together, or eagles, or crosses, and so on.

ORLE Fr. *Orle*; Ge. *Innenbord*
One of the sub-ordinaries. A band set a little way inside the shield and following its edge all the way round. Any charges placed all around the shield, in the position an orle would occupy, are blazoned as 'in orle'. A much narrower band in the same position as an orle is called a 'tressure', sometimes shown as double.

PAIRLE Fr. *Pairle*; Ge. *Deichsel*
A conventionalised bishop's pall, like the letter Y; a shield so partitioned is blazoned as 'tierced in pairle'.

PALE Fr. *Pal*; Ge. *Pfahe*
One of the ordinaries, being a vertical band down the middle of the shield. If the surface is divided in this way with an equal number of alternately tinctured bands, it is blazoned as 'paly'. The diminutive of a pale is a pallet.

PALL: see Pairle

PASSANT Fr. *Passant*
Walking. Used for beasts of prey, which are always depicted side view,

usually with the dexter forepaw raised. If the creature is looking out of the shield at the viewer it is blazoned as 'passant guardant' and when looking backwards over its shoulder it is 'passant reguardant'. Stags and similar creatures when walking are blazoned as 'trippant'.

PATE, PATY
Synonymous with formy.

PATONCE (CROSS) Fr. *Enhendée*
A cross with the ends of the arms splayed into three points.

PELLET: see Ogress

PIERCED
When an inanimate charge is perforated by, for example, a hole, so that the tincture of the field shows through.

PILE Fr. *Pile*; Ge. *Keil*
One of the ordinaries, being a wedge-shaped figure normally issuing downwards from the top edge of the shield. It can, however, issue from elsewhere. More than one are blazoned 'pily of two' or 'three', or 'two piles' or 'three piles'.

PLATE Fr. *Plate*; Ge. *Silberne scheibe*
A silver roundel, derived from the silver coin mentioned by Shakespeare. When the field is strewn with them it is 'platy'. Should be depicted flat.

POMME
A green roundel. The origin of the term is self-evident, if a trifle indigestible.

POTENT (CROSS) Fr. *Potencé*; Ge. *Krückenfeh*
A cross with the ends of the arms crutch-shaped, like the letter T. In the early Middle Ages this kind of cross, of which the best known example is in the arms of the Latin Kingdom of Jerusalem, was blazoned as a 'cross billetty'.

PROPER
Used of all animals and plants which are depicted in their natural or correct colours. In the Middle Ages people seldom distinguished between beasts or birds of the same species. For example, the missel thrush, fieldfare, redwing and song thrush were all lumped together as a throstle or thrush. Nowadays it is safer to blazon the creature by its colloquial name, followed by its scientific name in parentheses, for example, 'a song thrush (*Turdus philomelos*) proper'; thus, the creature can be identified in any language. Our predecessors were careless naturalists, being mostly town-bred monks stuck in an unfamiliar countryside.

QUARTER Fr. *Franc-quartier*; Ge. *Freivierted*
The quarter part of a shield. 'Quartering', however, denotes the inclusion in a shield of arms of the arms of heraldic heiresses, and the number of 'quarterings' can exceed four.

QUATREFOIL Fr. *Quatrefeuille*; Ge. *Vierblatt*
A conventionalised four-petalled flower, or group of four rounded leaves, radiating from a common centre. It may be of any tincture.

RAMPANT
Of a beast which is depicted standing upright on its left hind foot with its other three legs in the air, as if about to savage an enemy. Two lions rampant facing each other are blazoned as 'combatant'. In the early Middle Ages all lions were depicted rampant; when they were walking they were called leopards.

RED: see Gules

RESPECTANT
When the gentler beasts and birds are facing each other they are blazoned as 'respectant'.

RISING Fr. *Essorant*; Ge. *Aufflugend*
A bird about to take wing is thus blazoned.

ROUNDELS: See under Bezant, Hurt, Ogress, Plate, Pomme, Torteau

SABLE Fr. *Sable or Noir*; Ge. *Schwarz*
The colour black. The abbreviation is 'sa'. Regarded by some early writers as a humble colour, but the Black Prince's 'Arms for Peace' were black, and he was far from being humble. Lamp black is the most suitable paint.

SALIENT Fr. *Sautant*; Ge. *im sprung*
In the act of springing, depicted with both hind feet on the ground and both forepaws raised. A horse in this position is blazoned as 'forcene'.

SALTIRE Fr. *Sautoir*; Ge. *Schragen*
One of the ordinaries, shaped like the letter X.

SEGREANT
Term used for a griffin when rampant.

SEJANT Fr. *Accroupi*; Ge. *Sitzender*
Used of a beast sitting on its hindquarters.

SEMÉE, SEMY Fr. *Semé*; Ge. *Besät*
Term to denote a field strewn or powdered with small charges.

SILVER: see Argent

SINISTER Fr. *Sinistre*; Ge. *Links*
The side of the shield towards the left of the man holding it; thus to the right when viewed from in front.

SLIPPED
A leaf and/or flower with part of the stalk or twig attached is blazoned thus.

STATANT Fr. *Posé*; Ge. *Stehender*
Standing, with all feet on the ground.

SUPPORTERS Fr. *Tenants*; Ge. *Schildhalter*
The human, natural, or fabulous creatures which stand on either side of a shield of arms and support it by holding it.

TORTEAU O.Fr. *Tourtel*
A red roundel. From late Latin *torta*, and French *tourteau*, a round reddish-coloured cake. In early heraldry it could mean any roundel.

TREFOIL Fr. *Tiercefeuille*; Ge. *Dreiblatt*
Three-leaved charge with a short stalk, probably derived from the clover (*Trifolium repens Linn.*), or the wood-sorrel (*Oxalis acetosella Linn.*), but now drawn in a stylised way. The shamrock which St Patrick traditionally used to illustrate the Trinity.

TRESSURE Fr. *Trécheur*; Ge. *Doppelter innenbord*
A diminutive of the orle, often found doubled. In the case of the Royal Arms of Scotland, for instance, the double tressure is enriched with fleurs de lys which point in opposite directions alternately, and it is blazoned as *A double tressure flory counter flory*.

UMBRATED
Used of a charge which is shown only in outline, with the field showing through. A very rare and ghostly charge.

UNDY Fr. *Ondé*; Ge. *Wellengeteilt*: see Wavy

UNGULED Fr. *Onglé*
See under Armed. Term used when blazoning the colour of the hooves of ungulates.

VAIR Fr. *Vair*; Ge. *Feh*
This was a fur much favoured in the Middle Ages by the nobles and great

merchants, and consisted of the skins of a kind of squirrel, bluish-grey on the back and white underneath, sewn together to produce an alternate blue and white pattern. This was imported mainly through the Crimea (a trade in which Marco Polo's father was engaged), and, as it was therefore costly, it became a status symbol.

VERT Fr. *Sinople*; Ge. *Grün*
Green; the abbreviation is 'vt'. Regarded in the Middle Ages as symbolic of jollity and youth. Permanent green or viridian green are normally used, and both may be lightened with a little white.

VESTED Fr. *Paré*; Ge. *Bekleidet*
Clothed.

VOIDED Fr. *Vidé*; Ge. *Ausgebrachen*
Term for a charge with part or most of the centre removed.

VOLANT
Flying.

WAVY Fr. *Ondé*; Ge. *Wellengeteilt*
An undulating line or the edge of an ordinary drawn thus.

WILD MAN, *also known as a* **WOODHOUSE** *and* **WOODWOSE**
Used in fifteenth- and sixteenth-century heraldry as badges, or supporters of shields, and later more extensively as crests and in arms. Usually depicted as a naked, hairy man, wreathed about the loins with leaves. Popular in the Middle Ages as a figure in pageants.

WYVERN Fr. *Dragon*; Ge. *Drache*
The dragon was originally a peculiarly dangerous kind of flying serpent, with bat-like wings, long serpentine neck and tail, rather small body and two stumpy legs. In the early fifteenth century the four-legged dragon appears. 'Wyvern', derived from O.Fr. *wyvre*, var. *vivre*, which meant 'serpent', was only another name for the dragon or flying serpent. By the sixteenth century the name wyvern came to be applied by the English to the two-legged creature, and the four-legged one took the original name; but until Tudor times both sorts were called dragons.

NOTES

CHAPTER 2: THE LANGUAGE OF HERALDRY

1 Coll. Arms MS., Norf. XVI, p.46.
   This is illustrated in colour in O. Neubecker and J.P. Brooke-Little, *Heraldry: Sources, Symbols and Meaning* (Macdonald & Jane's, 1976), p. 95.

2 Sir Thomas Innes of Learney, *Scots Heraldry* (Edinburgh: Oliver & Boyd, 2nd edn, 1956), should be consulted on the Scottish practice as regards differencing.

3 Kenneth M. Setton et al., *A History of the Crusades* (University of Wisconsin Press, 1969), vol. II, p. 47.

4 J.E. Morris, *The Welsh Wars of Edward I* (Oxford University Press, 1901; reprinted 1968), p. 97.

5 Sir Harris Nicolas, *History of the Battle of Agincourt* (London, 1832; reprinted Tabard Press, 1970). Appendix viii, p.35, from Coll. Arms MS., L.5, ff. 102-4.

6 Anthony Wagner, 'The Swan Badge and the Swan Knight', *Archaelogia*, vol. 97 (1959).

7 Sir William H. St John Hope, ed., *The Last Testament and Inventory of John de Veer, thirteenth Earl of Oxford* (Oxford University Press, 1915).

8 Brit. Lib. Cotton MS. Nero D.I, f. 171. See also *CEMRA*, pp. 1-2, and 'The Matthew Paris Shields', ed. T.D. Tremlett, in *Aspilogia* II, *Rolls of Arms Henry III* (Society of Antiquaries, 1967), pp. 36-57.

9 Brit. Lib. Harl. MS. 4205. See also *CEMRA*, pp. 92-3, and Richard Marks and Ann Payne, *British Heraldry* (British Museum Publications, 1978), p. 46.
10 Brit. Lib. Add. MS. 48976 (English version), and Coll. Arms MS. Warwick Roll (Latin version). See also *CEMRA*, pp. 116-20.
11 See Rodney Dennys, *The Heraldic Imagination* (Barrie & Jenkins, 1975), p. 61.

CHAPTER 4: HERALDRY AND THE KNIGHT

1 C. Stephenson and F.G. Marcham (eds and trans.), *Sources of English Constitutional History* (Harrap, 1938), p. 85.
2 Prof. David C. Douglas, *The Norman Achievement 1050-1100* (Eyre & Spottiswoode, 1969), pp. 7-8.
3 K.R. Potter (ed. and trans.), *Gesta Stephani* (Nelson, 1955), p. 24.
4 Rosalind Hill (ed. and trans.), *Gesta Francorum et Aliorum Hierosolimitanorum* (Nelson, 1962), pp. 70-1.
5 A.R. Wagner, 'Heraldry' in: *Medieval England*, ed. A.L. Poole (Oxford University Press, 1958), vol.I, pp. 338-52.
6 D.L. Galbreath, *Manuel du Blason*, new and revised edn Léon Jéquier (Lausanne: Edn Spes, 1977), pp. 244-5.
7 Villehardouin and de Joinville, *Memoirs of the Crusades* (Everyman's Library, no. 333), pp. 140, 160, 174.
8 Brit. Lib. Add. MS. 42130, f. 202ᵛ.
9 Buccleuch MS. Wrythe Garter Book, f. 151.

CHAPTER 5: 'WHAT DO THEY MEAN?'

1 This is discussed more fully in Rodney Dennys, *The Heraldic Imagination* (Barrie & Jenkins, 1975) pp. 68-9.
2 Brit. Lib. Cotton MS. Nero C.III, and Bodleian Lib. MS. Eng. Misc. D.227. See also Dennys, op. cit., pp. 76-9.
3 Coll. Arms MS. C.7, f. 114.
4 *Aspilogia* II, p. 51, has a most useful note on the origin of these arms.
5 Coll. Arms MSS. 1st H.7, f. 62ᵛ; Philpot P.b.22, f. 10.
6 Coll. Arms MS. 2nd H.5, ff. 116ᵛ-118. These arms are illustrated in Dennys, op. cit., p. 149.
7 Coll. Arms MSS. R.20, f. 168; Philpot P.b.22, f. 10ᵛ.
8 Coll. Arms MSS. WZ, f. 231; EDN.57, f. 301; I.9, f. 84.
9 Coll. Arms MSS. Grants IV, pp. 280-4; Misc. Grants II, f. 269.
10 *Cal. Pat. Rolls Hen. VII*, vol. ii, pp. 75, 145, 219, 365.
11 A.B. Emden, *A Biographical Register of the University of Oxford to A.D. 1500* (Oxford University Press, 1957). *The Dictionary of National Biography* got him wrong.

12 Coll. Arms MS. Vincent 169, ff. 133 and 146.
13 Coll. Arms MSS. EDN.55, f. 45; Camden's Grants I, f. 4ᵛ; II, f. 4ᵛ; III, f. 13ᵛ.
14 Coll. Arms MS. C.22 part 1, f. 17ᵛ.
15 Joseph Foster, *Alumni Oxonienses* (Oxford University Press, 1891).
16 Coll. Arms MS. Grants CXI, p. 142.
17 Coll. Arms MS. Grants CXLI, p. 301.
18 Coll. Arms MS. Grants CXXXVI, p. 67.
19 Coll. Arms MS. Grants XX, pp. 39-44.
20 Coll. Arms MS. Bath Books, vol. IV, pp. 101-4.
21 Coll. Arms MS. Grants XX, pp. 261-4.
22 Coll. Arms MS. Grants XXIV, pp. 281-4.
23 Ibid., pp. 71-4.
24 Coll. Arms MS. C.22, part 2, f. 267ᵛ, Visitation of Somerset in 1623.
25 Coll. Arms MS. Grants LVI, pp. 288-9.
26 Ibid., pp. 290-2.
27 Coll. Arms MS. Grants XCV, pp. 253-4.

CHAPTER 6: ATTRIBUTED ARMS

1 Brit. Lib. Seals xxxvi, 243.
2 Bodleian Lib. MS. Douce 180, ff. 78-88, The Douce Apocalypse.
3 Sir Thomas Malory, *Le Morte d'Arthur*, ed. Sir John Rhys (Everyman's Library, no. 45, reprinted 1947), p. 1.
4 Brit. Lib. Add. MS. 34648, and Harl., MS.6097, John's Treatise on Arms.
5 Bibl. Nat. Paris, MS. Fr.5936, Prinsault's Treatise.
6 Geoffrey of Monmouth, *History of the Kings of Britain*, trans. Sebastian Evans, Rev. Charles W. Dunn (Everyman's Library, no. 577), p. 188.
7 J.E. Morris, *The Welsh Wars of Edward I* (Oxford University Press, 1901; reprinted 1968), p. 97.
8 R.L.P. Milburn, *Saints and their Emblems in English Churches* (Oxford: Blackwell, 1961), p. 109.
9 J.G.O. Whitehead, 'The Arms of the Confessor', *The Coat of Arms*, vol. VIII, no. 63, pp. 266-71, discusses the attributed arms of the Christian West Saxon Kings.
10 Myles Dillon and Nora K. Chadwick, *The Celtic Realms* (Weidenfeld & Nicolson, 1967), covers the history and culture of the Celtic peoples from their prehistoric origins to the Norman Conquest; also Nora K. Chadwick, *Celtic Britain* (Thames & Hudson, 1963). I have relied largely on their excellent and most readable books, but alas fall far behind them.
11 Major Francis Jones, Wales Herald Extraordinary, *Report on the Welsh*

Manuscripts contained in the Muniments of the College of Arms (London: privately produced, 1957), p. 2.

12 J.G. Edwards, 'The Normans and the Welsh March', *Proc. Brit. Academy*, vol. XIII, pp. 155-77.

13 J. Horace Round, 'The Origin of the FitzGeralds', *The Ancestor*, no.2, pp. 91-7.

14 Giraldus Cambrensis, *Expugnatio Hibernica* ed. and trans. A.B. Scott and F.X. Martin (R.I.A., Dublin, 1978), p. 169. I am indebted to Major Michael Maclagan, Richmond Herald of Arms, for drawing my attention to this passage.

15 Major Francis Jones, 'Welsh Heraldic Studies', *The Coat of Arms*, vol. V, no. 33, pp. 349-53. This is essential reading for anyone interested in Welsh heraldry.

16 Dillon and Chadwick; op. cit., contains many references to Cunedda and his descendants, as does Leslie Alcock, *Arthur's Britain* (Harmondsworth: Penguin, 1973); also Nora K. Chadwick, *Celtic Britain* (Thames & Hudson, 1963). Professor Alcock suggests that Cunedda and his tribesmen may have been transferred by Magnus Maximus shortly before he denuded Britain of troops in his unsuccessful bid for the imperial throne in A.D. 383, but he also discusses alternative later dates in great detail. R.G. Collingwood, *Roman Britain and the English Settlements* (Oxford University Press, 1937), like the other authorities, considers that it was done under Stilicho. As Professor Alcock says, 'Dyfed and Gwynedd are the only two kingdoms in western Britain in which we can trace dynastic origins with any degree of confidence.'

17 Including the two compilers of this book. The 'gateway ancestor' for most British families is Humphrey de Bohun, Earl of Hereford and Essex (died 1322), and thence through Miles of Gloucester and Bernard de Neufmarche, one of the Norman adventurers, who conquered the Welsh kingdom of Brecheiniog (Breconshire) and married the granddaughter and eventual heiress of Gruffydd ap Llywelyn, King of All Wales.

18 Major Francis Jones, 'Arms of the XV Noble Tribes of North Wales', *The Coat of Arms*, vol. V, no. 36, pp. 89-94; also 'The Royal and Noble Families', *Royal and Princely Heraldry in Wales* (Tabard Press, 1969), pp. 10-17.

CHAPTER 7: THE LOCOMOTIVE MERMAID

1 Bodleian Library MS. All Souls Coll. 6, f. 71; English, Salisbury, c. 1250. Also Brit. Lib. Add. MS. 24686, f. 13; Latin, c. 1284.

2 Bartholomaeus Anglicus, *De Proprietatibus Rerum*, trans. John of Trevisa (London, 1825), chapter xviii, pp. 345-6.

3 Bibl. Nat. Paris MS. Fr. 25526, f. 110, Guillaume de Loris and Jean de Meung, *Roman de la Rose*, French, mid-fourteenth century.
4 Brit. Lib. Harley MS. 4379, f. 32ᵛ.

CHAPTER 8: THE HERALDRY OF HAITI

1 Sir Harry Luke, 'Monarchy in Haiti', *Jamaican Historical Review*, vol. I, pp. 121-36, gives a good account of the history of this time; while George Bellew, 'Strange Heraldry for a Negro Aristocracy', *Illustrated London News*, March 31st and June 16th, 1934, discusses the armory.
2 Comte de Limonade, *Rélation des glorieux evénemens qui ont porté leurs Majestés Royales sur le trône d'Hayti* (Haiti: P. Roux, 1811). This rare book gives a remarkably full account of the establishment of the Kingdom of Haiti and its civil and military organisation. One wonders if the Comte de Limonade may have been one of the architects of the Kingdom of Haiti. Almost all that follows in this chapter has been taken from this work. It is an interesting fact that Henri Christophe's name is spelt throughout the book as Henry.
3 This edict is not printed by de Limonade, op. cit.
4 Coll. Arms MS. JP., 177. In the description of the arms, particulars of the grantees in brackets are taken from de Limonade, op. cit., pp. 68-73.

CHAPTER 9: THE ARMS OF THE KINGDOM OF JERUSALEM

1 Kenneth M. Setton et. al., *A History of the Crusades* (University of Pennsylvania Press, 1955–62), vol. I, pp. 236–42; and Steven Runciman, *A History of the Crusades* (Cambridge University Press, 1951), vol. I, pp. 106–10.
2 Setton, op. cit., pp. 241–2. A slightly different translation of this passage is given in Régine Pernoud, *The Crusades* trans. Enid McLeod (Secker & Warburg, 1962), p. 25.
3 *Gesta Francorum et Aliorum Hierosolimitanorum*, trans. and ed. Rosalind Hill (Nelson, 1962), p. 2: *Gesta Francorum* for short.
4 *The Alexiad of Anna Comnena*, trans. E.R.A. Sewter (Harmondsworth: Penguin, 1969), p. 314.
5 D.L. Galbreath, *Papal Heraldry*, ed. Geoffrey Briggs (Heraldry Today, 2nd edn, 1972), p. 2. The whole of Chapter I is well worth reading.
6 Rodney Dennys, *The Heraldic Imagination* (Barrie & Jenkins, 1975), p. 26.
7 David C. Douglas, *William the Conqueror* (Eyre & Spottiswoode, 1964), pp. 187–8.
8 *Gesta Francorum*, pp. 91–2.

9 *Aspilogia* II, p. 12, for a useful discussion of these arms. See also Paul Adam-Even, 'Contribution à l'héraldique de L'Orient Latin', *Etudes Héraldiques Médiévales*, p. 7, which is important.

10 Sir George Hill, *A History of Cyprus* (Cambridge University Press, 1948), vol. II, p. 41.

11 Ibid., vol. II, p. 221, where there is an excellent line drawing of the coin and the impaled arms.

12 *Aspilogia* II, p. 36, although elsewhere (p. 23) Matthew Paris gives the arms as *Or, a cross argent*.

13 *Aspilogia* II, pp. 169–70.

14 *Aspilogia* II, p. 76.

15 T. Rylance, 'The Latin empire of Constantinople. Do we read rolls rightly?', *The Coat of Arms*, N.S. vol. IV, no. 113, pp. 240–2.

16 W. de G. Birch, *Catalogue of Seals in the Department of MSS. at the British Museum* (Trustees of the British Museum, 1894), vol. I, no. 2459; also Brit. Lib. Seals LIV, 71.

CHAPTER 10: THE LEOPARDS AND THE LILIES

1 L. Bouly de Lesdain, *Les plus anciennes armoiries françaises* (Archives Héraldiques Suisses, vol. V, 1897), pp. 69–79, 94–103.

2 John of Marmoutier, *Chroniques de Comtes d'Anjou et des Seigneurs d'Amboise*, ed. Louis Halphen and Réné Poupardin (Paris, 1913), p. 179. This is discussed more fully in Rodney Dennys, *The Heraldic Imagination* (Barrie & Jenkins, 1975), pp. 29–30, 133.

3 Francis Sandford, *Genealogical History of the Kings and Queens of England* (London, 1707), p. 50.

4 *Aspilogia* II, p.29.

5 Ibid., p. 117.

6 *Northamptonshire Record Society Transactions*, vol. IV, p. 24.

7 Sandford, op. cit., p. 55, has good engravings of Richard's first and second Great Seals.

8 *Itinerarium Peregrinorum et Gesta Regis Ricardi*, ed. Stubbs, Rolls Series (London, 1864), vol. VI, p. 197.

9 Sandford, op. cit., p. 55.

10 *Aspilogia* II, p. 130.

11 Ibid., p. 21.

12 Mr Adrian Ailes has kindly let me see a thesis he has recently completed for Reading University, in which he argues the contrary case very persuasively. It is to be hoped that one day this will be published.

13 I have discussed this in more detail in *The Heraldic Imagination*, pp. 60–1. See also Gerald J. Brault, *Early Blazon* (Oxford University Press,

1972), pp. 209–10, under *fleur de glaieul* and *fleur de lis*, in which the origin of the French royal arms is discussed.

14 Corpus Christi College, Cambridge, MS. 26; also *Aspilogia* II, p. 67. The three banners illustrated are those of the Order of the Hospital of St John of Jerusalem, the Knights Templar, and the Oriflamme of France.

15 Mrs Janet de Gaynesford has drawn my attention to the fact that similarly quartered arms of Henry IV were erected on the Castle of Rhodes.

CHAPTER 11: RICHARD II AND HERALDRY

1 A. R. Wagner, 'The Swan Badge and the Swan Knight', *Archaeologia*, vol. XCVII, pp. 127–88. Compulsory and compulsive reading for any armorist.

2 N. Denholm-Young, *The Country Gentry in the Fourteenth Century* (Oxford University Press, 1969), p. 146.

3 Patent Roll, 13 Ric. II, p.i, m.37; also *Cal. Pat. Rolls Ric. II*, vol. IV, p. 72; also Sir Anthony Wagner, *Heralds and Heraldry in the Middle Ages* (Oxford University Press, 1939), pp. 66, 123.

4 *Froissarts Cronycles*, trans. from the French by Sir John Bourchier, Lord Berners (Oxford: Blackwell, 1928), vol. II, part iv, p. 1050. See also J. Horace Round, *Peerage and Pedigree* (Nisbet, and St Catherine Press, 1910), pp. 353–6.

5 Johannis de Trokelowe, et al., *Annales Ricardi Secundi*, ed. H. T. Riley (Rolls Series, 1866), p. 223, *et adderet scuto suo arma Sancti Edwardi*. I am much indebted to my colleague Mr Michael Maclagan, Richmond Herald of Arms, for drawing my attention to this and the following reference.

6 M. Douet d'Arcq, *Collection de Sceaux* III (Paris, 1868), no. 10193. This is also mentioned in J.H. and R.V. Pinches, *The Royal Heraldry of England* (Heraldry Today, 1974), p. 104, but in this case the label is said to have been of three points, each charged with three torteaux. I have not seen the original seal. However, it does not effect the question of the Confessor's impalement.

7 *Cal. Pat. Rolls Ric. II*, vol. V, p. 350.

8 Lewis C. Loyd and Doris M. Stenton (eds), *Sir Christopher Hatton's Book of Seals* (Oxford University Press, 1950), no. 387.

9 W.H. St John Hope, ed., *The Stall Plates of the Knights of the Order of the Garter 1348–1485* (Westminster: Archibald Constable Ltd, 1901), plate xxx.

10 Ibid., plate lxxvi.

11 Coll. Arms MS. Heralds, vol. III, f. 1014; also F. Sandford, *Genealogical*

History of the Kings and Queens of England (London, 1707), p. 234; and Coll. Arms MS. Vincent's Presidents, p. 164; and Brit. Lib. Cotton MS. Titus C.l, f. 404.

12 H. Stanford London, 'Officers of the College of Arms and their Predecessors in Office', *The College of Arms*, Sixteenth and Final Monograph of the London Survey Committee (1963), from which the information on these Officers of Arms is derived.

13 F. Sandford, op. cit., p. 124; and W. de G. Birch, *Catalogue of Seals in the Department of MSS. at the British Museum* (Trustees of the British Museum, 1894), vol. III, p. 110.

14 F. Sandford, op. cit., p. 124; also Birch, op. cit., vol. III, p.108.

15 *Rotuli Parliamentorum*, vol. III, p. 355.

16 Sandford, op. cit., p. 124; and Coll. Arms MS. Vincent 88, f. 89. Round, op. cit., pp. 355–60, discusses the question of the Confessor's arms. I am greatly indebted to Mrs Marie Louise Bruce for calling my attention to several references to the bearing of the Confessor's arms.

17 Sandford, op. cit., p. 125; also Pinches and Pinches, op. cit., p. 46.

18 Sandford, op. cit., p. 210; also Coll. Arms MS. Vincent 88, ff. 123, 180.

19 St John Hope, op. cit., plate xxx.

20 Coll. Arms MS. Vincent 88, f. 180.

21 St John Hope, op. cit., plate lxxvi.

22 Douet d'Arcq, op. cit., no. 10193.

23 Birch, op. cit., vol III, no. 12681.

24 J. H. Wylie, *History of England under Henry IV* (London, 1898), vol. IV, p. 173. I am indebted to Mrs Marie Louise Bruce for drawing my attention to Wylie's references.

25 Birch, op. cit., no. 12685.

26 Wylie, op. cit., vol. IV, p. 174.

CHAPTER 12: THE WARS OF THE ROSES AND THE TUDORS

1 Philippe de Commynes, *Memoirs*, trans. Michael Jones (Harmondsworth: Penguin, 1972), p. 89.

2 'Gregory's Chronicle', *The Historical Collections of a Citizen of London* (Camden Series, 1876), ed. J. Gairdner, quoted by J.R. Lander, *The Wars of the Roses* (Secker & Warburg, 1965), p. 120.

3 V.H.H. Green, *The Later Plantagenets* (Edward Arnold, 1955), p. 332, quoting a contemporary chronicler.

4 J. Horace Round, 'The Arms of the Kingmaker', *The Ancestor*, vol. 4, pp. 143–7, and vol. 5, pp. 195–200. See also Sir Anthony Wagner, *Historic Heraldry of Britain* (Phillimore, 1972), pp. 57–8, and C.W.

Scott-Giles, *The Romance of Heraldry*, Dent, 1929; reprinted 1957), pp. 131–5.

5 N. Denholm-Young, *The Country Gentry in the Fourteenth Century* (Oxford University Press, 1969), p. 20n.

6 C.W. Scott-Giles, *Shakespeare's Heraldry* (Heraldry Today, 1971), p. 147.

7 Lander, op. cit., p. 119, quoting 'Gregory's Chronicle', op. cit., p. 211.

8 This is discussed more fully by Paul M. Kendall, *Richard III* (Sphere, 1972), pp. 215–23.

CHAPTER 13: THE HERALDIC CONSEQUENCES OF RICHARD II

1 J.D. Mackie, *The Earlier Tudors* (Oxford University Press, 1952), p. 16.

2 J.G. Russell, *The Field of Cloth of Gold* (Routledge & Kegan Paul, 1969), pp. 6–7. See also Kenneth Pickthorn, *Early Tudor Government, Henry VIII* (Cambridge University Press, 1934), p. 45.

3 Francis W. Steer, *Henry Howard the Poet Earl of Surrey* (privately printed, 1977), for the best monograph on this brilliant and wayward Renaissance character.

4 *Letters and Papers of Henry VIII* (H.M.S.O., 1867–1910), vol. XVIII, nos 315, 351.

5 Brit. Lib. Harl. MS. 1453.

6 Coll. Arms MS. Vincent 18, 'Knights of the Garter', f. 198.

7 Coll. Arms MS. M.9, 'Coats of Arms of Noblemen and Knights temp. Hen. 8 and Edw. 6', f.4.

8 Roy Strong, 'Some Early Portraits at Arundel Castle', *The Connoisseur*, vol. 197 (March 1978), pp. 198–200.

CHAPTER 14: THE ARMS OF THE CONSTABLE AND THE MARSHAL

1 Francis Sandford, *Genealogical History of the Kings and Queens of England* (London, 1707), pp. 125, 229.

2 Coll. Arms MS. M.10, 'Coats in Colour', f. 129^b.

3 Sidney Painter, *William Marshal* (Baltimore: The John Hopkins Press, 1933), has a useful account of the early members of this family, as well as being a most readable biography of William Marshal, to which I am indebted for much of what follows. Also A.L. Poole, *Obligations of Society in the XII and XIII Centuries* (Oxford University Press, 1946), p.39, for their Somerset holding.

4 Sir Anthony Wagner, *Heralds and Heraldry in the Middle Ages* (Oxford University Press, 1939), pp. 26, 130, quoting the metrical biography written shortly after William's death: Paul Meyer, ed., *L'histoire de*

Guillaume le Maréchal (Paris: Société de l'histoire de France, 1891), tome i, p. 36.

5 Sir Anthony Wagner, *Historic Heraldry of Britain* (Phillimore, 1972), p. 39.

6 Meyer, op. cit., lines 1381–1512, quoted by Sidney Painter, op. cit., p. 24.

7 *Aspilogia* II, p. 8. Also Wagner, *Historic Heraldry of Britain*, p. 39.

8 *Aspilogia* II, pp. 18, 116, 132. In the 'Liber Additamentorum', the shield for Earl Bigod (MP.II, no. 12) is shown separately from that for *Comitis Marescallis* (MP.II, no. 18).

9 Coll. Arms MS. L.10, f. 31.

CHAPTER 15: THE EARL MARSHAL AND THE COURT OF CHIVALRY

1 The most important works which discuss the position of the Earl Marshal and the Court of Chivalry, and which are still available, are G. D. Squibb, *The High Court of Chivalry* (Oxford University Press, 1959); Sir Anthony Wagner, *Heralds and Heraldry in the Middle Ages* (Oxford University Press, 2nd edn 1956), and *Heralds of England* (H.M.S.O., 1967).

2 *A Verbatim Report of the Case in the High Court of Chivalry of the Lord Mayor, Aldermen and Citizens of Manchester versus The Manchester Palace of Varieties Ltd, on Tuesday 21st December 1954* (The Heraldry Society, 1955), pp. 55-61. This will be referred to for convenience as the 'Manchester Corporation Case'.

3 Squibb, op. cit., pp. 152-3.

4 Coll. Arms MS. I.25, ff. 128-9.

CHAPTER 16: THE HERALDS AND THE COLLEGE OF ARMS

1 The Original Royal Charter of 1483/4 is now in the British Library, Cotton MS. Faustina E.I, fo.23. A précis is printed in *Cal. Pat. Rolls, 1476-85*, p. 422. See also Sir Anthony Wagner, *Heralds of England* (H.M.S.O., 1967), pp. 129-32.

2 The original Royal Charter of 1549 is now in the College of Arms. A précis is printed in *Calendar of Patent Rolls, Edward VI*, vol. 2, 1545-9, p. 203. See also Wagner, op. cit., pp. 100-1.

3 The original Royal Charter of 1555 is now in the College of Arms. A précis is printed in *Calendar of Patent Rolls, Philip and Mary, 1555-7*, p. 31. See also Wagner, op. cit., pp. 182-3.

4 The full minutes of the Chapter meeting at Rouen are printed as Appendix XII in Hugh Stanford London, *Life of William Bruges* (Harleian Society, 1970), pp. 98-107.

5 Anthony R. Wagner, *The Records and Collections of the College of Arms* (Burke's Peerage, n.d.) is an indispensable guide to the College library.

6 *State Papers (1) 73*, fo. 193. See also Wagner, *Heralds of England*, op. cit., p. 161.

7 Wagner, *The Records and Collections of the College of Arms*, op. cit., is invaluable for the Visitations.

8 Brit. Lib. Add. MS. 3744, The Sloane Tract. Complete text ed. by C.R. Humphery-Smith, 'Heraldry in School Manuals in the Middle Ages', *The Coat of Arms*, vol. VI, pp. 115-23.

9 Coll. Arms, Hare's MS. I, R.36, ff. 148ᵛ-150.

CHAPTER 17: GRANTS OF ARMORIAL BEARINGS

1 Sir George Sitwell, 'The English Gentleman', *The Ancestor*, no.1 (April 1902), pp. 58-103. This is still one of the most important contributions to any consideration of this very difficult subject. See also N. Denholm-Young, *The Country Gentry in the Fourteenth Century* (Oxford University Press,1969), and Anthony Wagner, *Heralds and Heraldry in the Middle Ages* (Oxford University Press, 2nd edn 1956), both of which are essential reading in this context.

2 G.E. Cokayne, *The Complete Peerage*, vol. XII (St Catherine's Press, 1953), pp. 434-54.

3 N. Denholm-Young, op. cit., p. 139.

4 *Cal. Pat. Rolls*, 17 Ric. II, p. 1.

5 Rodney Dennys, *The Heraldic Imagination* (Barrie & Jenkins, 1975), pp. 62-4, discusses Bartolo in more detail.

6 The passage in question is quoted in Sir George Sitwell, op. cit., p. 86. See also Rodney Dennys, op. cit., pp. 76-82, and p. 50.

7 Wagner, op. cit., pp. 79-80, 163.

8 Ibid., pp. 9-10, 79.

9 G.D. Squibb, Norfolk Herald Extraordinary, 'Heraldic Authority in the British Commonwealth', *The Coat of Arms*, vol. X, no. 76, pp. 125-33. A most valuable and thoughtful article on this very difficult subject. See also J. Michael Crawford, 'Some Views on English and Scots heraldic authority outside the United Kingdom', *The Coat of Arms*, N.S. vol. II, no. 102, pp. 157-62. An interesting article which seeks to refute some of the tentative suggestions put forward by Mr Squibb, but, to my mind, not wholly convincing. Nevertheless, an important contribution to the debate.

10 G.D. Squibb, letter, *The Coat of Arms*, N.S. vol. II, no. 104, p. 231.

CHAPTER 19: OVERSEAS WORK OF THE HERALDS

1 Coll. Arms MS. Foreign Arms, vol. 2, pp. 119-21.
2 Ibid., vol. 2, pp. 143-5.
3 Ibid., vol. 2, pp. 146-7.

CHAPTER 20: THE HERALDS AND THE ORDERS OF CHIVALRY

1 Eric Christiansen, *The Northern Crusades* (Macmillan, 1980), pp. 70-88, for a most useful discussion of the monastic knighthood of the twelfth and thirteenth centuries.
2 One of the best accounts of knighthood and of the way in which it was regarded in the Middle Ages is that by Ramon Lull (born *c*. 1235, martyred 1315), which was first published in English by William Caxton, *c*. 1484, as *The Book of the Order of Chyvalry*, ed. A.T.P. Byles (*E.E.T.S.*, vol. 168, 1926).
3 Sir Ivan de la Bere, *The Queen's Orders of Chivalry* (Spring Books, 1961), pp. 43, 125.
4 Ibid., pp. 99-129. There is much of interest in this chapter on the Order of the Bath.
5 Ibid., pp. 135-6.
6 There is a most useful article on knighthood in all its European forms by Weatherley, 'Knighthood', in *Encyclopaedia Britannica*, 11th edn (1911), pp. 851-67.

CHAPTER 21: PARLIAMENTARY DUTIES OF THE HERALDS

1 Sir Anthony Wagner and J.C. Sainty, 'The Origin of the Introduction of Peers in the House of Lords', *Archaeologia*, vol. CI, pp. 119-50. This is essential reading on the subject, and the footnotes are invaluable.
2 See Sir Anthony Wagner, *Heralds of England* (H.M.S.O., 1967), pp. 72-7, for a discussion of these rights of the heralds.
3 Wagner, op. cit., p. 76.

CHAPTER 22: THE CEREMONIAL DUTIES OF THE HERALDS

1 Constance Bullock-Davies, *Menestrellorum Multitudo* (University of Wales Press, 1978), discusses in fascinating detail the organisation and activities of the 'minstrels' in the Court of Edward I, as revealed by a study of the Wardrobe accounts for the Feast of the Swans in 1306.
2 Fritz Kern, trans. by S.B. Crimes, *Kingship and Law in the Middle Ages* (Oxford: Blackwell, 1948), pp. 12-13.

3 F.M. Stenton, *Anglo-Saxon England* (The Oxford History of England, Oxford University Press, 1943), pp. 542-4. *Early Medieval Kingship*, eds P.H. Sawyer and I.N. Wood (University of Leeds, 1977), is invaluable for any study of the very early aspects of kingship and the inauguration of kings; also Kern, op. cit.
4 *London Gazette*, 1952, pp. 757-9.
5 Based on the printed Ceremonial used at the time.
6 *London Gazette*, 1952, p. 911.

INDEX